THUNDER
AND
LIGHTNING

THUNDER AND LIGHTNING

A NO-B.S. HOCKEY MEMOIR

PHIL ESPOSITO
AND PETER GOLENBOCK

TRIUMPH
BOOKS
CHICAGO

Library of Congress Cataloging-in-Publication Data

Esposito, Phil, 1942-
    Thunder and lightning : a no-B.S. hockey memoir / Phil Esposito with
Peter Golenbock.
        p. cm.
    Includes index.
        ISBN 1-57243-539-9 (hard)
            1. Esposito, Phil, 1942- 2. Hockey players — Canada — Biography.
I. Golenbock, Peter, 1946- II. Title.

GV848.5.E68A35 2003
796.962'092 — dc22
[B]

                                                                2003053362

This book is available in quantity at special discounts
for your group or organization. For further information, contact:

Triumph Books
601 South LaSalle Street
Suite 500
Chicago, Illinois 60605
(312) 939-3330
Fax (312) 663-3557

Published simultaneously in Canada by McClelland & Stewart Ltd., Suite 900,
481 University Avenue, Toronto, Ontario, Canada M5G 2E9.

Printed in Canada
ISBN 1-57243-539-9
Typesetting by M&S, Toronto
Design by Kong Njo

Contents

Preface *by Peter Golenbock*   vii

Introduction   1
1.   I was born in Sault Ste. Marie   7
2.   When I was a boy   14
3.   In 1960 I tried out   21
4.   At the end of the 1961-62 season   28
5.   Linda and I got married   35
6.   The Blackhawks had a great team   45
7.   The next day I got a call   53
8.   Harry Sinden   64
9.   Those Bruins teams   73
10. After the hockey season   83
11. One of the worst things   91
12. In July 1972   98
13. The Russians   108
14. Linda had come to Russia   120

15. When the 1972-73 season began   122

16. I was traded   129

17. I played in the Canada Cup   144

18. It became too difficult   153

19. Wayne Gretzky   157

20. After my retirement   164

21. When I took over   175

22. In the middle of the 1986-87 season   186

23. The tension and the pressure   198

24. The morning after I was fired   206

25. During the summer of 1990   216

26. I went to Jamaica   223

27. The Japanese   231

28. We had a lot to do   239

29. The tension between Crispy and me   245

30. During the 1993-94 season   254

31. At the end of June 1994   259

32. In early August 1997   271

33. My guess was   277

     Index   284

Preface

YOU ARE ABOUT TO READ one of the wildest autobiographies ever written by one of the greats of any game. It's honest and funny and at times more than a little ribald, but when you're done you'll appreciate and admire Phil Esposito for not having hired a PR agent or a spin doctor to help you decide he is perfect in every way.

He could have done that. He also could have spent half this book writing about his many accomplishments on the ice. And he would have been justified. Esposito was the greatest center ever to perform in the National Hockey League. A hulking presence, he would plant himself in front of the goal, wait for a shot or a pass, then muscle the defenders out of the way as he wristed the puck into the net. The image of Esposito lodged in front of the net waiting to strike, endures like that of Bobby Orr charging up the ice or Wayne Gretzky stickhandling around a defender. Phil is the standard by which all other centers are measured.

During his Hall of Fame career, Espo hit the back of the net a remarkable 717 times. When he retired at the end of the 1981-82 season, he was the second-highest scorer in the history of the National Hockey League, behind another legend, Gordie Howe. His 873 assists were third-highest at the time of his retirement.

Esposito, the first player to score more than 100 points in a season (126 in 1968-69), was at his peak during the 1970-71 season, when he set the NHL record for most goals scored in a season. The old record, held by Bobby Hull, had been 58. Esposito astounded the hockey world by scoring 76 goals and also getting credit for 76 assists to break the season points total with 152.

It was during this historic season that the bumper sticker, "Jesus Saves, But Esposito Scores On the Rebound," became popular around Boston and northern New England.

His prowess was no fluke: in the next four years Esposito scored 66, 55, 68, and 61 goals. During one ten-year period, Espo averaged an incredible 54 goals a year. He was an NHL All-Star eight years in a row.

In 1972 Esposito gained immortality when Team Canada took on the Soviet national hockey team. When the Soviets took a lead in games at the beginning of the series, it was Esposito who inspired his teammates to restore the honor of Canada.

After a blockbuster trade to New York in 1975, he led the Rangers into the finals of the Stanley Cup playoffs in 1979. He retired after playing 1,282 games in eighteen seasons with the Chicago Blackhawks, Boston Bruins, and New York Rangers. In the spring of 2002 Canada Post issued a postage stamp in Phil Esposito's honor.

But in preparing this book, aside from a few of his more memorable goals, Phil didn't want to talk about his hockey accomplishments nearly as much as about the fun he had putting on the skates and the equipment and playing the game. Being a player meant belonging to a team, hanging out with the guys, chasing the girls, heading for the bar. Phil loves to talk about his teammates. You'll get a look at his Blackhawks, Bruins, and Rangers as never before. Phil Esposito has always lived life to the fullest, and it is this that makes him most proud – and most interesting.

After he retired as a player, he became a broadcaster, the general manager of two NHL teams, and an owner for a short time before the deep pockets screwed him out of his ownership position. Phil happily provides details of all the drama, triumphs, and setbacks that have marked his career as an NHL executive.

After he was fired as GM of the Rangers in 1989, he was success-ful against long odds in founding the Tampa Bay Lightning hockey franchise. It remains his proudest accomplishment in the game.

Phil's intention in writing this book was to give hockey fans a bang for their buck.

"I intend to talk about *everything*," he told me the first time we met. Phil is a natural storyteller. Little is sacred to him, and if the joke is on him, so much the better.

His fans are sure to be enthralled by what he has to say about teammates, opponents, agents, team brass, and the NHL in general.

"I may never get another job in hockey," says Esposito. "But I don't care."

And yet hockey, whether it knows it or not, needs Phil Esposito. In a sport where most of the executives are almost invisible, Espo brings color, Sturm und Drang.

"The game should be exciting," he says.

No one could love the game more. Espo exhibits that fierce passion for it every single day. Shamefully, he no longer has an executive role with his baby, the Tampa Bay Lightning, but his thoughts are often with the team. He plots how he could make it better. The Bolts will always be Phil's team. He feels about it the way proud parents feel. New ownership has hired Phil to do the color for Lightning broadcasts, but he is like Napoleon at Elba, a general in exile.

Working with Phil this past year has been one of the pleasures of my career. As great a player as he was, that's how humble and decent and caring he is. I am honored to have had the privilege of knowing him.

I want to thank Mike Rees, my longtime friend and ally in the Little League wars, for introducing Phil and me. Since Phil lives in Tampa and I live in St. Petersburg, Mike figured the geography made for easy access. Mike also thought we'd make a good team. I also want to thank Henry Paul for his friendship and input and Peggy Sills and Ellen Brewer for their diligent tape transcriptions. It goes without saying, many thanks to editors Jonathan Webb and Mitch Rogatz for being so supportive throughout the entire process, and to copyeditor Peter Buck for his careful attention to detail.

Lastly, I want to thank my wife, Rhonda, and my son, Charlie, for making my life as full as it is. As Phil says, As long as you're having fun, what else could a guy possibly want?

PETER GOLENBOCK

Introduction

AFTER I SUFFERED a severe knee injury during the first playoff game against the Rangers in 1972-73, I was taken by ambulance to Massachusetts General Hospital in Boston. I had medial-collateral ligament damage. The next morning I was operated on. The surgeons transplanted ligaments from my elbow.

I remember coming out of the operation looking at the TV to learn we had lost the series to the Rangers and were eliminated.

The next day at about eleven in the morning Bobby Orr and a couple other of my Boston Bruin teammates came to see me. They said they were going to come back that night and take me to a party. I was game.

My wife at the time, Donna, said to me, "How are you going to do that? You can't walk."

I said, "Don't worry. These guys just had a few drinks. They aren't going to do anything."

But I was very wrong about that.

That night, around seven-thirty, the door to my room flew open, and there in a hospital gown, mask, and cap stood Bobby Orr. With him were Wayne Cashman, Kenny Hodge, Dallas Smith, Freddie O'Donnell and our trainer, Johnny "Frosty" Forristall.

Bobby said, "Wappo, we're taking you to a party."

"Whaaaaaat?" I said. "How are you going to do that?"

1

He said, "Don't worry about it. We're taking you."

I was in a full cast from my groin to my toes. My leg was in traction, up in the air in a sling. I was wearing only a hospital johnny and a sheet.

"Are you crazy?" I said. "What are you guys doing?"

Donna kept repeating, "What are you guys doing?"

They said, "Relax."

"Hon, it's okay," I said.

You might ask how they planned to get me out of there. Bobby had a friend who was a private detective. His job was to create a diversion. He went to the nurses' station and flashed a badge and said, "Where is the guy who got shot?"

The nurse said, "Nobody on this floor got shot."

He said, "Somebody got shot. And I want to see him." So while the boys came for me she was preoccupied making phone calls trying to find out if someone on the floor had been shot.

They wheeled the bed, levers, ropes, and all, into the hallway. There was an elevator across from my room, and when it opened, they pushed me in. They bribed the elevator operator, who was looking at us wide-eyed, to take us down to the basement.

When the elevator doors opened, they pushed my bed into the corridor. They pulled the sheet up over my head. Only my leg was visible. Donna was running beside me, and I could hear her saying, "Oh my God. Oh my God. Are you all right, Phil?"

I kept saying, "Yeah, yeah," and Bobby was saying, "Wappo, we got you. Don't worry. No problem." From under the sheet I could hear people in the corridor say, "Hey, that's Bobby Orr."

When we reached the exit, the guys couldn't get the bed through the doors because a metal post ran down the middle, so Dallas Smith, Kenny Hodge, and Freddie O'Donnell began rocking the post, and they ripped it right out of the cement! They wheeled me onto the street and into the cold Boston night.

Off we went toward a club Bobby owned called the Branding Iron, which was about a half a mile from the hospital. It was early

April in Boston, and I was freezing my balls off. As they wheeled me down the middle of Cambridge Street, I could hear horns beeping. Donna was trying to keep me covered with a blanket as we flew along.

Bobby kept asking, "Are you all right, Wappo?" I said, "Yeah, are we there yet?" Bobby said to me, "Wappo, put your left hand out. We're making a turn." Like an idiot I put my hand out. I said to myself, What am I doing?

By the time we got to the club, one of the wheels of the bed had broken, so the guys had to carry the bed inside and up twenty stairs to the party. I could see the veins sticking out of their necks, because the bed was heavy and I was not a light guy. But they got me up there and set me down in the middle of the bar.

Bobby yelled out, "Okay, the party can start now!"

They put bricks under the broken wheel, Bobby gave me a beer, one of the other guys gave me another beer, and Eddie Johnston grabbed a stinky provolone cheese and put it right between my legs. Guys would come over, cut off a slice of the cheese and eat it.

Meanwhile, the TV was on in the bar, and there was a news flash that said, "Phil Esposito has been kidnapped from Mass General Hospital."

Bobby said, "I guess I better call the doctor."

I said, "Yeah, Bobby, you better."

So he called Dr. Carter Rowe, the man who had operated on me, and told him I was okay.

Dr. Rowe said, "Listen, Phil has to get back. He just had a very serious knee operation, and if he falls he may never walk again, let alone play. We'll send a ambulance."

Bobby said, "No, we took him. We'll bring him back." And Bobby and the guys carried that bed all the way back to the hospital.

They got me back to my room and, to make a long story shorter, it cost me over $3,800 for a new bed and a new entrance door.

A little while later Bobby said, "Did you pay the bill?"

I said, "Yeah, I paid it."

He said, "What a great party, huh?"

I said, "You asshole."

And he left, laughing.

———

I have had one overriding philosophy in my life, which is to have as much fun as possible. When I played for the Boston Bruins during the glory years when we were perennial Stanley Cup contenders, most of my teammates felt that way. The spirit of fun and craziness, as much as anything else, made us the team we became. We were devil-may-care. We never held anything back, on the ice or off.

I remember one time when Wayne Cashman, my linemate and friend, was pulled over by the cops in Lynnfield, Massachusetts, for driving after having had a little too much to drink. When they gave Wayne his one phone call, he used it to call a local Chinese restaurant!

I lived nearby. One of the officers called me. He said, "Phil, we have Wayne here."

I said, "I'll come and get him."

He said, "He's pretty drunk, so we're going to leave him here in the tank for a while."

I went over to make sure Wayne was all right, and when I walked in, he was sitting in a cell with two officers eating Chinese food.

I asked, "What's this?"

One of the officers said, "We told him he had one phone call, and he called Kowloon." This was a great Chinese restaurant on Route 1 where we all went. He had ordered forty dollars' worth of food, and he and the cops were sitting there eating it.

Wayne said, "Espo, come on in and have some Chinese food." So I sat with them, and later I took him home. The cops were great that night. They protected us. Wayne was a sick bastard! We had so much fun.

Another time Wayne and I were in Oakland and we went into a sex shop, where we bought some toys. Wayne bought a doubleheader dildo. It was about three feet long, and he put it in his pants and went into a bar. The girls were sitting there watching, and he pulled up his cuff pretending he was scratching his leg like it was itchy, and that big dildo was sticking out at the bottom.

One girl screamed, "Oh, my God!" and we all broke out laughing. Cash said, "It pays to advertise."

As we rode on the bus from Oakland to the San Francisco airport, Cash decided to get rid of it, so he threw it out the window at a passing car. Can you imagine what the driver must have thought when that thing hit the windshield?

I asked him, "Why didn't you take it home to your wife?"

Wayne said, "Shit, no. She'll throw me out and keep the dildo!" We were so young and crazy.

━━━━━━

When Peter asked me if I was interested in writing a book about my life, I told him I didn't know if we could print some of the things I did and some of the things that happened. He said that if I told the truth, I could tell it all. I said, "That's the way I want to do it. I don't know how to do it any other way."

After beginning my life in a small town in Canada, I went on to become at one time the all-time single-season goal-scoring leader and the all-time single-season points leader. I was hired to run one NHL franchise, and I founded (and managed) another National Hockey League franchise, the Tampa Bay Lightning.

But I've also suffered disappointments and defeats. As a player I was traded, a shocking, humbling experience at the time, from my beloved Boston Bruins to our hated rivals, the New York Rangers, and twice I was fired as a general manager, first by the Rangers and then by the Tampa Bay Lightning. I was also divorced twice. Nothing, however, hurt me more than my having founded the Lightning and having the fat cats with more clout, power, and money take my team away from me.

Through it all, though, I feel if I can have fun every day, I have succeeded in life. I have lived a full life – several lives, in fact, as you will see, and in this book I will try to tell you about it as honestly as I can. If I have offended anyone, tough shit. I'm not sorry.

I'm now going to order in some Chinese food. Pull up a chair and make yourself comfortable.

1

I WAS BORN IN SAULT STE. MARIE, Canada, where three Great Lakes, Michigan, Superior, and Huron, join. When I was a young boy Sault Ste. Marie was a small town, and we never left our neighborhood. In those days we lived in the all-Italian west end. My friends in the neighborhood were Gino Cavacuello, Donny Muscatello, Clem Giovanatti, and Ross Hryhorchuk, an honorary Italian. Their relatives came from Italy to Ellis Island, and somehow, from there, they got on a boat going up the St. Lawrence, and wherever they found work, they stopped. Some of them stopped in Toronto, some in Hamilton, because it was a steel town, and some in London, but my relatives kept on going until they got to Sault Ste. Marie. It's a twin city to Sault Ste. Marie, Michigan. We used to throw rocks across to the American side. Little did I know I'd be spending my whole life in the United States and loving every minute of it.

I couldn't wait for the wintertime and the snow to come so I could play hockey. When I was four and my brother Tony three, my dad would make a little rink in our backyard, and we'd skate around. My old man put double runners on my shoes and pushed me out there.

I wish I could talk to my dad now, because there is so much I'd like to ask him. My dad told me he got kicked out of hockey because he punched a referee, and that it was during the Depression so he couldn't play any more, couldn't go to school any more. My old man was in the twelfth grade at age thirteen. He was highly intelligent. But he had to quit school to get a job.

He got a job at Algoma Contractors, which was owned by my mother's father. It was a company that collected the excess slag from the steel plant and took it to be recycled.

My grandfather, who was about six-foot-four, 280 pounds, was a huge man and a mean, sadistic bastard. He once put a clothespin on my penis. He held my hands and laughed. My grandfather would put dollar bills on a clothes-line, and we'd jump and try to get them, and he'd pull them away and laugh.

One time he got some glue and put it on his best friend's bicycle seat, and when the guy stuck there he had to take his pants off to get off the bike.

Even though my father worked for his wife's father, he started as a welder. He had a job. That was it. He was just a common employee. You have to fend for yourself in life. My dad had a job. But he was very smart, and he designed the separating plant, which had this huge magnetic belt that all the leftover steel would stick to, and he also designed the crushing plant, where the stones would go on and get separated into half-inch slag and three-quarter-inch slag.

My dad wasn't an alcoholic, but sometimes he drank, and I thought it had a lot to do with the fact he was working for my grandfather and then for my uncle and my mother's brother, and my grandmother was a pain in the ass too.

We called her Mamone. I'll never forget one time, when I was about seven years old, my grandmother came over to the house and in Italian started yelling at my dad. I didn't understand what she was saying. But my father told her, "Leave this house now. And if you don't fucking leave, I'm going to throw you the fuck out of here." He turned to my mother and said, "I am so tired of your family. I have had it." And when she began defending her mother, he said, "Why can't you defend me?" That started a knock-down, drag-out fight between the two of them.

My dad could be mean, and when he got drinking, he would get more mean. I remember once he threw an ashtray at my mom, and then he started going after her. I jumped right on his back and held on to his neck, and he was trying to fling me off. My feet were flying, but I wouldn't let go. I was shouting, "Stop it! Stop it!"

I don't want to paint my dad as a bad guy, because he wasn't. He and my mother sacrificed a lot so Tony and I could play hockey. Dad came to every one of my hockey games. He never said a word, until the end of the game, when if I scored he'd say, "You should have had two." To my last game, he was never satisfied with anything I did. At least he never told me he was.

———

Since the time I was a little boy, my old man gave me every opportunity to play hockey. I remember waking up at three in the morning, and Tony and I would look out the window and there he was flooding the yard to make a rink or shoveling the rink to get the snow off. I have fond memories of him doing that. He'd go back to bed and get up again at six to get ready for work at seven. As he was leaving to go, Tony and I would be out skating on the rink.

Tony and I got along pretty well. I always was the kind of kid who wanted to go outside to play. But he would say no.

"Why not?"

"I just don't want to."

I love the guy to death because he's my brother, but his ways sometimes just pissed me off. I remember during the summer we'd get a broomstick and one of my mother's Tupperware cups, and we'd play home-run derby. If it was a windy day, that cup would go all over the place, and if I beat him, he wouldn't play with me for

another week or so. But that's Tony. If he couldn't win, he didn't
want to play. He had to be the best.

That's why he doesn't play golf. It's why he won't play in Old-
Timers hockey games. If he can't play his best, he doesn't want to
play at all. But he was a goalie, and there is a difference. A lot of
goalies won't put the pads on and play in these charity games.

I'm entirely different. I know I was a good player, so for me to
play in a charity hockey event, what's the difference how well I play?
Tony asks me, "Don't you feel like an old fool?" My answer is, "Tony,
it's fun to go out and skate and play these charity games. Nobody's
going to get hurt."

So sometimes I don't understand him. He gets stubborn. And
for Tony, nothing is ever good enough. And I don't understand that.

When we got older, we'd wake up and skate until our mom
yelled out, "It's eight-thirty." Then we'd come in and get dressed for
school, which was right across the street. At dinnertime, which in
America is called lunch, we'd have an hour and a half, and we'd eat
as fast as we could and skate the rest of the time. We fooled around
with a puck and stick. I always skated with a stick. I don't even know
whether I can skate without one. You get a balance with a stick, like
a third leg. And we'd go back to school, and after school we'd skate
again until my dad would whistle us for supper at five o'clock. We'd
come in, and Mom would put newspaper on the floor, and we'd eat
with our skates on.

My dad came home at four, and every day we ate at five, because
he'd be really, really furious if the food wasn't on the table after he
came home. He would be like a bear.

My dad had a temper. I remember one time Tony was pushing
his spaghetti away with his fork. He said, "Aw, spaghetti again?" My
old man was holding his fork, and he threw the fork at Tony and it
stuck in his forehead. As my brother pulled the fork out, my father
said, "If you ever, *ever* push food away again, that will be the end of
you, pal. Don't you ever do that again. Now sit down and eat your

damn spaghetti, and eat it now!" Holy Christ, he was miserable when it came to food.

Truth be known, my dad was a foodaholic. He died because he ate so much food. He was very overweight. Later on, after he had a stroke – he had it at fifty-five and died at sixty-two – he would hide salami and pepperoni in the couch. My mother would never know, and when she left the room he'd take it and bite into it, and he'd say to me, "If you squeal, you're in trouble." He couldn't even walk then.

But let me tell you what my dad did when I was nine years old: There was a guidance counselor at school by the name of Mrs. Cunningham, and every month she would ask, "What do you want to be when you grow up?" I'd say, "I want to be a hockey player." That went on for months, and finally she got really angry with me. She sent a note home demanding my parents come and see her.

The three of us went into her office. I was petrified. I figured my father was going to kill me because I wanted to be a hockey player, and I had gotten in trouble for it.

Mrs. Cunningham said, "All the other children want to be doctors or lawyers or work in the steel mill. Phil says he wants to be a hockey player."

My father said to her, "So what's the problem?"

"Your son refuses to tell me what he wants to do when he grows up," she said.

He looked at me. "Is that true?"

"No, Dad," I said. "I want to be a hockey player."

"See what I mean?" she said. "Hockey is a sport, but it's just a sport. What does he *really* want to do?"

She looked at me again.

"I want to be a hockey player," I said.

My dad looked at her and said, "May I ask you a question?"

"Sure," she said.

"What is wrong with him wanting to be a hockey player?" he asked.

My father rose dramatically in my estimation. He could do little wrong after that. He could bust my face up if he wanted to.

"That's not realistic," she said.

My dad said, "Why not, if that's what he wants to do?"

"I think that's terrible," she said. And she never asked me about it again.

I didn't like school to begin with. I could not understand why I was learning about the fifteenth century. "Who gives a shit about what happened then?" I said.

One time I was playing baseball. I could really hit the ball, and during a game I hit a ball and broke a window of the King Edward School. I was called in and scolded by one of the teachers for breaking the window. I told him it was an accident, that I had broken it during a game, but he didn't care. I got a reprimand.

I was so angry at the teacher that at night I and the rest of my gang, who were called the Skulls, went out and threw stones at the school and broke about twenty windows. They all knew it was me, and this time I got myself in real serious trouble.

My dad had to pay for all the windows. He wasn't very happy with me. But after I did it, I told him why I had done it. I never asked Dad how much the windows cost. All I remember was that he didn't give me a beating. And that taught me a lesson. If I ever got in trouble, I was going to tell him right away.

At school they gave me the strap. You put your hands out, and the principal took this big horse strap, fourteen inches long and thick, and whacked your hands. I got ten on each hand. Goddamn, he hurt my hands. They were all swollen.

I was always the leader of the pack. The Skulls were the same guys I played sports with, Gino Cavacuello, Donny Muscatello, Nicky Kutcher, and Benny Greco. (Not Clem Giovanatti, because he was a brain, a smart guy, all the time better than us in school.) We wore black leather jackets. Elvis Presley was just coming in.

We weren't bad, nothing like the gangs of today. Mostly it was harmless fun. On Halloween one of the things we used to do was turn over garbage pails. I don't know why we did that.

We had a neighbor, an old guy, a miserable son of a bitch who was always yelling at us. One night we put dog shit in a paper bag, put it on his porch, and set it on fire. He came out, and he started stomping on it, and the shit was squirting all over the place. It was gross, but we were laughing like crazy.

He said, "I'll get you, Esposito. I know it's you."

I figured I'd better tell my old man, because if I didn't, the old guy would come to the house and I would really be in trouble. I told him, and because I told him, Dad was okay with it.

When I was fourteen years old, I finally did something I couldn't talk myself out of. There was an alley that ran behind our house, what we called the laneway, and one day I borrowed my dad's truck, and I drove Tony up and down the laneway.

Then we decided to get a little braver. One night after my parents left for the movies, Tony and I took Dad's '56 Mercury Monarch, put our sister, who had been born just a few months before, in the back seat, and went cruising.

Mom and Dad came home early, because my dad hated the movie, I guess. We were gone, and so was the Monarch. They were frantic with worry.

When we returned, I saw Dad's truck, and I knew I was in trouble. I didn't know what to do, so I sent my brother into the house with my sister. My dad came out, and when he saw me, he screamed, "You dirty son of a bitch. You little bastard." He started chasing me, and I ran, boy. I ran. We ran around the block, and when he got close he kicked me in the ass, and I kept running.

When I finally came home, my brother was hiding under the bed. I tried to hide too, but my dad grabbed me by the foot, yanked me out, and what a beating he gave me! That was the first time my nose was broken. He had to make sure I would never do that again. Because I was crazy. I was fourteen. I didn't have a license, but I *loved* to drive.

2

WHEN I WAS A BOY, I rooted for the Detroit Red Wings. Detroit was 365 miles away so they were the closest NHL team to us. I loved the Red Wings. Gordie Howe was my hero. Even though I was from Ontario, I hated the Toronto Maple Leafs with a passion. The story around Sault Ste. Marie was that the owner of the Leafs would never let an Italian play for his team. But Alex Delvecchio played on the Red Wings. Still, Gordie Howe was the man, and I wore number 9 until I was twelve, when my dad got five hundred dollars from the Chicago Blackhawks. He signed what they called a C form, which said if I ever made the pros, I would play for Chicago. Angelo Bombacco, a scout for the Blackhawks, arranged it.

After that I only wore Blackhawk sweaters, which I still think is the neatest sweater in all of hockey. It is absolutely gorgeous.

I wore number 7 all through high school and the minor leagues because of Mickey Mantle. I loved Mickey Mantle. He was *the* man. We didn't even have a television until 1958, so I would listen to the Yankees games on the radio. I'd sneak out of the classroom during the middle of the World Series, and I'd be gone for ten minutes. I'm sure the teacher knew what I was doing. "It took you this long to go to the restroom?" I'd say, "Ah, er, ah." I never knew what to say.

At home we had a Philco, and on Saturday nights my family would sit around that radio listening to *Hockey Night in Canada*. My dad would sit with us, unless he went and played cards with the boys. He would make a huge pizza and pop popcorn, and we'd listen to the hockey game until it was time for bed.

For us, hockey was a year-round activity. We always had ten or twelve kids to play, always enough. In the summer we played street hockey in running shoes. We played adjacent to the church, and we often broke the church windows. Monsignor O'Leary would get so mad at us!

We'd steal wooden horses and put them at both ends of the street so the cars couldn't get through. For a while we used two shoes or two bricks to mark the goal, but when the ball went through, it went down the street, and somebody would have to run and get it – over and over and over. We didn't have any money, so with my dad's help we built our own nets with two-by-fours and chicken wire. In the wintertime we'd carry those nets onto the ice. God, the kids today miss out on so much. Today you can go and buy a net with mesh for twenty bucks.

I never wanted to leave any game I was playing. When I was ten, I was playing hockey in the street when my appendix burst. But I wouldn't quit. I was hurting and throwing up all over the place, and finally I just collapsed. My mother threw me into the car, took me to Dr. Guardi who lived five doors down. He told my mother to get me to the hospital immediately.

They took my appendix out, and I remember when I came home from the hospital I had to sit by the front window watching my brother and the other kids play.

When I was eleven or twelve, we would go over to the King Edward School, build an ice rink, long and not very wide, and we'd play hockey. An older man by the name of P.J. Heaney would come over to where we were playing, and he would teach me how to stickhandle and pass the puck. Kids today don't have a clue about stickhandling. When you stickhandle, you don't have your head down. You have to be able to see the puck out of the corner of your eye. That's why Wayne Gretzky and Mario Lemieux were so good. Gretzky used to see the ice better than any human being I ever saw play hockey. Until someone else comes along, he was absolutely the smartest hockey player ever. People ask me, "Why couldn't anyone hit him?" You can't hit what you can't catch – not that he was fast, but he was so smart. Even when he lost a step when he got older, mentally he was just as sharp.

Not skating with his head up has been Eric Lindros's biggest problem. He goes across center ice with his head down. No one took the time to teach him when he was young because he was so much bigger than everyone else that if they hit him, he'd just run them over and he wouldn't get hurt. Now that he's a grown man and he's playing against grown men who are just as big as he is, he's getting nailed and suffering concussions. I would not be surprised if his coach tells his teammates, "Don't pass to Lindros across the middle of the ice," because he's going to get nailed again, and when that happens, that might be the end of his career.

At night we couldn't see the puck, and if it went into a snowbank we'd go crazy trying to find it, so instead we played a game called pump, pump, pullaway. One kid would get in the middle of the ice, and everyone else would go down to one end, and they'd yell, "Pump, pump, pullaway." Everyone would start skating, and the guy in the middle would start chasing after them. You would deke and dive and miss tags, and the idea was to be the last player not tagged. And quite often, I was that last guy. That game helped me with feinting and stickhandling. I always wanted to play pump, pump, pullaway.

After it got dark, my old man would whistle, and as soon as he whistled, not only would Tony and I go home, but all the other kids would go too. Everyone in the neighborhood knew it was the signal to go home.

"Guys, see you tomorrow night at five-thirty." And the next night we'd all be back out there playing pump, pump, pullaway. God, it was a fun time.

We even found a way to play hockey at night in the house. My mom would put flannel diapers on Tony's and my elbows and knees, and she would put wax on the basement floor, and she'd say, "Go ahead, boys, play hockey." And we'd play on our hands and knees and wax the floor. A lot of times, she'd be the goalie. The puck would be my dad's wool sock. We'd use our hands and hit the sock at my mother down in our basement. And we'd shine the floor for her!

I remember Mom and Dad, my Uncle Edward and Aunt Margaret, and Uncle Danny and Aunt Joyce used to have parties down in the basement. Tony would go upstairs and go to sleep, but I'd sneak down and sit right at the top of the stairs and listen to the music. I love Cole Porter and those romantic songs of the forties. I'd listen for hours to the music and their laughter, and I'd watch the dancing and everyone having a good time.

When I hit puberty, all of a sudden I became very shy, especially with girls. Jesus, I was shy with girls! When I was sixteen years old I went to Sault Collegiate High School. One time we were supposed to get on a bus to go to a cottage thirty minutes away for a school party. A couple of girls I really liked, Janie Quitanen and Bonnie Miron, were going to be at that party. But I felt awkward, geeky, out of place, and all of a sudden I felt the need to get away from there, and I ran all the way home.

I told my mother, "I can't do it. I don't want to be there." I know a lot of people don't think I'm shy, but I can get shy sometimes. I get insecure.

But it really bothered me because I didn't know what was wrong with me. I knew I loved sex, like every other teenage boy. One time when I was twelve this girl came over to our clubhouse, and we were kissing and fooling around, and she pulled her pants down and asked me to have sex with her. I did what I could. Another time my dad had a babysitter for us who was a lot older, and Tony and I tried to make her. So my shyness had nothing to do with sex. I was just shy about going to parties. And I could never speak in front of people. God forbid I had to get up and speak in class.

One time I went on a camping trip with my brother, and I called my mother and asked her to come and get me. I told her, "I don't want to stay here in the sand and the dirt, and I don't want to eat pork and beans."

After she picked me up, my old man said, "You big baby. You couldn't stay there?"

I said, "I didn't want to stay there."

My mother said, "If he doesn't want to do it, he doesn't have to."

Good hockey equipment was expensive. The first pair of skates my dad got for me were size 12, even though I had a size-8 shoe. I would put five or six pairs of his socks in there to fill up the space. My old man couldn't afford new skates. My feet were going to grow, and we got what we got.

Mom got catalogs from Sears and from Eaton's, and we'd tie them to our shins with rope to use as shin guards.

When I was eleven, twelve, thirteen, Angelo Bombacco would call us over, and we'd go to the back of his sporting-goods shop and he would give us hockey sticks and pucks. A couple of times he gave me a pair of hockey gloves. Angelo would do this for all the kids. His partner never knew. Angelo was that type of guy.

When I turned fourteen I played bantam hockey. The city of Sault Ste. Marie was divided into zones. Tony and I played for Zone 7. This was after we tried out for the Algoma Contractors Blackhawks team, which my uncle sponsored and Angelo Bombacco ran, and we didn't make it.

I'll never forget that tryout. I skated around the ice maybe twice, and if you went on skating ability alone, I was in deep trouble. At fourteen years old, I was five-foot-eleven but skinny as a bone, and awkward. I never was a great skater. Even after I made pro, reporters would write, "Esposito has to beat his man twice before he gets down to the other end." I never looked like I was going fast. But Gordie Howe didn't either. And try to keep up with him. Holy cripe! You couldn't do it. Gordie was unbelievable.

And so Jimmy "Chubby" Sanko made it, but I and a bunch of other kids were told to go and sit on the bench. We sat and watched the rest of the practice, and we were never asked to come back out and skate again.

Terry Murphy, who was one of the coaches, skated over to us and said, "Sorry, boys, we can't use you. Try again next year."

Angelo told me, "You aren't going to make the team." This was after Angelo had gotten me that C-form contract with the Blackhawks. I was good enough for the Chicago Blackhawks, but apparently I wasn't good enough for the Algoma Blackhawks. I didn't understand getting cut. My uncle owned the company, and my father worked there, and I couldn't make the team? I haven't gotten over that to this day.

So I had to play for Zone 7. We didn't have a company name, because we didn't have a sponsor. We had to supply our own equipment. Johnny "Clipper" LaNoche was our coach. Benny Greco was on the team, and so was Nicky Kutcher. We made it to the playoffs, but we couldn't beat the Algoma Contractors.

I remember a game we played against them. It was snowing outside, but we played in the Memorial Gardens, which was Sault Ste. Marie's indoor rink. An Algoma player, Paul Krumpetich, shot one from the red line and scored on Tony. That day they scored two from the red line, and I was furious. After the game, I said to Tony, "Are you blind? What's the matter with you? How could that happen?"

All the way home, pulling our equipment on a toboggan, I called him all sorts of names. I hollered, "You blind son of a gun. What's the matter with you? Are you blind?" It's one of the things I did that I regret to this day. Tony never said a word to me.

When we got home, I was still ranting and raving. I told my mother what had happened. She said, "I think we ought to get Tony's eyes checked."

It turned out that he was almost legally blind. He could see up close, but he couldn't see far away. And from that day on, Tony played with glasses and a baseball catcher's mask, and he was unbeatable.

At the end of the year the Algoma Contractors were headed for the all-Ontario midget finals. They were allowed to add four or five players to their roster, and Angelo Bombacco chose Tony and me. And we became the stars of the team. Tony was named the MVP of the tournament. Angelo has a scrapbook, and in it is a picture of me playing in that tournament with a caption, "Phil Esposito – most likely to turn pro."

Which surprised me, because no one had ever said anything like that about me before. Of course, the news accounts would also talk about the gangly, slow-skating Phil Esposito with a lot of skill. I was like Emmitt Smith. They said he was small and slow, and all he could do was score touchdowns. The criticism of my skating ability stopped after the Canada-Russia series in 1972. Before that I was always being compared to Bobby Hull or Bobby Orr. When we played the Soviets, neither Hull nor Orr were on the ice. And I became the difference. But that was a whole lot of years to have to listen to that bullcrap.

━━━

When I was seventeen my neighborhood team won the all-Canadian juvenile championships. We were all Italians. Pat Nardini and Tony Esposito were in the net. Our defensemen were Roger Desordo, Chester DePauli, Louie Nanne, Carlo Longarini, and Clem Giovanatti. One line was Chubby Sanko, Esposito, and Richard Lachowich – how the hell Lachowich made the team I'll never know! The second line was Harvey Barsanti, Lorne Grosso and Jerry Bombacco. The third line was Donny Muscatello, Fuzzy Pezzuto, and Chuckie Frayne. The coach was Abbie Naccarato. The trainer was John "Clipper" LaNoche. The manager was Angelo Bombacco. The stick boy was Norman "Sockeye" Ciotti. All Italians. And we won it all! What a team!

We beat Owen Sound, which is in Ontario, 11-0 in both games. We were an awesome team. Twenty of the players on the team should have ended up in the pros, but a lot of them didn't get there because they didn't have the courage or the chance to leave home.

After the last game of the hockey season, we would always have a party at our house. Even after I made it to the NHL as a player I would hold a party for the team. You have a couple of beers and let it all blow out.

When we held the party for the 1960 Algoma championship team we were all over sixteen, and we were driving, so my dad took the keys to everyone's car and he said, "Okay, I'm going to let you guys have some beer. But nobody's going to drive. You're all staying here tonight." My sister has a picture of Fuzzy Pezzuto, a little guy, sleeping in a dresser drawer. Another guy slept in my closet, another one in the bathtub – out cold. Four of us were lying in the bed – out cold. We were all plastered. Of course, it took only about three beers to get us drunk. My old man wouldn't let anyone leave. Everyone stayed and had a great time.

3

IN 1960 I TRIED OUT for St. Catharines in Junior A. I was eighteen years old. I went with Richard Lachowich, Jimmy Sanko, and Benny Greco. We made the team, but then one night we went out partying and came back around two in the morning. Kenny Hodge had a room at the top of the fire escape, and so we climbed up, rapped on his window, and he opened it and let us in.

We said, "Hodgie, don't you goddamn squeal on us."

We left his room and started walking down the corridor to get into our room when we were spotted by Bob Wilson, the Blackhawks' chief scout.

Wilson didn't say anything. He just turned and walked away, and we went to our room.

I said, "Boy, are we in trouble! We are in *big* trouble."

Richard said, "I don't think so. We'll be all right."

I said, "No. We're in trouble."

The next day Wilson called us in. He said he was sending Richard Lachowich and me to see the general manager over in Niagara Falls, another Junior A team run by a guy by the name of Hap Emms, who later became general manager of the Boston Bruins. Basically, because I was out after hours, the Blackhawks were giving up on me. Niagara Falls was owned by the Boston Bruins, and if I had made the Niagara Falls team, I would have joined the Bruins organization. Back then, there were thousands of kids in junior hockey and only six NHL teams. If they let you go, they didn't give a shit. It was a numbers game.

Richard and I went to Niagara Falls for a tryout. We got on the ice, skated around, and it was like that first tryout with the Algoma Contractors. After we skated two or three times, Emms said to us, "Listen, you two, if you're not good enough to make the St. Catharines team, what in God's name makes you think you can ever make my team?"

We didn't say a word.

"I want you to get off this ice and get the hell out of here," he said.

I said to him, "Why did you invite us to come play here?" But he never answered, and we left.

Several years later, after I made the Chicago Blackhawks, Emms did everything he could to stop the Bruins from trading for me. Milt Schmidt, who made the trade, later said to me, "It's a good thing I didn't listen to him. That fucking Hap Emms didn't know shit!"

So we went back to St. Catharines, and this time Wilson said, "You guys have two choices. You can go home, or you can play for either London, Ontario, or Sarnia, Ontario, in Junior B."

We found out that London had a horseshit little rink and were dead last the year before. Sarnia was a nicer town, so we decided to go there. Sarnia paid us ten bucks a week.

In 1960 there were four or five hundred junior hockey teams all across Canada. Every province had its own league. You couldn't be older than twenty to play. At the end of the season you played in a round-robin tournament for the Memorial Cup.

While I was playing for Sarnia, I attended St. Theresa's Catholic High School. I was in grade thirteen, which in Canada was the last year of high school or the first year of college in the States.

Halfway through the school year we were playing in Tillsonburg, which was about three and a half hours from Sarnia, and we didn't get home until four in the morning. The next morning I had to write an English exam. It was about nine in the morning, and I put my head down on the desk and fell asleep.

The nun woke me up and said, "Esposito, wake up and write your paper." I got mad, and I wrote on my paper, "I don't know nothing." And I signed it and put it down.

She said, "Leave this class." And I got up and left.

The next day I went back to class, and the Mother Superior – the principal of the school – called me into her office.

She said, "What are you doing? Why are you at this school?"

I looked at her and said, "I don't know. I'm supposed to go to school, so I'm at this school."

She asked, "Why are you here?" Meaning in Sarnia.

"I came here to play hockey."

She said, "We don't want any hockey bums in this school."

I said, "Well, Sister, I didn't come all this way to go to school. I came to play hockey. So you can stick your school." And I got up and left, and I never came back.

I told Richard Lachowich what had happened, and he said, "My God, Phil, your dad is going to kill you!"

"I know," I said. "I know." I was more afraid of my father than anything else. I figured he was going to beat the shit out of me.

I was out of school three months before I had to tell my dad. I didn't want to tell him. He was sending me ten dollars a week to go with my ten dollars a week from the hockey team.

But when we made the playoffs, he and Angelo Bombacco came down to see me play. They took Richard and me out for dinner.

Dad said, "How is school going?"

I said, "Dad . . . it's not. I got kicked out of school about three months ago."

Dad looked at Angelo and said, "The little son of a bitch. I knew it. I just knew it."

He looked at me, and I thought, Here it comes. I was waiting for the left hook.

But he said, "You better make it in hockey, son, because if you don't, you're going to be working in that steel plant for the rest of your life. If that's what you want, fine." And that was the end of it. He was with Angelo, and we were in a restaurant, and that night I scored 12 points in the game, and we won 15-3. I had played one of the greatest games I had ever played in my life.

But to this day I can hear him say, "You better make it in hockey."

That summer I went home and worked in the steel mill. I would be covered with dust and dirt, and when he'd see me, sometimes he'd say, "Hey, you like sucking the dust? You better make it in hockey." And he'd walk away.

———

I scored 47 goals and had 61 assists in 32 games for Sarnia, and after my breakout season I went to rookie camp for the St. Catharines

Blackhawks in the summer of 1961. I was nineteen, too old to be playing Junior A, I figured. I told myself I didn't have a chance in hell of making the team, and so I came to camp weighing about 228 pounds, and with nothing to lose. I just went out and had a good time.

Kenny Campbell was the coach and general manager of the team and a scout for the Blackhawks. One day he called me over and said, "Don't you want to play? Don't you want to play on this team?"

I said, "Yeah, I do."

He said, "Put some effort into the workouts. I mean, you're not even trying."

I said, "I am trying, but I'm not good at the drills. If we scrimmage and play games, I'll do a lot better."

It was true. I didn't like drills. I didn't want to do them. I didn't have a passion to do them. I wanted to play. I would rather have scrimmaged. Let's play hockey.

Rudy Pilous, who owned the St. Catharines Blackhawks, was coaching the Chicago Blackhawks that year. We were skating through drills, and I wasn't doing much. Then when we started to scrimmage, I started playing hard, and I scored a couple of goals.

Rudy said, "Hey, you! Fatso."

I said, "Me?"

He said, "Yeah, you. Come here."

I skated up to the boards. He was seated on the players' bench. He said, "You want to make this team?"

"Absolutely. I want to play hockey."

He said, "How much do you weigh?"

"Two-eighteen. Maybe two-twenty," I said.

He said, "Do you think you can get down to two hundred pounds?"

"I guess."

He said, "I'll tell you what: you go home now, you come back for the big camp in October, and if you're at two hundred pounds, I'll give you a contract and sixty bucks a week."

I left on the train for the Soo that afternoon. I had about five weeks to lose twenty pounds. I told my dad what the deal was. I really watched what I ate. My mother cooked me a lot of round steak because it doesn't have any fat on it. I didn't eat pasta. I cut out the bread. When I returned for the big camp, I got on the scale.

I weighed two hundred and one and a half.

Pilous called me in after practice. He said, "You didn't get to two hundred."

I said, "Yeah, but I'm at two hundred and one. Come on."

"I'll tell you what I'll do," he said. "I'll give you $57.50 a month. I'm taking $2.50 off because you're a pound and a half over."

"I'll take it," I said.

I scored 32 goals and had a hell of a year at St. Catharines. But I almost quit before I got started.

I didn't play much the first three or four weeks, and when I played, Ken Campbell put me at left wing. I would go to him and say, "Am I going to play, Ken? I gotta play."

He'd say, "Yeah, yeah, you'll get your opportunity. Don't worry about it." Like they always do.

About three weeks into the season I called my dad. I said, "I think I'm coming home. I'm not playing, and I don't want to lose my seniority at the Algoma Contractors." Which would mean that instead of working my shift from seven in the morning to three in the afternoon, I'd have to work from three in the afternoon until eleven at night, which would pretty much keep me from being able to play softball and have a couple of beers with the guys.

I decided that after the next game I would tell Kenny I was quitting. We were playing an exhibition game against Port Colborne, guys aged twenty-one to thirty-five who couldn't make it in the pros who were just playing intermediate hockey and having a good time. The center on our first line was Ray Cullen, a good guy who today lives in Boca Raton and owns car dealerships all over the place. Ray got hurt, and Kenny Campbell put me at center, and in that game I scored four goals. From that moment on, I played center, and I never looked back. Our left winger was Jack Stanfield, Freddie's older brother. Jack now runs Liberty Television out of Dallas. Fred was also on that team, along with Kenny Hodge and Dennis Hull.

At the end of that season in St. Catharines, I lost the scoring championship to Terry Crisp on the final day when he scored 15 points in one game against the London Knights. Terry had a player on his line by the name of Dubois, and God, could that kid score goals. Terry had three or four goals, and he had assists on seven or eight of Dubois's goals and a couple more assists, and he beat me out for the scoring championship by a couple of points.

I had come within one game of quitting. I had already told my father my intentions. I often think of the players with talent who don't make it because they don't get a break. When I talk to kids at banquets, I tell them, "You just can't give up. If it's what you want to do and you feel it in your heart, you've got to go for it. You can't give up until you have exhausted every possible avenue." I almost gave up, and I hadn't exhausted all my avenues. If Ray Cullen hadn't gotten hurt, today I would be living in the Soo weighing about 290 pounds working at the steel plant. I'd be getting my retirement pay and spending a week in Florida every year.

While I was playing for St. Catharines that year I also suffered one of my most embarrassing moments. I went to a YMCA dance, and during the evening I was dancing with Sandra Coleman, a classmate of mine at St. Catharines school. Sandra was beautiful. Her mother once said to me, "Don't call her Sandra. Call her *Saun*-dra."

Sandra – *Saun*-dra – and I were slow dancing to "It's All in the Game," by the Platters. I was holding on to her pretty close, swaying back and forth to the music, when she leaned back and said, "Do I dance like a flat tire?"

I said, "Excuse me?"

She repeated, "Do I dance like a flat tire?"

I said, "No, I think you dance great."

"Then will you kindly lower your jack," she said.

I had a hard-on, and I guess she was feeling it. Needless to say, it went down pretty quickly. I was so embarrassed, I didn't know what to do, and I just left.

4

AT THE END OF THE 1961-62 SEASON at St. Catharines, we played the Hamilton Red Wings in the semifinals. Hamilton had Paul Henderson and Ronnie Harris. During one of the playoff games in Hamilton, I went to jump over the boards to get back onto the ice. The boards were very high, higher than any I've seen before or since, and my foot got caught on the top of the board. I went down face first, and as I fell, I put my hands out, and I broke my left wrist.

I played the last five playoff games with a broken wrist, which was an incredibly stupid thing for me to do – it could have cost me my career – but I was a kid, and I didn't want to sit.

After we lost to Hamilton, I was called up to the Sault Ste. Marie Thunderbirds, a professional team in the Eastern Hockey League, to play through to the end of the season. From the EHL you can go right to the National Hockey League.

I shouldn't have played. I should have let my wrist heal. But this was a once-in-a-lifetime opportunity, so instead of resting, I came home and played in front of my dad and everybody in town.

When I arrived in Sault Ste. Marie, I didn't tell anybody my wrist was broken. I figured that if they found out, they wouldn't let me play.

The Thunderbirds had a player by the name of Jimmy Farrelli, a tough son of a bitch who took a liking to me. I told Jimmy about the broken wrist, and Jimmy showed me how to file the cast down so the shaft of the stick would fit in perfectly. I couldn't shoot very well, but I could pass the puck and stickhandle. Jimmy played the wing, and he would take the faceoffs for me.

We played against a big red-headed guy by the name of Jack Bownass, who tried to beat the shit out of me. He started pounding on me. Farrelli came to my rescue. He and Bownass had one of the best fights I've ever seen in hockey.

After we got back to the bench, I thanked him. He said, "That's okay, kid. Maybe one time when I'm in trouble you can return the favor."

We played the Kitchener Rangers, led by player-coach Red Sullivan, a center. Red had played for the New York Rangers and was on his way down. During the game he and I had a faceoff, and after I beat him to the puck, he slashed his stick across my ankles.

"What's the matter, kid, can't you take it?" he said.

Farrelli skated over and said to Sullivan, "Red, you do that again, and you'll deal with me." Red never bothered me again.

I played six games for Sault Ste. Marie. I didn't score a goal but had three assists. It was quite an experience to play pro hockey in front of my family and friends in my hometown.

Before the 1962-63 season I signed my first contract with the Blackhawks. Tommy Ivan, the Blackhawks' general manager, was in a hotel room in St. Catharines, and about ten of us who were waiting to go in and see him were sitting in the hallway on the floor.

While we were sitting there, Johnny Brenneman, one of my teammates, said to me, "Phil, I think I'm in trouble."

"Johnny, what happened?" I said.

He said, "I put my tongue down my girl's throat and I think she's pregnant."

"Are you kidding?" I asked.

"No," he said.

Johnny was really naive. He was seventeen, younger than we were. I explained to everyone sitting there what Johnny had done. For two days we told him, "You're in real shit, man." We would wag our tongues at poor Johnny, tormenting him.

It was finally my turn to go in to see Tommy Ivan. He had his glasses at the end of his nose, and he was reading. "Okay, son," he said, "how'd you like to turn pro?"

I had played six games with Sault Ste. Marie with my cast on. I said, "I'd like that. Playing pro hockey is what I want to do."

"We'll give you thirty-eight hundred dollars to play and a thousand to sign."

I said, "Fine." No questions asked.

I called my dad and told him.

He said, "Congratulations."

I said, "I don't know when I'm going to get the thousand, but when I get it, it's yours. Buy a boat or do whatever you want with it."

Dad loved to fish. A lot of times after he came home from work, he and Tony and I would get in the car and drive to Echo Bay, and for two dollars we'd rent a boat for a couple of hours and fish for perch, pike, and pickerel. We'd come home at night with twenty perch and a pike or two and my mother would clean them, and we'd eat them. Tony loved to fish more than I did. I had ants in my pants. It was easier for Tony to sit there.

I was really hoping in 1962 that I could play the whole year for the Sault Ste. Marie Thunderbirds, because I was engaged to my high-school sweetheart, Linda, and it would have been great for both of us to be able to live at home while I played.

Linda was in Tony's class, and best friends with Marilyn, who became Tony's wife. I actually took Marilyn to a movie once. I really don't remember meeting Linda. She and I just sort of knew each other from the beginning.

Our family had moved down to Shannon Road, and Linda had moved to McNab Street, up on the hill. I asked her out, and we went to a couple of dances together, and one thing led to another. She was tiny and very pretty, and a nice girl, and she could always make me laugh. She still gives me a shot every time I see her.

But before the 1962-63 season began, it was announced that the Sault Ste. Marie Thunderbirds were moving to Syracuse. That meant that Linda and I had to be apart again. And it turned out we couldn't draw flies in Syracuse.

We were scheduled to play a game against Ottawa, who had Jacques Laperriere and Cesare Maniago and a lot of great players. Before our game they scheduled a kids' game. There must have been seven hundred people in the arena, the parents and friends of the kids playing.

During their game I ran out of the dressing room in my long underwear. I went up in the crowd and yelled, "Don't go away! We're going to play next. Please stay."

Our coach, Gus Kyle, came out and yelled at me, "Esposito, get back in that dressing room."

I said, "I was just trying to get them to stay." And about 450 of them did stay. That was the largest crowd we had that season.

One of my teammates on Syracuse was Merv Kuryluk, who like most of the guys were a lot older than I was. Another teammate was Donnie Grosso, who came from the Soo with me. We called him Count Dracula, Count Chocula. He and I used to go out a lot. The three of us loved to gamble. Nick Polano, who once worked for Calgary, and Milan Marcetta also played cards with us. Gus Kyle called us the Chinese gamblers.

We would stay up all night playing cards. Kyle would say, "You fucking guys, you sleep all day and you wait for the night so you can get up and gamble." We played a game called bicycle one, two, three and another game called hi-lo, where if you had six-low, you could declare both ways. I lost a lot of money playing cards. We were kids. I was twenty.

Donnie Grosso and I lived together in a small apartment in Syracuse. While we lived there this young girl just sort of camped out in front of our apartment. She was all over me. She came to the bars with me. But she was young – she told me she was eighteen, but I suspected she was younger. At the time Steve Lawrence sang the song, "Go Away Little Girl." I knew I had to break up with her because I was having some pretty vivid thoughts about what I wanted to do with her, and knew it was wrong. I didn't know how to tell her we should stop seeing each other.

Donnie said to me, "Phil, she's too young." Then he said, "She's gorgeous though." She had a great little body.

We went out one night to the bar, and I said to her, "Listen, I want you to hear something." I put a dime in the juke box, and I played the song. She looked at me and started crying.

"Why would you do this to me?" she asked.

"You're way too young," I said. "I don't know how old you are."

She said, "I'm eighteen."

"No, you're not," I said. "I know you're not."

"I'm close," she said.

"You're too young," I said. "So just go away. Leave me alone. I just can't handle this."

She would call our apartment at all hours. She drove me crazy. Then halfway through the season we were told that because of poor attendance, we were moving to St. Louis. I was relieved, because I was getting away from her too.

We snuck out of town and moved to St. Louis and became the St. Louis Braves.

I drove from Syracuse under cover of darkness with one of my teammates – it was either Richard Lachowich or Jimmy Sanko – and we drove through the Soo just after Christmas and stayed for a week. Linda and I got engaged. I gave her a ring on New Years' Eve. Then I drove to St. Louis for our January 3 opener. Linda did not go to St. Louis with me.

In St. Louis, we played in an arena where the soot was falling from the ceiling. You'd cough on a towel, and it would be black. But I liked the building. Our dressing room was great. I had a great, great year in St. Louis. I scored 36 goals and had 54 assists that year, finishing with 90 points.

I remember one game we played against Omaha, a Montreal farm team that had moved from Ottawa. Cesare Maniago was their goalie, and Bob Plager, Barclay Plager, and Jacques Laperriere were their top players.

We were two men short. I got the puck in my own zone and started stickhandling up the ice. I beat one defender, and I beat another one. I looked around, and I had to beat the defender I had beaten the first time, and then I had to beat the second defender again, and I went in and scored against Maniago. When I came to the bench, Gus Kyle said, "That's one of the most beautiful goals I've ever seen scored in my life. You had to beat the same guys twice." I thought back to when I was playing midget and juvenile hockey, and they'd say, "The trouble with Phil is he has to beat the same guys twice."

I said to myself, "Things haven't changed much, have they?"

I played center with a winger by the name of Alain "Boomer" Caron. We played great together, and that year he scored 61 goals to lead the league and had 36 assists for a total of 97 points.

When I signed that year to play for the St. Louis Braves, I was making the minimum, twenty-five hundred dollars, but I lost fifteen hundred of it playing poker. At the end of the season I came back to the Soo owing Donnie Grosso fifteen hundred dollars, and I had to borrow the money from my dad and Uncle Danny, the younger brother of Nick, who owned the steel mill and the Contractors. My Uncle Danny and Aunt Joyce were my mom and dad's best friends. They would dance and laugh and drink and have a great time together.

Linda and I were supposed to get married in June, but because of the money I had lost gambling, we had to put it off. I didn't tell her the reason, but I told her, "We can't get married until August. I have to make some money during the summer."

I lived at home and worked at the steel mill. I operated a trackovator, a steel bulldozer on tank tracks. I drove it toward the open-hearth furnace, and a man in asbestos would take the excess hot lava coming out of the opening and, using a big bucket, put it on the truck.

I also drove Euclids, gigantic trucks. The tires are as tall as you are. You have to climb up into the truck, which hauls heavy-duty hot metal. It was a dangerous job. I once saw a man – his name was Enos Finos, a big, tough son of a gun – get run over by one of those trucks and get squished like a grape. It was awful. He was getting a piece of slag out of the way so it wouldn't rip the tires, but when you back up those trucks, you can't see because there is no mirror on the right side.

My cousin, Joe DiPetro, was backing up the truck, and it was very loud, and he didn't hear anything when he ran right over Enos.

Another employee who worked on the conveyor belt separating the slag lost his balance and fell on the belt. He went right into the hole and was smothered to death.

The entire operation was dangerous. One time a big chunk of molten steel fell out of a bucket and landed between my fuel tank and my back tires. I tried to rock the truck to get it away from there, but it was stuck. It wouldn't move. As I looked down, I could see the rubber inside the tire treads starting to burn. And the fuel tank was starting to turn red.

I got out of that truck and ran.

My father, who was a general foreman, said to me, "Where are you going?"

"It's going to blow," I said. "It's going to blow."

I wasn't away twenty seconds and then – BOOM!

Dad said to me, "That piece of equipment was your responsibility. You should have figured a way to get that truck out of there. Do you know how much that truck costs? Two hundred and fifty thousand dollars." And he laid me off on the spot.

That night when he came home, he said, "Son, that truck was your responsibility, but I'm glad you got out."

I ended up getting four days off without pay, which was fine, because I was able to play softball four days in a row.

When my brother came home from college in the summer, where did he work? While I was out in the shit, he was in the office. Tony had gotten a scholarship to Michigan Tech. The college boy got to work in the air conditioning. When my first daughter, Laurie, was born on August 14, 1965, I wasn't at the hospital with Linda. I was working my shift at the steel plant. We were living with my parents at the time. I ended up working in that steel plant until I was thirty years old.

5

LINDA AND I GOT MARRIED on August 19, 1962. I don't remember much about it, because I was pretty much hammered. So were Jerry Bombacco and my brother. The night before, we had a bachelor party at home. We drank and shot the shit. There were no girls around. We got really drunk. Before the ceremony I cut my throat so badly shaving that it looked like I needed stitches. I had toilet paper all over my face because of the nicks.

I never questioned getting married. I was sure I was doing the right thing when Linda walked down the aisle. She was petite, cute

as hell, beautiful, with big brown eyes. As she walked down that aisle
all I could think of was how gorgeous she looked.

———

I was invited to the Chicago Blackhawks' pre-season practice in the
summer of 1962. Linda stayed back at the Soo. Coach Billy Reay ran
a serious, tough training camp. We scrimmaged hard, but we didn't
have much fun. I wasn't made to feel part of the team by the older
guys. Bobby Hull treated me okay. So did Moose Vasko. Glenn Hall,
our goalie, didn't say anything. Stan Mikita, a centerman who was
very good on faceoffs and really smart at passing the puck, wasn't
friendly. Stan was later one of the first players to wear a helmet, a big
Northland Pro that looked like a football helmet. When I first knew
Stan, he was a little prick who never backed down from anyone. He
used to get the shit kicked out of him in fights on the ice. He always
had an edge, on or off the ice. He gave you the feeling he was better
than you. And when people do that to me, I tend to want to show
them. When I see Stan today in golf tournaments, he still has that
chip. Later in his career he changed his game to where he won the
Lady Byng Trophy as the most gentlemanly player in the game.

But when I arrived, Mikita didn't treat me very well and neither
did Pierre Pilote. Billy Hay treated me like I was trying to steal his
job. In practice he'd whack me in the ankles with his stick. It just
went with the territory. If you're a rookie, you're going to get
dumped on. I had to prove myself.

———

After going through the Chicago training camp, I played in a couple
of exhibition games, but they sent me back to the minors. I reported
to St. Louis for the 1963-64 season and Linda met me there.

That year Boom-Boom Caron and I were unstoppable. When I
got called up to Chicago on January 16, 1964, I was so far ahead in

the scoring race that I missed the last thirty-eight games and still finished third in the league with 26 goals and 54 assists for 80 points. Boom-Boom finished out the season with 77 goals and had 48 assists for a total of 125 points to lead the league.

I remember the last game I played for St. Louis. It was against St. Paul. Doug Harvey was player-coach for the Fighting Saints. I was standing in front of the net waiting for a pass when Harvey kicked my feet out from under me, and he said, "Welcome to the pros, kid."

On the next shift I beat him on a play and scored a goal, and I said, "Welcome to the minors, Doug." He was on his way down, and I was being a smartass.

In the third period I had a fight with Tracy Pratt, and we were both kicked out of the game when we wouldn't stop.

I was sitting in our dressing room when I heard the announcement, "Will the doctor please report to the St. Paul dressing room." I had broken Pratt's nose and jaw. I had a couple of black eyes, but I remember thinking it was worth it, that I had gotten him good.

That night Gus Kyle called me in the hotel room around twelve-thirty. "The Blackhawks want you to join them in Montreal tomorrow night," he said.

"Wow!" I said. "The Blackhawks in Montreal."

"Yes," he said, "we have a plane ticket for you tomorrow morning."

There were only twenty-seven games left in the season when the Blackhawks called me up, so Linda and I decided that she would drive home to the Soo.

I called all the guys to tell them I was leaving in the morning. I had never been on a plane before. At least five of them came to me and said, "You have to sit way in the back, right in the last row on the window. Sit in the corner, buckle your seatbelt and pull it real tight."

In those days we were flying DC-9s. If you sat in the back you felt the vibrations. You felt every bump.

But I didn't know that, and so like a dummy I requested a seat as far back as I could get.

I got a window in the last row. The plane took off, and all I could hear was the noise of the engine and all I could feel was the vibration! I was scared to death. There were people sleeping in the two seats between me and the aisle, so when I had to go to the bathroom, I couldn't get out, and I began cursing my teammates, because obviously this had to be the worst seat on the plane.

I was nervous and claustrophobic. I didn't even know you could turn the air conditioning on. It was one of the worst trips I ever took in my life!

When we got to Montreal, I got off the plane and made a beeline for the bathroom. I peed for two minutes.

When I met my Chicago teammates and told them where I had sat, Bobby Hull said, "Aw, Phil, they fucked you good."

I never sat in a window seat again. Whenever Bobby Hull and I flew together, he'd take the middle and let me take the aisle. If we went by train, he'd let me take the lower berth, and he'd go into the upper.

He'd say, "I don't care. I can sleep anywhere."

━━━━━━

When they brought me up to the Blackhawks, they sent Murray Hall down to St. Louis. He wore number 7, so I took his uniform number. I always tried to wear number 7. When I walked into the Blackhawks' dressing room, I found that my locker was between Bobby Hull's and Chico Maki's.

My first game, against the Canadiens, I sat on the bench until late in the third period when Chico was called for a ten-minute misconduct. Coach Billy Reay sent me out onto the ice, and I played center for three or four minutes.

Our next game was against the Detroit Red Wings in the Olympia. Back then the pre-game warm-ups were short. You would dress, go out on the ice, take a few shots at the goalie, and then you'd

Top left: My grandpa,
Anthony DiPietro.

Top right: Grandma Theresa,
who we called "Mamone."

Bottom: My parents, Frances and
Patrick Esposito, at their wedding.

Tony and me. He's five, I'm six.

Shoveling snow in front of Mamone's house.

My first Communion.

I became a member of the Sarnia Legionnaires in 1959. From left to right: two team officials, Chester DiPauli, Richard Lachowich, Jimmy Sanko, me, and the team president. I made ten dollars a week.

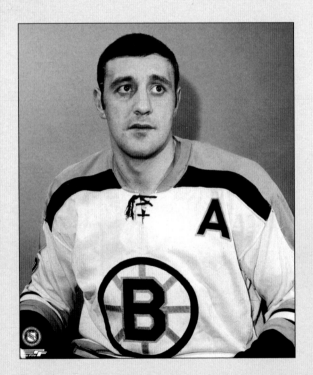

A Boston Bruin, 1967.
I had just arrived.

My first Stanley Cup, 1970.

Tony and me during the Canada-Russia War of 1972.

The Rangers were the last team I wanted to go to.

Donna and me
in Las Vegas.

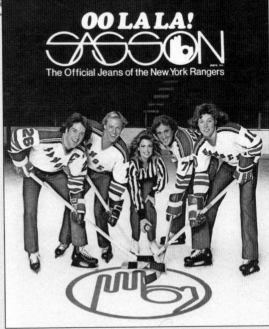

Dave Maloney,
Anders Hedberg,
Donna, me, and
Ron Duguay.
We had the look.

go out there and they'd dropped the puck. None of this twenty-minute warm-up like they have now.

Again, I didn't play at all the first couple of periods. I was sitting on the bench. I wore a size-12 shoe, and I had a size-10½ skate, and my feet would just kill me, so I was sitting on the bench with my skates untied. In the middle of the third period Reay all of a sudden shouted, "Esposito, get out there with Hull and Fleming, but let Bobby take the faceoff."

"Me?" I asked

"Yeah, you."

I tied my skates real fast and got out there.

"Billy said you should take the faceoff," I said to Bobby.

I took a position on the ice, and opposite me was Gordie Howe. Bobby yelled to me, "You got the old son of a bitch?"

I said, "Yeah, I got him. I got him." Gordie smiled.

I looked around me. On the ice were Bill Gadsby, a Hall of Famer, Alex Delvecchio, a Hall of Famer, and Ted Lindsay, a Hall of Famer. Glenn Hall, a Hall of Fame goalie, was at one end of the ice, and Terry Sawchuk, a Hall of Fame goalie, was at the other end. Pierre Pilote, a Hall of Famer, was out there, and so were Moose Vasko and Bobby Hull, a Hall of Famer.

I backed off and exhaled. I was very nervous.

The puck dropped, and Gordie Howe whacked me with an elbow right in the mouth at the bottom of my nose above my lip. He hit me so hard my teeth cut my lip. I still have the scar. I could feel the blood flowing.

I saw stars. I wheeled back, because tears were starting to form in my eyes, and I swung my stick at him. In those days we didn't swing at the head, we swung at the hips, and I smacked him, good.

The linesman got in between us, and I snarled at Howe, "You old fucking asshole piece of shit." I was bleeding like a sieve. In those days you didn't get stitches until after the game. I ended up with six stitches.

I went into the penalty box, and so did Gordie. Back then a cop or an usher sat between you and whoever was in the box from the other team. I went in first because I was from the visiting team. I had a towel, and I was patting my mouth, trying to stop the bleeding. Gordie was sitting there, and I looked past the cop and I yelled at him, "And you used to be my fucking idol, you asshole."

He turned and said, "What did you say, Wappo?"

I said, "Oh nothing, Mr. Howe. Absolutely nothing."

The next summer Gordie and I were sitting together on the dais of a banquet hall in Prince Edward Island, and he told me that if I hadn't responded to him the way I did, he would have owned me for as long as he played or as long as I played. He said he tested every rookie. He said, "You responded. You came back at me. And after that, if you noticed, I never bothered you again." Which wasn't quite true. He added that when I said to him he was my idol, he was flabbergasted, he didn't know what to say.

I scored my first goal in that game. Since I began playing hockey, I would study the opposing goalie during warm-up, the same way the goalies would study the shooters. I always tried to find spots where the goalie was vulnerable. Back then there were only six teams, and you could learn a goalie's tendencies if you paid attention.

I noticed that Terry Sawchuk had a habit of folding down on his right knee whenever a skater was coming in on him alone or if he didn't know where he was going to shoot.

I skated onto the ice with Reggie Fleming and Bobby Hull. Bobby took the puck at center ice and passed it up to me. I got a breakaway, and bore down on Sawchuk. When I saw him bend down on that right knee, I drilled the puck over his right shoulder into the upper left-hand corner for my first goal in the NHL.

You never forget your first goal. Many years later I was the color commentator for the New York Rangers when Reijo Ruotsalainen scored his first goal. Sam Rosen, who was my broadcast partner, said to me, "He's supposed to be the new Bobby Orr." I said, "Yeah, right,

Sam. The only thing they've got in common is that they both have two legs, two arms, and a friggin' head."

So Ruotsalainen scored his first goal, and after Sam announced that, I said, "Sam, he will never, ever forget that goal. That goal will be etched in his memory forever." Sam described the goal, and I repeated, "I can't believe it. This is a goal he will never forget. He'll never forget it for his whole life."

Sam still didn't pick up on what I was getting at. The play continued and there was another whistle, and I repeated, "Ruotsalainen scored his first NHL goal. He will never forget that, Sam."

Finally, Sam caught on. He said, "By the way, Phil, where did you score your first NHL goal?"

I said, "Sam, I can't remember."

Sam almost fell on the floor laughing.

━━━

That first year with Chicago I ended up with three goals, but I only got to play one shift a game. Every time you stepped out onto the ice, it counted as a full game. So I got into twenty-seven games, which turned out to be two games too many for me to qualify for the Calder Trophy for rookie of the year the following season.

After the season Bobby Hull said to me, "They made you play two extra games." I asked him what he meant. He said, "Next year, if you play good, you could have won rookie of the year. Now you can't."

I'm convinced that Tommy Ivan, the general manager, and Billy Reay, my coach, did this to me on purpose, keeping me from earning the twenty-five-hundred-dollar bonus in my contract for winning the Calder.

The next year I ended up with 23 goals, which was like hitting .300 in baseball in those days. I finished with 55 points, tenth in the league. Roger Crozier ended up winning the Calder, but I felt I would have had a shot at it. Roger had played goalie with me in

St. Louis, but he was behind Blackhawks goalie Glenn Hall, and no one was going to replace Glenn. Roger ended up going to the Detroit Red Wings.

That first year I lived on Wolf Road in Hillside, Illinois, near Dennis Hull and Doug Jarrett. After practice, the three of us would go to a bar half a block from my apartment called Doc Stimac's, where we drank beer and ate chicken wings. After we drank enough beer, we'd go back to one of our places and watch the Three Stooges from four to five in the afternoon. We'd make popcorn, watch the Stooges, and when it was over the other two would go home and have dinner with their wives. Then we might go back to Stimac's after dinner.

I hung out a lot with Dennis Hull, Bobby's younger brother. Dennis was a lot of fun. He was witty and funny. His wife was actually Dennis's best audience. One night we all went to a Christmas party and we got blasted. Before long, Dennis's wife said to him, "Dennis, you asshole, I'm leaving. You can stay."

It had snowed heavily and Dennis said to me, "Let's grab the back bumper of her car when she leaves and go skiing."

Just as his wife got in the car and started the engine, Dennis grabbed the back bumper and prepared himself to be pulled along by the car using his shoes as skis. But instead of going forward, his wife put it in reverse and backed up, and I could see Dennis sliding under the car when I yelled for her to stop.

She stopped just in time to keep him from getting run over. She got out of the car and helped us get him out from under the car. She said, "Get in the car, you stupid fool." Dennis was lucky he wasn't killed.

I learned a lot that first year. I got to go places I had never been. We went to Los Angeles to play a pre-season exhibition game. L.A. was in the Western Hockey League then. Howie Young, that lunatic, played for them, and I ended up getting a charley horse when I was whacked by Dougie Jarrett, him and his fat ass. Dougie got me real good. We didn't wear thigh pads like they do now. We had just a little nylon cloth in front, nothing in the back. Anyway, I got a charley horse, and I didn't want to tell my coach, Billy Reay.

Bobby Hull's mother-in-law lived in Malibu Beach not far from Doris Day, and Bobby said, "Come with me." I was twenty. Bobby was twenty-four. We went down to the beach and I tried to go in the water. My thigh was beginning to turn black and blue. I was really hurting.

Afterward we went over to Paramount Studios. We went to watch *Bewitched* being filmed. I met a girl on the show named Lisa Sharf. God, she was good-looking. I said to Bobby, "Man, I got to get a piece of that one, I'll tell you that!"

I talked to Lisa Sharf for about a half an hour, trying to get her to come to dinner. She wouldn't come. I didn't have any money. I was dressed in plaid slacks. I had a beard because we were bumming around and I hadn't shaved. I was limping.

Then out of the blue Elizabeth Montgomery came walking up. She was wearing a flowing, pink negligee for the shoot. Elizabeth was tall and beautiful. There was a glow around her. She was one really gorgeous woman. And for years after that I watched *Bewitched*, because she turned me on. I still watch the reruns.

When we got back to our hotel room, I found I could barely walk because of the charley horse. I said, "Christ, Bobby, my leg. I can't even bend it. How am I going to play?"

He said, "You better call Billy Reay and tell him you can't play."

"I don't want to do that," I said.

We had a few beers and we got to talking back and forth. He said, "Phil, you got to call him."

So I got on the phone and called Billy Reay's room, and I said, "Hey, Bill, Phil Esposito here. I got a pretty bad fucking leg right here!"

Well, when Bobby heard me say that, he started to laugh. And he started laughing so hard that he made me laugh.

Reay said to me, "What are you guys doing?"

"Bobby's laughing at me because I can't move my leg," I said. "Billy, I can't play today." Bobby was still laughing.

"You guys are drunk, aren't you?" Reay said.

"No, we're not drunk," I said. "Honest to God, I can't move my fucking leg."

"Then I'll send you back to Chicago."

I said, "No, no, no, don't do that. Come on. I've never been out here before. I'll try to play."

He said, "Fine."

I hung up the phone. Bobby was on his hands and knees, with his head on the bed, dying from laughter.

"What is so funny?" I asked Bobby.

He said, "'I got a pretty bad fucking leg right here?' Say what?"

"I didn't know what else to say."

To this day when Bobby Hull sees me, the first thing he says to me is, "I got a pretty bad fucking leg right here."

When we got back to Chicago from the road trip, they put me in the hospital, because I shouldn't have played on it. But Billy Reay had said he was going to send me back to Chicago, so I played. A calcium deposit started growing on my thigh. I was in that hospital quite a while.

———

Bobby Hull, as everyone knows, had the hardest slapshot of anyone playing hockey. One time Bobby hit me in the ass with a slapshot.

Bobby and I used to have a set play on faceoffs. Even though he was a left-handed shot, he'd line up on my left on the right side of the goalie as I drew on the backhand. He was very quick with the release. My job was to win the faceoff and head to the net. This one time, I did exactly that, and he nailed it and hit me right in the left cheek of my ass. Fortunately, he hit me with the flat side of the puck and not with the edge. I can't describe the pain to you! The doctor later told me that if it had hit me on the edge, it would have shattered my hip.

I skated back to the bench and sat down. I leaned on my right cheek, keeping my left cheek up in the air.

"Holy shit, does this hurt!" I yelled.

The trainer, Nick Garen, said, "What can we do?"

"I don't know what you can do," I said, "but it hurts."

Eventually the pain began to subside and I was able to go back into the game. After the game I could barely sit to take off my skates. I walked naked toward the shower into the little room with all the mirrors, and my teammates started laughing at me.

"What's the matter with you guys?" I asked.

They said, "Look."

I looked at my left buttock in the mirror, and I could see the faint outline of the Blackhawk imprinted on the cheek of my ass.

The next day the area from below my knee up to just above my hip on my left side was totally black and blue. It was so bad I had to have blood drawn with a needle.

6

THE BLACKHAWKS HAD A GREAT TEAM that year, the 1964-65 season, and we made it into the playoffs. I remember Billy Reay took the team to Rockford, Illinois, to get away from Chicago as we prepared for them. Bobby Hull, Chico Maki, a few of the other guys, and I went to this bar in Rockford, and I guess I was busting the bartender's balls, so the bartender said, "I'm not serving you any more."

"What's the problem here?" I asked.

"You're too drunk right now," he said. "I can't serve you."

Bobby Hull reached over and grabbed this guy with his right hand, lifted him up and over the bar, and said, "You better bring us some beer, or I'm going to whack you." Then he let go of him, and the bartender just sort of slithered back behind the bar.

Holy shit, I thought to myself, Bobby's strong.

Afterward, Bobby and I were walking back to our hotel, and we were pissed off, so we started throwing rocks. We were betting fifty cents on who could take a rock and break a street light. I won. We knocked a few out. Stupid! When I think about the things I did when I was young, I shake my head. It was just crazy stuff. But in those days there were only six teams, and the guys were very close. We're still close all these years later.

In the seventh and final game of the playoffs against Montreal, a game that was played in Montreal, we trailed 1-0 when I went out on the ice for a faceoff.

Bobby Hull said, "Don't let them win it clean, Phil."

"I won't," I said, "but goddamn, our defense has to jump in there."

I stood in the circle with Jean Beliveau, their Hall of Fame centerman, my idol. The official dropped the puck, and I didn't lose it 100 per cent clean, but I did lose it 80 per cent clean. The defense couldn't move in fast enough, and Beliveau went to the point with it, passing it back to Dickie Duff, who shot it in, and we were goners. We lost 4-0.

Man, that hurt. I blamed myself for our losing the Stanley Cup. Goddamn, I should have won the faceoff or at least tied it up – that was my job. But I missed it. Beliveau won it clean. And I stayed with him, like I was supposed to. Dickie Duff was right there and put it in. So mine was not the only mistake. Still, I lost the faceoff.

I had to live with that all summer. Oh man, I didn't like that. And then the following year Billy Reay wouldn't let me take any faceoffs. He would pull me off the ice and put in Stan Mikita or Billy Hay. I was really good on draws, but I didn't get another chance to show what I could do until I was traded.

I scored 23 goals my second year in Chicago with 32 assists to finish tied for ninth in the league in scoring. We went to the semifinals of the Stanley Cup – we lost to Detroit. Detroit was then beaten in the finals by the Canadiens.

The player I remember most vividly from watching that final series and later playing against him, was the Pocket Rocket, Henri Richard. That son of a bitch was the best centerman I ever played against. He was good on faceoffs. He was fast. The little bastard could score. He was a tough little guy, and I really respected him.

It was while I was with the Blackhawks that I began to get involved with the Players' Association. Ted Lindsay was the player who started it in the mid-1950s. He was with the Red Wings at the time. The association didn't have much clout because Gordie Howe refused to join. Gordie wouldn't buck Jack Adams, the Red Wings' general manager, or Bruce Norris, the team owner. In fact, Teddy Lindsay ended up getting traded from Detroit to Chicago because of his union activities. Bruce Norris considered Teddy a troublemaker, and got rid of him, though he got a couple of good players in return.

Norris traded him to his brother, Jim Norris, who owned the Blackhawks and a piece of the Rangers and Madison Square Garden. Jim Norris didn't care whether Lindsay was trying to start a union or not. Jim didn't give a shit what Lindsay was doing, because he was sure he was wasting his time. And to tell the truth, it was a waste of time, until Bobby Orr joined the league in 1966. Alan Eagleson was Bobby's agent. Eagleson had gotten his hooks into Bobby when Bobby was thirteen years old. Bobby then brought Eagleson into the organization. The story I heard was that Lindsay and Eagleson met, and Lindsay agreed to go along with his pension plan, and then almost every player signed up within the next two years.

In the beginning we paid three hundred dollars a year toward our pension, and the owners matched it. I started taking my NHL player's pension in July 2002. I played in the NHL for nineteen years, and I am now getting thirty-two thousand dollars Canadian. It's not very much, considering what the players are making today. But the current players don't care that a lot of the guys who busted their asses for them are living in poverty. And it's too bad.

———

In 1966-67, I scored only 21 goals, but I had 40 assists for a total of 61 points. Bobby Hull scored 52 goals that season, and I probably got 25 points assisting on his goals alone.

Bobby had come to Chicago in 1957 and quickly established himself as the best all-round player in the game. A good-looking man with a lot of charisma, he was called the Golden Jet. If he was playing today, he'd be as dominant as Barry Bonds or Tiger Woods are now in the world of sports.

I first met Bobby when I was seventeen years old. He came to the Soo to be the grand marshal at our Community Day Parade. He was twenty-two, already a Blackhawk and an All-Star.

After the parade they held a dance, and Linda and I went to it. Bobby asked Linda to dance with him. I could see he was three sheets to the wind.

She asked me, "Can I?"

"You don't have to ask me," I said. "If you want to dance with him, go ahead." I was pissed but I couldn't say no.

They went out onto the dance floor. A Canadian country singer by the name of Tommy Hunter was also at the dance, and it seemed to me that they wanted to pass Linda back and forth between them. Or maybe it was my paranoia or my Italian ancestry.

Finally, I walked out onto the dance floor, and I said, "That's enough. Come on, Linda."

Bobby said, "Relax, kid." He started laughing.

"Some day I'm going to tell you about this, you son of a bitch," I said. "You'll see. You're going to hear from me."

"Yeah? What are you going to do?" Bobby asked.

"I'm going to be playing with you, and I'm going to tell you about this one day," I said.

I didn't bring it up the following year at the Blackhawks' training camp. Bobby had befriended me. I figured he had been so drunk at that dance he didn't remember what had happened.

When I made the team the next year, Bobby and I would go out and have a few beers after practice. He said, "You know, you should make this team this year. You have Billy Hay, Stan Mikita, and Eric Nesterenko playing on the third line. You should make this team."

One night we had a couple of beers. I said, "Remember when you were in Sault Ste. Marie, you fucking asshole?"

"What are you talking about?" he asked.

"You messed around with my girl," I said. "She's my wife now."

"Linda?"

"Yeah, Linda."

"I remember her," he said. "Aw, we were just having some fun with her."

"You prick," I said. "You would have screwed her too, wouldn't you?"

"No, Phil," he said. "Absolutely no way. No."

"Bobby," I said, "you'd screw a snake if you could catch it. Who are you kidding?"

He laughed with that infectious laugh he has. We were always good buddies.

"I told you then I would bring it up to you," I said.

He said, "I do remember your saying you were going to be playing with me some day. Do you know how many kids have said that to me?"

I said, "Well, here I am, sucker."

———

In 1966-67, the Blackhawks finished in first place in the regular season, breaking the Muldoon curse. Pete Muldoon had been the Blackhawks' first coach, and when he was fired in 1927, he said, "The Blackhawks will never win a championship." So it took forty years before we finally we broke the curse. That year my 61 points put me seventh in the league in scoring. In three years I went from ninth to eleventh to seventh.

We went to the Stanley Cup semifinals and lost to the Toronto Maple Leafs with Terry Sawchuk and Johnny Bower, both Hall of Fame goalies. We didn't know which of those sons of bitches was older, but they played really well. They were the reason we lost – no doubt in my mind.

They beat us, and then they went on to beat the Montreal Canadiens for the Stanley Cup. It was the last Stanley Cup Toronto ever won. When the New York Rangers won in 1994, the Blackhawks gained the distinction of having the longest tenure without winning the Stanley Cup. The Hawks haven't won since 1961. The Rangers hadn't won it since 1940. When I later played for the Rangers, I can't tell you how many times I heard the chant, "Nineteen for-ty! Nine-teen for-ty!" I used to say, "Who cares? None of us was even born then. Who gives a shit about 1940?"

I didn't have a real good playoff series in '67. The Leafs' Pete Stemkowski and Bob Pulford, a hard-nosed centerman, were on me, and I didn't score any goals.

After we lost, we had a windup-of-the-season party. Bobby Hull and I got very drunk in the dressing room. I said to Bobby, "See those two guys over there?" meaning coach Billy Reay and general manager Tommy Ivan. "They've got a hell of a team here, but they're gonna fuck it up, guaranteed."

"Why don't you go over and tell them?" Bobby said.

I said, "I think I will." And I walked over, and I was saying, "We've got a great team here, you could almost have a dynasty, but you two are gonna screw it up," when Bobby came over and dragged me away from them. He was laughing, and I was laughing, and we took off.

"I opened my big mouth again." I said.

Afterward I said to Bobby, "Why did you let me do it?"

"I didn't *let* you do it," he said.

"Yes, you did," I said. "You pushed me to do it, you bastard." And Bobby started laughing again.

A day later I went to Tommy Ivan's office to get my expense money. I said to the secretary, "I'm here to see Mr. Ivan and get my expenses."

She buzzed him, and I could hear him yell, "You tell that son of a bitch I don't want to see him. I don't care about him. Just give him whatever he wants and tell him to get out of my sight. If I ever see him again, it'll be too soon."

I think I knew then I was not coming back. Six more teams were coming into the National Hockey League. There was going to be an expansion draft, so I felt I was going somewhere.

I figured what I had said to Ivan and Reay prompted them to trade me, but later I was told that Jim Norris, the Blackhawks' owner, didn't like the way I played. I was a big guy, but I was more of a finesse player than a tough guy, and Norris didn't think I played physical enough. Plus I had a little bit of a mouth, and I stood up for myself. I was told it was Norris who said, "Get this guy out of here."

Linda and I took off for our home in Sault Ste. Marie. I had bought a cottage in a place called Point DesChennes, also called Point Louise. I paid seventy-five hundred dollars, and I had to borrow the down payment from my Uncle Danny. On the front of the cottage was a carved plaque of a Blackhawk Indian.

While we were driving, I said to Linda, "I don't know for sure whether I'm going to be back in Chicago. And I don't know where we're going."

"I don't see a problem," she said. "Why don't we just stay home? You can go to work in the steel plant and forget about hockey."

As soon as I got home, I worked my shift at the steel plant like I always did in the off-season. I played softball in the evenings, went out afterwards with the guys for a few beers, had a great time, and then came home.

A couple of weeks before the expansion draft, which was held in June 1967, I was speaking at a banquet in Sault Ste. Marie. Jesse Owens was the main speaker, and a bunch of us were down in the basement of a friend of mine, Russ Ramsey, who ran the radio and TV station. Russ had sponsored the banquet, and we were visiting him.

Somebody said I had a phone call. Bobby Hull had called the house, and Linda told him where I was.

Bobby said, "Phil, they traded you. Did you know that?"

"To where?" I asked.

"To Boston," he said.

"You're kidding me."

I announced it at the party. There was a lot of media there, so in effect I announced my own trade. Of course, as soon as Mr. Ramsey found out, he had me go on the radio and talk about it.

Linda found out before I did. Neither Tommy Ivan nor Billy Reay called. Instead, their public-relations guy, a guy named Murphy, who we called Porky Pig because he dressed like a slob and looked like the cartoon character, was the one who called the house.

The trade was Kenny Hodge, Freddie Stanfield, and me to the Bruins for Jack Norris, Pit Martin, and Gilles Marotte.

I was in shock. I was no longer a Blackhawk. I was a Boston Bruin. You don't think that you're *ever* going to be traded – trust me, you don't.

I came home about one in the morning, and I walked to the front of my cottage and I took down the Blackhawk plaque. I brought it into the house.

"What are you going to do with that?" Linda asked.

I said, "I don't know yet."

I put it by the side of the fireplace. I didn't have the heart to throw it in the fire.

7

THE NEXT DAY I GOT A CALL from Milt Schmidt, the general manager of the Boston Bruins. I was still in shock. He called to welcome me. He said, "We're really happy to have you. We think you can be a great player for us, but you've got to get yourself in better shape and condition." All I could think to say was, "Thank you." I really didn't ask him any of the questions I needed to ask.

The next day I drove alone to Houghton, Michigan, for my brother Tony's graduation from Michigan Tech. I was having a great time, drinking a few pops with those college guys. My God, did they drink! I always wondered how they got through school. At the dormitory, if you opened the back window, all you saw were empty beer cans. This was college?

Milt Schmidt tracked me down on the phone at my brother's.

"Phil, Milt Schmidt here."

I said, "Hello, Milt."

"I want to talk to you a little bit more," he said. "You're up for contract, and we want to talk to you about that." I was making about $8,000 a year. He wanted to give me ten, and I wanted twelve.

"There's no sense talking about my contract," I said. "There are three things that I want from you. I want $12,000 a year."

"Impossible," he said.

I said, "I'm not even through with the other ones. I don't want to be bothered about my weight – not one iota."

"What are you talking about?"

I said, "From the time I've played in Chicago, I had to pay them ten dollars for every pound over 192. Every paycheck I was twenty or thirty dollars light because I could never get under 195. I want to play at my weight, and I want to be comfortable."

"I can't have you come in at 210 pounds," he said.

"Why not?"

"What do you weigh now?" he asked.

"About 205."

He said, "Will you come to camp at 205?"

I said, "Okay." That's why it said I weighed 205 in every Boston Bruin media guide and program. (That year I played at around 210, and I had the greatest year I could ever have.)

Milt wanted to know what the third thing was.

I said, "I have a wife and a child, and I want to make sure I live in a nice house. I don't know anything about Boston." Whenever the Blackhawks arrived in Boston, we took the bus to the Boston Garden, which was downtown. I never got to see the nice parts of the city.

"Are you going to rent or are you going to buy?" Milt asked.

"How am I going to buy? Are you going to give me a five-year contract for $100,000?"

"Are you crazy?" he said.

"Then how am I going to buy?"

"I understand that," he said. "We'll help you find a nice house."

"Okay, those are the three things."

He said, "I cannot say to you that we can give you $12,000. In fact, I won't. Ten is all you're getting."

"Well then, I'm not coming."

"Suit yourself."

"That's how I feel," I said, and I hung up the phone on him.

I went back to work for my uncle at the steel plant. I told Linda, "We're not going to leave Sault Ste. Marie. We're going to stay here." She was thrilled. And at that point my intention was not to go back to playing hockey.

After the NHL draft in June, I got another call from Milt.

"What are your plans?" he said.

"What do you mean, what are my plans? I told you what I needed. I'm not budging until I get it."

"What if we give you $10,000 and some bonuses?" he asked.

I said, "Bonuses?" I was smart enough to know how that game is played. I did it myself later when I ran the Rangers and the Lightning. You throw in bonuses for winning the Hart Trophy or the scoring championship, knowing the player can't possibly achieve that, just because the agent wants it, and knowing if you throw it in, the player thinks he's getting something of value.

I had no intention of grasping at thin air. I wanted something concrete. I told him, "Last year the Boston Bruins finished dead last. The Blackhawks went to the finals. My salary was $8,000 and I made $3,800 more from the playoffs. Add it up, and I made $11,800. All I'm asking for is what I made last year, because the Bruins aren't even going to make the playoffs."

"You don't have much faith in your teammates," he said.

"I don't even know my teammates," I said. "I just know what I know from playing against those guys."

"We've got Bobby Orr, who is going to be a great player."

"I played against him," I said. "He's a kid. He's not gonna carry the team."

"We have Johnny Bucyk and Gerry Cheevers and Eddie Johnston."

I said, "Well, shit, you had them last year, and it sure didn't friggin' do anything for you."

"I'll tell you what I will do," he said. "I'll give you $11,000, and if you score twenty goals I'll give you another $2,500. If you score thirty goals, another $3,000, and if we make the finals, you'll have another bonus coming."

I figured I could achieve those goals, and I said "Okay." (That year I ended up making $16,500 because I accomplished all my bonus goals except for our making the finals.)

My brother and his friends wanted to know what happened and I told them. I said, "Well, it looks like I'm going to Boston, guys." I added, "Okay, let's go out and celebrate!"

We played in a softball game. They had a keg of beer at second base and another at home plate. I said, "What is this?" Under the rules, if a player got to second base he had to drink a paper cup of beer. If he got home, he had to drink another paper cup of beer. A lot of runs scored. A lot of beer was drunk.

By the time one of the players got to third base he had no clothes on. The other players had ripped them all off.

Linda came up for the graduation ceremonies with Tony's girl-friend, Marilyn, whom he married that summer. Linda and I then drove back home together.

"I guess we're going to Boston after all," I told Linda.

She wasn't very happy about it. "I don't want to go to Boston. Why don't we just stay here?"

"Look, I want to go, and we're going to go," I said.

I had to go back and tell my uncle I was quitting the steel plant again. They threatened not to hire me back the next summer, because I was taking some guy's job and the union didn't like it. But they always hired me back. I worked in the steel-recovery plant another five years.

I drove by myself fourteen hours from Sault Ste. Marie to London, Ontario, where Boston had its training camp. I should have taken the American route, highway 75 to Detroit and then gone across to Windsor, but in those days we stayed in Canada, driving down Highway 17, which was a two-lane road all the way to Barrie, Ontario. It was a tough drive, but I had driven it a hundred times.

As I drove, I felt really nervous. I arrived in September for six weeks of training. I got to the hotel around three in the afternoon, and as I was checking in, I met the other guys. I was looking for Freddie Stanfield and Kenny Hodge, because I had played with them in Chicago. I met two new teammates, Ronnie and Danny Schock, and I met Milt Schmidt and the coach, Harry Sinden.

They assigned me to a room with Teddy Green. Teddy was the meanest, toughest son of a bitch, with whom I had had some altercations. He had kicked the shit out of me a couple of times, and now I was rooming with him. I thought, Geez, Teddy Green.

I went up to the room carrying my equipment bag. I opened the door. Green was lying on the bed. I introduced myself. He said, "I'm Teddy Green. Come on in and drop your stuff." We didn't shake hands. "I remember you from the Blackhawks."

"Teddy, you're one of the good players on this team," I said.

"Yeah, we've got a pretty good team," he said, "but to tell you the truth, we have a pretty cheap owner."

"Jesus, why does it make this team any different from any other?" I asked. And it didn't.

Greenie and I sat there and talked about the team. I asked him about different players. "How's Bobby Orr?" He said, "A great guy." After we talked for a while, we went over to a bar called the London House, which became our place during camp. Beer was fifteen cents a draft. You could put a buck on the table and get blasted.

I was impressed by the fact that almost all the guys were over there having a beer. There had to be forty guys drinking in there, and I got to meet them all. After that, I felt a lot better. I felt pretty good about the whole situation.

I got ready to go to the ice pretty early the next morning. Greenie said to me, "Where are you going?"

I said, "I've got to go. I have to get my sticks ready."

He said, "Aw shit, I'll see you over there."

I walked into the dressing room alone, and the first guys I met were Frosty Forristall, the equipment manager, and Danny Canney, the trainer.

Frosty said, "Hey, Phil Esposito, how the fuck are you, man?" He had that Boston accent. He said, "Man, you drive over here with your cah?" I said, "No, I walked over. They won't let us drive. They want us to walk."

He said, "Yeah, that's fucking Harry Sinden. He wants you to fucking walk." Every other word was "fucking." He said, "What do you need, kid? I got your hockey sticks. Chicago sent over whatever they had. I got to get you a pair of pants and shoulder pads." Frosty was terrific. So was Danny. They made me feel so at ease.

We were sitting there, and I was trying on all the equipment, getting ready to go out on the ice. All of a sudden, I heard, "Hi ho, hi ho, it's off to work we go . . ." The door flew open and this guy shouted, "Clear the track, here comes Shack."

It was Eddie Shack, who had been traded from Toronto to the Bruins the same day I was traded. When he walked in, Frosty said to me, "This fucking guy is a fucking lunatic."

"I know," I said.

"You haven't seen anything yet, Phil," Frosty said. "I've been on the phone with him. He's crazy."

Shack came around and said, "Hey, Phil, how are you? I'm Eddie Shack. We're gonna have a good time this year. We're gonna have a good team." Everyone was impressed with Shackie's attitude. He was the one who broke the ice for everyone. He was the one who said, "We've got a good team. Let's go to work."

We went out on the ice and had a great time. For the first three days of practice, we never touched a puck. We were so sore, especially those poor goalies who had to skate with all the equipment on. All of us had worked jobs in the off-season, especially the married guys. Everybody but Bobby Orr, who was only nineteen, but had gotten big money.

I would practice from nine to eleven in the morning, walk back to the hotel, usually with Greenie or Gerry Cheevers, have lunch, and rest until one-thirty. We had to be back to practice from two until three-thirty in the afternoon. Often I would stay after practice for about fifteen minutes and shoot pucks. If the goalies didn't want to stay on, I'd shoot into the open net.

I'd shower, and go to the bar at the London House and eat pickled eggs. I can't tell you how many eggs we ate and beers we drank. They also served pigs' feet, but I wouldn't eat that. We were all watching what we ate, because the coaching staff would continually yap about our weight. I wore a rubber jacket under my equipment to try to keep my weight down. Guys would even take Lasix – piss pills – to try to dehydrate themselves before the weigh-in.

After a few days in training camp we formed teams and played a round-robin tournament. The Green Bullets, which was Greenie's team, played against the Smithereens, which was Dallas Smith's team. There was also a Cheezie team and a Shackie team, led by Gerry Cheevers and Eddie Shack. Fourteen players to a team. We'd each put ten bucks in a pot, and we'd play for that. Then we'd take the losers' hundred and forty bucks to the bar and everybody would join in and drink and eat. It was great fun.

Linda came to join me in London, but I was spending all my time with the guys and very little with her. She probably would have been better off back home in the Soo. She left a few days after she arrived and went to stay with her parents near Toronto until camp was over. We probably should not have gotten married.

During training camp I fell in love with a college girl from London by the name of Shirley. We called her Mainsie. She was gorgeous. I really liked her a lot. She had a great sense of humor. She loved the song "Gypsy Woman," and we would play it and dance to it. She had a friend, Colleen Higgins – Higgie they called her – and she was gorgeous too. I won't tell you who the player was, because he's still married to the same woman, but he really liked her, and Higgie liked him. I think she ended up with Dougie Favell (who later played for Philadelphia). Boy, did Mainsie and Higgie like to party and dance and drink. They were fun. We had a blast with them, a blast.

Had Mainsie been more receptive to me, she was the type of girl I really would have gone for. My biggest problem was that I would fall in love with them. The other guys could find 'em, feel 'em, fuck 'em, and leave 'em, but not me. I don't know what it was, but I just seemed to fall in love with them. I treated them nice all the time. I guess I just didn't know what love was all about. I would argue and fight with the ones I loved, but the ones I didn't love I treated nicer. That's weird, isn't it?

Several years later, Mainsie drove from London to Detroit to see us play. I left her two tickets, and when she walked in, I hardly recognized her. She looked like "Two-Ton" Tony Galento.

I said, "Shirley?"

"That's right," she said. "It's Mainsie."

I said, "Come on, sit down."

She said, "Well, I need two chairs."

"What are you talking about?" I said.

"I need one for each cheek," she said. "Don't you see how fat I've gotten?"

"Well, yeah, you have gained some weight."

She said, "More to grab."

She was still hilarious.

I always looked forward to training camp. Most guys didn't, but I did. One time Gerry Cheevers and I walked to the rink. We were very sore. Cheezie and I were shooting the shit, talking about the other guys on the team, and as we were walking – Gerry saw it first – this little garter snake slithered in front of us.

"Holy shit, a snake," he said.

"Where?" I wanted to run.

Turned out we were both afraid of snakes. I was grabbing him, trying to get away, and he was pulling on me, trying to go in another direction, and we looked like something from the Three Stooges. When we got far enough away, we started to laugh.

"We can't tell anyone about this," I said.

Cheezie said, "Look at us. Two tough guys afraid of a little snake."

"I can't stand snakes, Cheezie," I said.

"Neither can I," he said.

For years we never told anybody. It was a private joke between us. We'd be on a bus going to a game, and he'd look at me, and I'd say, "Remember the snake," and then we'd laugh, because we didn't want the guys to know we were so chickenshit.

Gerry was such a character. Right after I was traded to Boston, we played the Montreal Canadiens, and we lost 6-2.

After the game all of us were sitting there with our heads down when Milt Schmidt came into the dressing room. He was kicking the lockers and punching the walls, throwing things, going crazy.

Gerry Cheevers was sitting kitty-corner from me beside the doorway leading to the showers and bathroom. He had his goalie pads and pants on, but he had taken his belly protector off, and he was sitting there with his fat belly hanging out, smoking a cigarette and drinking a beer.

Milt went around the room, giving it to the players. When he got to me, he said, "You wop bastard. You piece of shit. I should have left you in Chicago the way you play. I can't stand the way. . . ."

Then he got to Cheevers. During the game the Canadiens' J.C. Tremblay had flipped the puck from the red line, and it had bounced past Cheezie and gone in.

Milt said, "Cheevers, you must have felt like a complete asshole."

"No, Miltie," Cheezie said, "I didn't feel like an asshole at all." The room was silent.

Milt took two or three steps, turned around, and said, "You didn't feel like an asshole? Then how did you feel?"

Gerry took a hit on his cigarette and a sip of beer and said, "I felt like a queer."

Everyone looked at each other as if to say, What is he talking about? There was silence.

Milt said, "A queer? What do you mean?"

"Let me put it this way, Miltie," Gerry said as he took another puff and another sip. "If you had fifteen thousand people calling you a cocksucker, what would you feel like?"

Well, Jesus, we died laughing. The whole room broke up, and even Milt started to laugh. He couldn't help it. Milt then turned around and walked out. And we went on a roll, won the next bunch of games in a row.

After that game I figured, Whoa, we have a good bunch of guys here.

Gerry would tell jokes on the bus, plane, and train. In the Dean Martin–Jerry Lewis movies they always had this short, fat guy who would sit up front in the audience and laugh all the time. That's who I was to Gerry Cheevers. The guy made me laugh. He said some very funny things. We'd make up sports questions and play Jeopardy for hours. In those days we bused a lot, and playing games really helped make the time go.

Cheezie and I once picked the all-ugly team in the NHL. We picked Eddie Johnstone, who played for the Rangers, and Larry Keenan, who used to play for the Blues and the Sabres. We picked them because they didn't have any teeth. When they took their teeth out to play, man, they were ugly! Jimmy Roberts was on that team, too. He wasn't really ugly, but we picked him anyway.

I remember we picked the all-stupid team. Reggie Fleming was on it, because I said he wasn't very bright when I was with him in Chicago. They called Reggie "C.H." They kept calling him that, and I didn't know what it meant. Finally, I found out. It meant "Cement Head."

As we were picking the all-stupid team, Kenny Hodge asked us, "Who are you going to put at right wing?" Cheevers looked at me, and he gave me the eyebrows and said, "Ooh, I think Hodgie could make that team."

"No, no, come on, we can't do that," I said.

Cheezie said, "Okay, okay, but he's a close second."

We also picked the all-good-looking-wives team. Of course, we said we had to exempt our wives.

What made the Bruins special was that it was made up of a bunch of characters who could play. Garnet "Ace" Bailey was another one. He was the captain of the Ignorant Squad. Four of us – Johnny McKenzie, Cheezie, Ace, and I – belonged.

Throughout the year after the games fans and other people were constantly streaming in and out of our dressing room. Sometimes charities would bring in sick kids. Perhaps a kid would be wearing braces, and it broke our hearts to see this, but if you know anything about athletes, you know they have a way of making light of a sad situation. If they brought in a kid wearing braces, Ace would say to us, "He couldn't play on this team." Or he'd say, "Can't skate." And we would die laughing, because it was a way of relieving the tension.

One time a kid suffering from Elephant Man's disease (neuro-fibromatosis) came into the dressing room. He had a very large head, and Ace looked at him, and the three of us couldn't imagine what he was going to say. He whispered to us, "Can you imagine what would happen if you got a pin and stuck it in the kid's head? He would go around the room, *pssssssshhhhhhh.*"

I laughed, but I was appalled. I said, "Acer, that's the most ignorant thing I ever heard of in my life." And on the spot we made Acer the captain and MVP of the all-ignorant team. God, was he awful!

Acer didn't play regularly, but when he got in there, he played hard and well. Later he went to Edmonton and played wing on a line with Wayne Gretzky. Wayne and I have talked about him ever since he was killed on September 11. Acer was on the second airplane that crashed into the World Trade Center. I was in Los Angeles when it happened. At six in the morning I got up to go to the bathroom, and I turned on the TV set and they said, "Breaking News," and I sat on the edge of the bed and watched the second plane go into the tower. I was stunned. They started talking about terrorists, and later the names of the people on the two planes were scrolled at the bottom of the screen, and one was "Garnet 'Ace' Bailey." It was surreal. I just sat there all day. I never left my chair. Acer was something else.

8

HARRY SINDEN was the greatest coach I ever played for. He saw something in me that I didn't even know I had: my scoring potential. I knew I had hands, as they say, and I had developed the snapshot from watching Bobby Hull when I played in Chicago. By the time I arrived in Boston, the hooked sticks were becoming popular, and I was starting to get pretty good at snapping the puck.

It was in training camp my first year with the Bruins when Harry came to me and said, "I'm going to make you our scorer."

"That's all right with me," I replied.

He said, "I'm going to get you two players who are going to get you the puck."

I couldn't have been happier.

Harry put me on a line with Kenny Hodge and Ronnie Murphy, a veteran who had come to the Bruins several years before from the Rangers. Ronnie had played on a line with Johnny Bucyk and Don McKenney. He was a left winger, a smart player. But he would make me mad, because he didn't seem to give a shit whether we won or lost. If we lost, he'd say, "We have another one tomorrow night."

Meanwhile, if I had a bad game, I'd be furious with myself. I'd be bitching and moaning, calling myself names. Ronnie would say, "Kid, don't worry about it. You have another game in two days." His attitude was, who cares? It used to drive me crazy.

Hodgie and I had a great relationship right from the beginning. I knew him from junior hockey when I played in St. Catharines. He was fifteen then, a few years younger than I was. He was big and strong. He wasn't a regular, but a real good kid. If Hodgie had a fault it was that an opponent could talk to him and be nice to him, and Kenny wouldn't play as hard. If the opponent was an asshole and antagonized him, Hodgie would try to kill him.

Harry Sinden would say to me, "Park yourself in front of the net. That's where you're going to play, and we'll get you the puck. You're going to be our scorer." Every day at practice Murphy would pass me the puck, and Kenny would pass me the puck, and I'd practice snapping pucks at the goal.

Bobby Orr had been a rookie the year before, and he hadn't developed into a great player yet. He was only nineteen years old, but it would not be long before he would be able to carry the team. The only other twenty-one-year-old who did that was Wayne Gretzky. Even Mario Lemieux didn't do it. You've got to be surrounded by great players, and maybe Mario wasn't. On the Bruins, Bobby was surrounded by good guys.

When I came to the Bruins, Bobby was very quiet. He did come out with the guys for the most part, even though he was under-age, because the bartenders knew who he was and let him in. Every once in a while he'd get carded and have to go back to the hotel. Maybe they felt the police were watching. I don't know. Sometimes, when they wouldn't let him in, we'd all say, "Fuck you. We don't need this place. We'll go someplace else," and we would.

I remember that first year being in a place called Campbell's. Cheezie, Bobby, and I went on stage, and we sang "Ob-La-Di, Ob-La-Da" by the Beatles. Oh, were we bad! Bobby was single, and he was a lot younger than I was, so we didn't pal around all that much, but on the ice we really clicked. I really understood Bobby's game. I knew what he was going to do with the puck, and he knew where I was going to be, especially on the power play, when he would wind up and I would cut in front of him and shield the goalie, and he would fire that puck into the net.

Bobby Orr was the fiercest competitor I ever met. He *hated* to lose. My God, did he hate to lose. And if he didn't like what was going on out there, he would give you that Irish dirty look and, holy smokes, it could kill you. It was a mean look. Bobby could be mean.

Some of the Bruins would come to me and say, "Bobby hates me. He just doesn't like me at all." I knew how they felt. I knew Bobby was a good guy, but on the ice he could be cutting and merciless.

Bobby was single, and my first year as a Bruin he roomed with Eddie Johnston and Frosty Forristall. Boy, did they have parties in Boston. I didn't go to a lot of them. The married guys would come, stay a little while, and then take off. But I can tell you, their parties were wild. Bobby Orr was cute and a good guy, and a great player, and he could have gotten laid any time he wanted. Before he met his wife, there were broads coming out of his room at all hours of the day and night. And if he wasn't in the mood, he'd say, "Hey, why don't you go screw my buddy over there?" and they would. I thought Bobby was absolutely terrific. He didn't meet his wife, Peggy, until

1972. The first time I met her, I thought, What a beautiful, beautiful woman she is. And she was really nice too.

My first year in Boston, at forward we had Eddie Westfall, Johnny Bucyk, Johnny McKenzie, Ken Hodge, Freddie Stanfield, Eddie Shack – and don't forget Derek Sanderson. What a character Derek was! It was the first year of the amateur draft, and the Bruins took Derek. He was a rookie, and that year his job was to kill penalties. He played with Eddie Westfall and Wayne "Swoop" Carleton, who we got in a trade with Toronto. They were our checking line. We had Stanfield between McKenzie and Bucyk, and I played center with Tommy Williams and Kenny Hodge. That's all, just three lines. Everybody got to play a lot, and I loved it. I would find it hard to play in today's era of four lines, and so would Bobby. That 1967-68 season our power play was great and so were our penalty killers. We were a good solid hockey team.

On defense we had Bobby Orr, Ted Green, Don Awrey, Dallas Smith, and Gary Doak, and Gerry Cheevers played in goal.

Wayne Cashman came to camp but he was sent down to the minors after he broke his jaw. When Wayne drank, he became nuts. This night he was on the balcony of his hotel room on the second floor, and he was drunk. He tried to jump from his balcony to the next one over. He didn't make it.

We had some great nicknames on our team back then. Johnny McKenzie was "Pie," Bucyk was "Chief," Teddy Green was "Greenburg," even though he wasn't Jewish. We made him Jewish.

Let me tell you why Johnny McKenzie had the nickname "Pie." The story I heard was that the team was traveling by train, and Johnny was trying to get into the upper berth. His bare ass stuck out of the berth and was perfectly round, and the guys saw it and started laughing and said, "Look, his ass looks like a pie." Then Johnny stuck his head out, and he has a perfectly round head, and they said, "Shit, his face looks just like his ass, perfectly round, like a pie-face." And that's why they named him "Pie-face" or "Johnny Pie."

I remember going tuna fishing with Pie, Shackie, Chief, and Freddie Stanfield. We had the day off and left early in the morning and headed twenty-five miles offshore of Gloucester, where the "Perfect Storm" took place. The captain had a pink balloon for me, a black balloon for Freddie, a white balloon for Pie, a blue one for Bucyk, and a yellow balloon for Shackie. They would be out on the riggers, and we'd be sitting there playing cards and drinking, waiting for a fish to hit, and we were getting blasted.

We would rotate the balloons every fifteen minutes, and for hours we didn't get a single bite. If the pink balloon was out, it was my turn if we got action. The captain yelled, "I see fish." I perked up, even though I was pretty much hammered by this time.

Well, the balloon sank and bobbed back up, and I took the reel. As I sat in the chair I felt like I was pulling a log. I couldn't believe how heavy that fish was.

After about twenty minutes, my hands were bleeding, and my arms were sore, and the reel was smoking. Johnny Bucyk was getting water from the ocean and throwing it on my reel and all over me, and my crotch and balls were freezing! I bet you my dick shrunk to an eighth of a centimeter. At the same time, Shackie poured a beer down my throat.

Finally, the captain backed the boat up, and we gaffed the fish and took it on board. It weighed seven hundred pounds.

The next day at practice I was so sore I could barely raise my arms over my head.

We didn't want Harry and the other coaches to know we had gone fishing, so during practice I said to Shackie, "Give me a tap on my arm, 'cause I can't move my fucking arm, and I can't shoot." Shackie whacked me in the arm, and I pretended he had really hurt me, and I went into the dressing room and told Danny Canney, our trainer, what we were doing. He said, "Okay, okay, I'll get you out of it." He told the coaches, "Phil has a bad bruise. He can't come back for practice. We're going to try to do everything we can to get him ready for the game tomorrow."

The next night I played, and I was fine.

Later on we did the same thing when Eddie Johnston got into an argument in the bar in London, Ontario, and broke his hand.

It was a stupid fight. I was sitting between Kenny Hodge and Jimmy Harrison, who said, "Pass the salt."

Hodgie said, "You got a broken arm? Get the salt yourself."

Harrison said, "You fucking asshole," and he grabbed the salt and threw it at Hodgie.

"Will you two guys stop?" I said. I looked at Kenny. I said, "Stop." And as I was doing that, Harrison reached over to nail Hodge and punched me instead. Hodgie then started in, and Eddie Johnston tried to break it up.

Harrison said something really bad to Eddie, and Eddie said, "You fucking creep," and whacked him. Later he came into my room and said, "My hand is swollen."

We didn't want the coaches to know, so the next day on the ice during practice Shackie snapped one at Eddie. He went to stop it with his blocker, and he hollered, "Jesus Christ," then went into the dressing room and never said anything. They had his hand X-rayed and found it was broken. He said the puck got underneath the blocker. That wasn't it at all.

Eddie missed about four weeks. If management had found out, they wouldn't have paid him. But that was the kind of team we had. We covered for each other. And our trainers covered for us too.

━━━━

That first year in Boston I ended up second in the league in scoring, behind Stan Mikita. We finished the regular season in Boston, and after the game was over I was in the lead. But Stan was still playing, because it's an hour earlier in Chicago. He ended up scoring three points in the game, and he beat me out for the scoring championship. I really would have loved to have won it.

In 1967-68 the Bruins finished third in the league and made the playoffs for the first time in nine years. We played the Montreal Canadiens in the opening series and lost in four straight. We couldn't score against Gump Worsley. But we knew things would be different the next year.

After one of the Montreal games, we took the bus to Dorval Airport. After you walked in the front door, it was a long walk to U.S. Departures. Harry Sinden stopped to get a drink at a water fountain. I wanted to get a drink too, and I stood behind him. When he turned around, I said, "Harry, if we keep progressing like we're doing and the nucleus of the team stays, in three years we're gonna win the Stanley Cup."

He said, "Phil, we're getting close."

Tommy Johnson, our traveling secretary, was standing with us, and he said, "From your lips to God's ears."

———

Midway through that 1967-68 season, Harry Sinden sent Ronnie Murphy down to the minors and replaced him with Tommy Williams, who had played on the American Olympic team in 1960. Williams was later traded to the Minnesota North Stars, at the end of the 1968-69 season, and Sinden replaced him on left wing with Wayne Cashman. I don't know why Harry put him there. Wayne was a right-handed shot, and he had played right wing in Junior A. But Cash was so good in the corners and so good in that off wing that he could play either side.

Wayne would say to me, "Throw it in my corner and get the fuck in front of the net."

"I will be there, Wayne," I would say. "Have no fear."

With Wayne on one side and Hodgie on the other, my job was to skate to the hashmark area in front of the net. They would get me the puck, and I would snap it into the net.

Our team also improved as Bobby Orr improved. By the 1968-69 season, Bobby had become the most dominant defenseman ever to play the game. He played thirty-five to forty minutes every game. And when Bobby was on the ice, I would tailor my game to fit his. Normally I liked to carry the puck up the ice. When Donnie Awrey and Teddy Green were on defense, I'd go deeper into my own zone, and I'd bring it up. But when Bobby played, he wanted to carry it, and I let him. I don't think anyone even noticed I was doing this. With Bobby back there, I didn't have to come back so deep.

Bobby was amazing. God blessed him with talent, and then a few years later his knee was wrecked. And that was too bad. In those days you didn't have the arthroscopic surgery you have today.

My second daughter was born during that season on February 12, 1969. I was on the road when Linda gave birth. When I called the hospital, Linda told me she had named her Carrie Lynn. Several days later, after we returned to Boston, I went to the hospital and drove them home to Braintree. Harry Sinden had promised me a nice place to live, and he kept his word. He had traded Don McKenney to Toronto, and he arranged for me to rent McKenney's house for the season.

In the 1968-69 season I broke the 100-point mark. I attribute a lot of my success to positioning myself in the right spot. Offense is positioning, just like defense. And the asshole coaches nowadays don't believe it. It's getting yourself in position and counting on your teammates to get you the puck. People would say, "He's a garbage collector." Well, I scored a lot of goals in front of the net because I positioned myself properly, and I'm proud of it. I could score, but I could also play defense if I had to. A lot of times I didn't have to. If you have the puck, you don't have to play defense. What part of that doesn't anyone understand? Coaches today always say, "Defense first. Defense first." Why? Why would you take a big kid like me and make me into a defensive specialist? For the coach's ego? Because a coach would rather lose 1-0 than get beat 5-1? That is stupid. If you lose, you lose. Who gives a shit what the score is?

In the 1968-69 season I ended up with 49 goals and 126 points. I scored my 100th point in Boston against the Pittsburgh Penguins goalie Joe Daly. No one had ever scored 100 points before. Up to then the most points scored in a season was 98 by Bobby Hull in 1961-62. That was the year he scored 50 goals and had 48 assists.

We were short-handed, and I took a great pass from Bobby Orr, stickhandled through guys, faked the goalie, and put it in the net. The crowd in Boston was chanting, "Espo, Espo, Espo." They just kept going on and on. I had never heard noise like that in my life. It was wild. I can feel the emotion right now when I talk about it. There is no film of it. Channel 38 in Boston didn't tape the game. Don Earl was the TV announcer, and the radio play-by-play guy was Bob Wilson from WBZ.

My contract called for me to get a huge bonus if I reached 50 goals. I would have made $10,000, almost as much as my salary. It was a big deal for me, and I did it, I scored the fiftieth goal against the Rangers in Boston. The goal judge put the light on, but the referee, Vern Buffy, ruled that it hadn't gone in. I liked Vern, but that night I called him every name in the book. I had some personality, but I put it on a little too. I always felt I was an entertainer as well as a hockey player. I always wanted the fans to be able to say, "That Phil Esposito really puts on a great show."

That year I won my first scoring championship – the first of six in a row. I got the tag "the Babe Ruth of hockey" for two reasons.

They said I was built like him, and I was the first player to hit 100 points, like the Babe was the first to hit 60 home runs.

Not long after the season was over the owner of the Bruins, Weston Adams, Sr., called me into his office. Mr. Adams was the sort of person who would fumble you for a dime for a cup of coffee. When we practiced at Harvard he would show up in an old brown coat and an old brown hat. But he loved his team, and the players knew it.

I wondered what he wanted to see me for. I had made 49 goals, so I knew I wasn't going to get my $10,000 bonus. And I didn't have a bonus clause for making 100 points.

I went into his office, and he said, "I'm going to do something for you. I'm going to give you a $10,000 bonus. For what you did, you didn't make enough money." And he handed me a check for $10,000. It was a significant amount of money. It meant for the first time I didn't have to work for my uncle during the summer if I didn't want to.

In 1968-69 we played ten playoff games, and though the Bruins lost I scored 8 goals and 10 assists for 18 points. I led all scorers, but we still hadn't won the Cup.

9

THOSE BRUINS TEAMS were the greatest I ever played with. Part of the reason we were so successful was that the organization did everything it could to make us feel comfortable. I believe that a good dressing-room environment – the trainers, the equipment guy, the doctors, the dressing room itself – will contribute four or five wins, eight to ten points, a year.

If the trainers and doctors do their jobs right, a player will return sooner from an injury. If the equipment guy makes sure the equipment for the player is absolutely right, the player will feel good about himself. And if the equipment guy can crack a joke at the right time and relieve tension, he'll make the players perform that much better. In Boston, Frosty Forristall was the best I ever saw at doing that. He could also give you a kick in the ass if he had to.

I used to have a ritual. Between every period I'd put powder on my hockey stick. I'd powder the whole blade including the black tape so the puck wouldn't stick to the snow and ice on the blade.

This day I was playing horseshit, and I came in after the second period and I said, "Frosty, powder the stick for me, will you?"

"Fuck you," he said. "Powder it yourself."

"What did you say to me?" I said.

"Fuck you," he repeated. "Powder it yourself. The way you're playing, you can powder it yourself."

I growled, "Powder the goddamn stick." He did, but he got his message across.

I went out that third period and scored two goals, and I never forgot it. This was early in my career in Boston, and after that I'd say, "Everything okay, Frost? Everything good?"

"Keep going, baby," he'd say. "Keep going. You're doing it." Or he'd say, "You're not into it, man. You aren't." He'd do the same sort of thing with the other players, loosen them up or let them know they weren't going all out, and it was an important part of our winning.

We also had a wonderful traveling secretary. Tommy Johnson had been a great player with Montreal. He was traded to the Bruins in 1963. Then Chico Maki of the Blackhawks kicked him in the heel with his skate. It wasn't on purpose, but it severed Tommy's tendons, and he could never play again. He still walks with a limp.

I never could figure out what Tommy actually did. We always said he had the best job in hockey. He never did shit and got paid. I'd say to him, "Tommy, I want your job."

The clubhouse environment was so important. If you're a coach, you want the guys going out for a beer after practice or a game. We did that. We were good on and off the ice. We partied, boy. We had a *good* time. If we had been more disciplined, it's possible we could have won four or five Stanley Cups in a row. We were that good. We were cocky, arrogant, but we backed it up.

Gerry Cheevers and I had a routine. Just before the opening whistle I would skate over and give him a tap on his pads with my stick, like you're supposed to, and he'd say, "See you after the game, hey, Phil?"

"Absolutely," I'd say.

One time we were on a flight back to Boston from Vancouver. Some of us were sitting in first-class, and the rookies and bench guys were sitting in the back because the airline didn't have enough first-class seats. We didn't have a game for two or three more days, and we were drinking our brains out.

Carol Vadnais went into the cockpit, took his teeth out, and put on the captain's cap. He stuck a big cigar in his mouth and went back and opened the drapes between first-class and coach, and he said to everyone, "Guys, the whirlpool up here is terrific. Anybody want to go for a swim?" He was hysterical.

Another time in our hotel room on the road Cash and I were half in the bag, and we tried to wrestle Hodgie, who didn't drink like we did. Hodgie literally flipped us around. We were giggling like schoolgirls. He grabbed the mattress, put it on top of us, and pinned us both. Kenny Hodge wasn't a real good fighter, but he was one of the strongest guys I ever met in my life.

Off the ice and sober, Cash was a pussycat, but on the ice he could be downright mean. Cash was a very sensitive guy, but when he was drinking he became a little bit crazy. When he drank, his inhibitions left him. Whatever his most deep-seated demons were, that's what he became. Cash had a great career, but if he had stayed away from the craziness a little more, he would have been a Hall of Famer. Of our group of crazies, Wayne was the Most Valuable Crazy.

Cash, Mike Walton, who was called "Shaky," and I once were sitting at a table at the Hofbrau in Oakland having lunch and drinking beer. Shaky went to grab one of Cash's french fries, and Cash stuck a fork right into his hand.

Blood was pouring out of the four holes in the back of Shaky's hand. Everyone was shocked.

"You crazy son of a bitch," Shaky said. "What are you doing to me?"

"Nobody touches my food," Cash said. "Take anything you want, but don't touch my food or my beer."

Mike got the nickname "Shaky" before he came to the Bruins. He was one of the most anal people I ever knew. He was so neat and meticulous that he'd hang up roommate Gerry Cheevers's clothes for him. And if you farted in front of him, he'd go crazy.

Shaky was a little crazy, that's why we called him Shaky. He *was* a little shaky. He was one of the big drinkers along with Cash and myself. He would drink rum like it was water. He'd get a quart of Pepsi, pour half of it out, fill it with rum, and sit on the plane drinking what everyone thought was Pepsi. I couldn't drink like that. No sir. I drank beer.

Derek "Turk" Sanderson was another of the great Bruin characters. We were at the Hofbrau in Oakland at the bar on another night, and all of a sudden I hear *smack*. A girl had slapped Derek right across the face. Turk looked at her, turned around to me, and said, "Okay."

"What happened?" I asked him.

"Well," he said, "I asked her if she wanted to go to bed with me, and she looked at me as though she wanted me to go away. So I said, 'I guess a blow job is out of the question, huh?'"

So she slapped him.

Derek and I roomed together on road trips, for a time. He smoked cigarettes non-stop and it would drive me crazy. He was *always* puffing away.

One night we were lying in bed watching TV, and his bed was closest to the bathroom. He sat up and hawked and spat a glob of mucus onto the bathroom floor.

"Christ, Derek, what are you doing?" I said. "You're spitting on the floor."

He said, "So?"

"I have to walk there," I said. "I'll have to go to the bathroom and take a shower."

"Phil, you're right. I'm sorry," he said.

A few minutes later he hawked again, and this time he spat on the wall. He turned to me and said, "You don't walk on the fucking walls, do you?"

What was I supposed to say? I couldn't believe it. But that was Derek. He was something else. Whenever I made speeches, I would say, "Derek Sanderson is the type of guy who sends himself a telegram of congratulations on his birthday."

The 1969-70 season was pretty much a runaway for the Boston Bruins. One incident marred it. We were playing an exhibition game in Ottawa before the season. Teddy Green, who with Dallas Smith was our second-best defenseman behind Bobby Orr, was on the ice, and Teddy was one tough son of a bitch. We were playing the St. Louis Blues, and Teddy and Wayne Maki started high-sticking each other right in front of our net, really pushing and shoving, when Maki turned around and with two hands just cranked Teddy over the head with his stick. Teddy dropped to one knee and started to convulse. His whole face was contorted. Stuff was coming out of his mouth, and blood was flowing out of his head. He was looking up at me, as if to say, What happened?

We all went after Maki. Johnny McKenzie tried hard to get him. Pie would have speared him, because he was mean with a stick. Maki skated back to the glass, and he started swinging his stick to keep us away. They opened the door behind the net that they used to bring in the Zamboni and escorted Maki off the ice and out of the arena.

We finished the game, and afterward we were told that Greenie was in the hospital for surgery, that it was touch and go whether he would live. Bobby Orr and Eddie Johnston, who were his closest friends, stayed with him all night. They came back and said the surgery was a success but that Teddy would never be able to play again and would be paralyzed on his left side. We didn't know if he'd ever be right again.

That was a real downer. We saw first-hand how easily and quickly it could all go.

I got hit in the head with a stick only once. This was during the 1971-72 season. We were playing Minnesota, and I was skating, and an opposing player lost his footing and his stick accidentally whacked me in the back of the head. I had to have twenty-five stitches. I didn't miss much of the game, but when I went to Mass General the next morning the doctor told me I had an aneurysm. I could feel it. He said he would have to take it out.

"Freeze it," I said. "I have to play tonight."

"You can't possibly play," he said.

I said, "I have to play tonight. Give me a local anesthetic, otherwise I won't be able to play."

He stuck needles in my head, froze it, sewed it back up, and said, "If you feel okay, I guess you can play."

"I'm playing," I said. I took four aspirins, and I played.

In the opening round of the playoffs in 1969-70 we were set to play the New York Rangers. We knew that if we could beat the Rangers, we would win the Cup. No other team would be a match for us.

While I played, the Rangers-Bruins rivalry was the fiercest I experienced. We did not like New York, and they didn't like us. That stemmed from the Bambino, Babe Ruth, and the Curse of the Bambino on the Red Sox. As most sports fans know, the Red Sox traded Babe Ruth to the Yankees in 1920, and legend has it the Red Sox were cursed by Babe's departure, fated never to win a World Series again. In fact, since 1918, they have not won another World Series. So Boston hated New York, and New York hated Boston.

We had the best team in the world. We had Bobby Orr on the point, and we had Gerry Cheevers, who next to Patrick Roy was the greatest money goaltender of all time. It didn't matter if you won 5-4, as long as you won. Gerry was that way, and so was Patrick.

Johnny Bucyk, the Chief, was our captain. He played on a great line with Freddie Stanfield and Johnny McKenzie. Hodgie, Cash, and I had a great line. And Derek Sanderson, Eddie Westfall, and Wayne Carleton were on the third line. And if Carleton wasn't in there, we had Ace Bailey or Donnie Marcotte. We had a hell of a team. One guy would get hurt, and another would fill in.

Our power play was terrific. If you committed a penalty, you paid for it. They didn't keep stats the way they do now, but I'd venture to say that we scored on one out of every three power plays. We were awesome at it.

For the power play, we had Freddie Stanfield and Bobby Orr on the points, and I would play center between Chief and Pie. When the second unit came on Freddie and Orr would stay out there, and I'd play between Hodgie and Cash. Later on, after Freddie was traded to Minnesota, and Carol Vadnais became the point man with Bobby.

We beat the Rangers in six games. We were tied two games apiece, and then we won the final two games. We then swept the Blackhawks and swept the St. Louis Blues for a total of ten straight wins.

My brother Tony was in the net for the Blackhawks. If it weren't for him, we'd have killed them even worse. Bobby Hull and Stan Mikita were still playing for Chicago, but we were a better hockey team. We were really, really good.

After sweeping Chicago, we went up against Scotty Bowman's team in St. Louis. The first game was an easy 6-1 win. After we led three games to none, the Blues were facing elimination, and that's when a team usually plays its best. When you're playing in game seven, both teams are facing elimination, so the motivation is even, but in this case the Blues had their backs against the wall, and we figured they'd come out fighting.

If we had lost, we would have had to go back to St. Louis, and that was something none of us wanted to do. We were behind 3-2, and there was a faceoff to the left of Blues goalie Glenn Hall. I won the draw, the puck bounced, and I got it, took a stride to my left, and snapped a shot. It went in the net, and the game was tied.

When I scored, I said to Hodgie, "We got these guys. We are not going back to St. Louis."

The game went into overtime. In the dressing room, before the extra period, I turned to Derek Sanderson, who sat beside me, and I said, "We can start partying now. Why do we have to wait? These guys can't beat us. Why are we prolonging the agony? Let's bury the sons of bitches."

Derek said, "I'm getting the goal – me. Don't worry about it. I'll take care of it."

"Okay, Derek," we said. "Sure." Every guy felt the same way. We wanted to end the series right then.

Harry Sinden came into the dressing room, and he said, "Derek, your line starts." St. Louis was starting Red Berenson's line, their scoring line, and Derek's was our checking line.

At the opening faceoff, I was sitting on the bench and turned to

Hodgie and said, "I really wish we would have started, because I know we would have scored this first shift. Hodgie, I feel it."

"We'll get 'em when it's our shift," Hodgie said.

Harry came over and said, "Espo, your line is next." We were up, ready to go in, when the puck went into the St. Louis zone and came around, and Donnie Awrey went into the corner and poked at it with his stick. He was starting to skate backwards because he didn't want to get trapped. The puck went down and around in the corner and banged off Derek. Just as Bobby Orr took off for the net, Derek took control of the puck and passed it to him, and bang, the game was over. And in my mind I can still see that famous picture of Bobby flying through the air.

I tried to jump from the bench onto the ice, and I caught my foot and fell headfirst onto the ice and cut my chin. By the time I got to the middle of the ice, Bobby was at the bottom of the pile. I weighed 225 pounds, and I jumped on top of that pile, and I could hear defenseman Gary Doak, that lovable sick bastard, a guy who grumbled all the time, yelling, "Jesus Christ, get off of me." You'd be playing, and you could hear Doakie on the ice yelling, "Blaving, get the duck over here, you sons of meeches." I'd wonder what he was saying. I'd be on the bench, and he'd lean over and say, "Jesus Rice, pucka tippa over der." You'd say, "Okay, Doakie." I'd turn to Kenny Hodge and say, "What did he say?" Hodgie wouldn't know either.

The highlight of the evening came when Bobby Orr went and got Teddy Green and brought him down onto the ice. Greenie had been paralyzed on his left side, and his mouth was still twisted a little bit. His hair was still cut off. He came onto the ice, and we all gathered around Greenie, and he was crying, and we were all crying.

I scored 13 goals and 14 assists in the fourteen Stanley Cup games that year. That year, we were the best hockey team in the world. Winning that Stanley Cup was the ultimate. We were not only the kings of New England, but we were the kings and queens, queens and kings. We were the top dogs. Understand that the Red Sox, by winning the pennant, had won the Impossible Dream in 1967. They were pretty much it, until we won the Stanley Cup in 1969-70. We absolutely took over the town, and for the next three or four years, we were on top of the world there.

And from 1969-70 through 1974-75, we were the most influential hockey team in the United States. Because of us, hockey in Massachusetts started to flourish. No longer was it just a Michigan game. We influenced everyone because we were the flamboyant Boston Bruins. We were compared to the Oakland Raiders, the New York Yankees, and even the St. Louis Cardinals Gashouse Gang. The Gashouse Gang of hockey – that was us.

The city of Boston threw us a party and held a parade. We partied all night. None of us got any sleep. We were hungover, and then we got into the cars, and we were cheered in a parade by millions. I have never seen so many people as were at that parade.

I sat in a car with Teddy Green, Bobby, Chief, and the Stanley Cup. One girl ran up to our car, lifted up her skirt, took off her panties and threw them at us. Bobby grabbed them, the pig. We said, "Here, Greenie, take a whiff." Other girls were showing us their bras and their breasts. It was wild.

After the parade, we all went up to the stage where Mayor Kevin White got up and made a speech. It was televised, and while he was talking Johnny McKenzie took a mug of beer and poured it over Mayor White's head. Kevin White was a great sport. He started to laugh. Pie was laughing. Kevin White, in his Boston accent, said, "I will get you back, Pie."

We had a wild party at one of those restaurants on a paddle-wheeler in Swampscott. In the middle of the celebration my wife, Linda, came over and said, "Phil, I want to go home." So we left. In the middle of our Stanley Cup celebration.

10

AFTER THE HOCKEY SEASON ended each year a bunch of us would go golfing in Pompano Beach or Hollywood or West Palm Beach. I remember after we won the Cup in the spring of 1970, during a party, the guys said, "We have to go to Florida."

After I went home with Linda, some of the guys came over to continue the celebration, and the next morning I woke up on my lawn holding the Stanley Cup. Two days later I was in Pompano, staying at Bobby Orr's condo with Eddie Johnston. Our trainer, Frosty Forristall, also came down and joined us. I called Linda and said, "If you want to come down, come down." She and a group of the other wives came down later.

Before they came, we played golf and drank. There were women all over the place. Around the pool . . . ooooh, Jesus. Bobby Orr was single then, and all he had to do was crook his finger and the girls would come running. Eddie Johnston also was single then. Popsy Johnston was smooth. He was a great guy who you could count on.

Bobby Orr and I weren't close the first few years because of Alan Eagleson. I remember a Halloween party in the basement of Kenny Hodge's house when Bobby and I had words with each other, and they were not nice words. Bobby was not a jovial drinker, and we didn't agree about Eagleson, who was Bobby's agent and business manager. I didn't like Eagleson from the word go. I thought he was a crook and a liar. His court conviction for fraud proved years later how right I had been.

Bobby was all for him, so my second year in Boston I hired him to be my agent. I made $23,000, and I took $12,000 home, and $11,000 was deferred, and he invested it in a Carl Brewer car wash without asking me first. Brewer played for the Toronto Maple Leafs, and I didn't like him at all. He would hold me and punch me. Brewer cut the palms out of his gloves so he could hold you and keep you from shooting the puck and not get caught by the referee.

When I found out what Eagleson had done, I told him I wanted my money back. He said, "You'll be sorry you're doing this." And that scared me, because he had a lot of power.

But from that day on, that hurt Bobby's and my relationship off the ice. On the ice Bobby respected what I did, and I felt the same way about him, even though I didn't like Eagleson.

———

In 1970-71, I scored 76 goals and had 76 assists for 152 points. At the time the record for goals scored in a season was 58 by Bobby Hull. I was in Los Angeles in early March when I scored goals 59 and 60. And I still had a lot of games left.

My historic moments rarely came in the Boston Garden or in the traditional arenas like in Toronto's Maple Leaf Gardens or the Montreal Forum. In this case I was in Los Angeles, home of the Kings, owned by Jack Kent Cooke at the time. The Kings were drawing flies.

Someone said to Cooke, "There are a lot of Canadians in Los Angeles."

Cooke replied, "Yes, they moved here to get away from hockey."

There were a lot of reasons why I scored as many goals as I did with the Bruins, and one of the big ones was Bobby Orr. Simply put, he was the greatest player I was ever with on the ice. Is he the greatest player of all time? You could argue that. My feeling is you cannot compare players who play different positions. To me, Bobby was the greatest defenseman of all time, and Wayne Gretzky was the greatest forward. At the time they said I was the greatest centerman.

If I was, it was also because of my linemates Kenny Hodge and Wayne Cashman. In 1970-71, Cash, Hodgie, and I set a record for the most points scored by one line. That year when I scored 152 points, three of my teammates, Bobby Orr, Johnny Bucyk, and Kenny Hodge, also scored over 100 points. At the end of the season the Bruins presented the four of us with 18-karat-gold hockey pucks. Gold wasn't even on the market yet. At one point gold reached $970 an ounce. The puck weighed close to six pounds and was worth about $90,000. I remember my old man saying, "What are you going to do with that solid-gold puck?"

"What do you mean?" I said.

"Can you eat that puck?" he said. "Sell it. Get a lead puck and plate it with gold, and no one will know the difference."

I never did sell it. Donna has it. I'll get to her shortly. Donna has most of my trophies and plaques in her garage, but she won't let me go in there and get them.

I gave the stick with which I scored my 500th goal to Walter McKechnie, a player with me on the Bruins. He has it in his bar in the Georgian Bay area in Ontario, Canada. He tells me it's his most prized possession, and it makes me feel good that he really cherishes it.

I never cared about any of it. I always said, my memories are in my heart and in my head.

My brother Tony, on the other hand, has a room filled with souvenirs. His wife, Marilyn, did that.

Only much later, four or five years after I retired, did I start to say, "Gee, I wish I still had some of that stuff."

After the season when I broke all the scoring records, Linda told me she was fed up with hockey. She said, "Why don't we go back to Sault Ste. Marie? You go back to driving a truck, and we'll go back to a simple, beautiful life."

I looked at her like, Are you nuts? But looking back, maybe she realized she was losing me, and this was her idea of how to keep us together. The truth is I never treated Linda very well. I messed around on her from the first day of marriage. I was not a good husband or a good father. My family didn't come first. Hockey always came first. I loved hockey more than anything else. I feel bad about that, but I couldn't help myself. I loved playing. I cannot explain how much I loved to play hockey.

I hated practicing. I couldn't wait until we scrimmaged and began playing again. Nothing could ever equal that. Playing hockey was better than the best sex I ever had. Even when I go on the ice today in the Old-Timer celebrity games, I feel that way.

I don't like putting the equipment on. It takes a long time. I'm stiff. My hip and back hurt. But once I get on the ice, everything melts away. I don't feel any pain. Then after the game, I'm dying again. But I just love playing. It was one reason I was so successful – I just loved doing it. Any chance I got, I played. Ask my brother. When I was a kid I'd say to him, "Let's go and play street hockey. Let me shoot pucks at you. Let's go play baseball with Tupperware cups." The idea was to try to swing at the little containers and hit home runs. And sometimes he wouldn't want to play, and I would get mad at him. I'd say, "Why do you want to just sit in the house?" He'd say, "I don't want to play." I would get very mad at him.

———

In 1970-71 we faced the Montreal Canadiens in the first round of the playoffs. We were the better team, no doubt about it. That year we were the dominant hockey team, but the Canadiens have something on the Boston Bruins when they play them in the playoffs. I don't know what it is, but they always seem to beat the Bruins. They did it again in 2002 when they had no business winning.

We faced goalie Ken Dryden in that series. The Canadiens signed Dryden as a junior, and he played spectacularly that year. I don't think he played that well again the rest of his career. He is very tall and big, and he had a great team in front of him his entire career. Against him, I took sixty shots, and I was only able to score three goals.

The series went to seven games. The season came down to that last game, and we blew it. We were ahead 5-3 in the third period, and they beat us 7-5. John Ferguson scored a couple of goals, driving to the net and poking in rebounds. Henri Richard, that little bugger, God, he was good. Henri was the most underrated player on the Canadiens. He could skate, shoot, pass, and score.

Jean Beliveau and Serge Savard were unbelievable. Serge shot from the point, and one of their forwards tipped it in to take the lead. We panicked, and they beat us.

We should have won five Cups in a row.

After the loss, I was depressed for weeks, because we never should have lost to those guys. We should have won another Stanley Cup. It took a while to get over it.

———

After that season I got a huge raise. I became one of the first players to earn a hundred thousand dollars a year. I turned thirty years old. It was the first year I didn't work at the steel plant during the summertime.

I bought myself a thirty-three-foot Egg Harbor boat. My two buddies Jerry Bombacco and Matt Ravlich and I cruised on it all the way from Boston to Sault Ste. Marie. We went from Old Saybrook, Connecticut, to Queens, where we stayed in the marina near

LaGuardia airport, and then we left and went up the Hudson River through the Erie Canal to Buffalo, across Lake Erie, and crossed a little bit of Lake Michigan to Sault Ste. Marie.

My brother Tony couldn't come. He wanted to come, and it's too bad he didn't, but his wife was pregnant, and she would have killed him. We had a blast. The entire trip was 1,242 nautical miles. We went a hundred miles a day, sun-up to sundown, and we'd dock the boat and party, go to a bar to see if we could get lucky. Matt and I went to the bars and found them. Jerry never did. Jerry was loyal to his wife, which was good, because he could take care of things. But Matt and I were pigs.

I didn't drink while I was running the boat. No way. I would not even drink a beer until we stopped, and then I'd have my share.

A highlight of the trip was going up the locks of the Erie Canal. You can only go five miles an hour in the canal. Going that slow I felt like Humphrey Bogart in *The African Queen*. It was hot, and I sped up the boat, and I got stopped and threatened with a fine. It cost me a couple of hockey sticks.

When we came to a lock, we'd have to hook up the rope, and Matt would go to the bow, and Jerry would be on the stern, and I'd have to steer a little bit. If the locks were going down, Jerry would jump on, and if it was going up, we'd have to tighten the rope to a steel ladder until we got to the top. It was quite an experience.

We ran into a sailor we called the Old Man and the Sea. He had a boat with one little sail, and he told us that every year he'd go from Florida to Boston, and this time he was sailing all the way to Buffalo. Which was why we ran into him.

During the trip one of my engines went, and we found this mechanic with no legs. He fixed the engine, and I gave him $350.

One evening I pulled in and I said, "Is this Vermilion, Ohio?"

"No, this is Sandusky," the guy said. "Vermilion is thirty miles back."

I said, "No shit. I missed it."

I gassed up every day. I loved running that boat.

We had fifty miles to go. Even though it was sunny that morning, small-craft warnings were up. I said to the dockmaster, "I don't understand."

"They have heavy seas out on Lake Michigan," he said.

"How far is Presque Isle?" I asked.

"About fifty miles across," he said.

We had been gone eleven days, and I figured it was time we got home. I was impatient. I looked at Jerry and Matt and said, "It's eight in the morning. If we leave now, we can be home by one in the afternoon. What do you think?"

Well, we took off, and halfway there the waves were pounding over the bridge, which was sixteen feet up. I was at the wheel, and I got cuts all over my knees from banging them on the boat from the motion of the waves. I thought the boat was going to break in two.

I said to Matt, "Get on the C.B. radio and call the coast guard." I was quartering the boat.

"Ghost card. Ghost card." Matt said.

I said, "Matty, it's *coast guard.*"

"Yeah, yeah," he said.

A big freighter came by. On the radio one of the sailors said, "Don't worry. You guys are fine. We've spotted you. We're going to notify authorities." And they left. Forty-five minutes later, still nothing.

All our maps and charts were blown overboard, along with a television set and my hockey equipment, my sticks and the stuff I was going to take home to practice with. I was panicking. I had Jerry get the life preservers ready and pulled out the life raft.

"I don't know where we are," I said.

Finally, I saw land. I remembered from the map that there was a channel leading to Presque Isle, but if you missed it, you faced rocks and disaster. Jerry and Matt were screaming at me to land the boat.

"I can't go in there. I don't know where the channel is," I said.

Out of the blue I saw a little dot coming toward us. It was the coast guard. We got them on the radio. We were at Presque Isle. They said, "You can follow us in."

When we finally docked, Jerry Bombacco, who is one of these Italian guys with dark skin, was white. He was down in the salon wearing three life preservers, one on each leg and one over his back. I looked at him and started to laugh. You know how it is after a fright. We couldn't stop laughing. I asked him about the three life preservers.

"You fucking guys," he said, "don't you think I know you? You'd have taken these life preservers from me and let me drown. And I have rations." He showed us a packet of red licorice in his pocket.

Out on the deck sat the huge life raft, opened. And you can't fold those things back up.

Ah, Jesus Christ, I thought.

When we got on land, we found a bar and called the women. Jerry would not ride on the boat the last ten miles. "No way," he said. "I'm driving home with my wife."

Linda drove over with Jerry's wife to meet us. I said to her, "Come with us on the way home." She said, "No way." She never wanted to go on the boat. She got seasick. Linda drove home with the Bombaccos.

After they left, Matt and I were giggling and laughing very hard. We started to drink, but we couldn't get drunk, no chance. We had been too frightened.

The next morning Matty and I cruised a couple hours up to Sault Ste. Marie, and I docked the boat up by my cottage in my uncle's spot on the lagoon. It had been quite a trip.

I had a good time with that boat, but boats are too expensive to maintain, and it takes forever to go anywhere, and everybody else has a good time. I hired a captain to run it back to Boston, and then I sold it.

11

ONE OF THE WORST THINGS I ever witnessed in my life occurred during the 1971-72 season. We were staying at the Chase Plaza Hotel in St. Louis. Shaky Walton and Bobby Orr were rooming together, and Eddie Johnston was in a room on one side of them, and Cash and I were in the room on the other.

I don't know how it started, but a water fight escalated to the point where we were filling large garbage cans with water, going out onto the balconies, and throwing the cans of water at each other. I had an empty garbage pail, and I snuck around and surprised Shaky. He thought I was going to throw water on him and tripped and went backwards right through the plate-glass window of his balcony. The glass shattered, and he was impaled by hundreds of shards of glass. They stuck out of every part of his body.

If it wasn't for Kenny Hodge's quick thinking and the fact that Shaky was very drunk, which slowed his metabolism and prevented him from bleeding to death, Shaky would have died. Kenny got a towel, made a tourniquet, and started pulling the glass shards from his body. While he was attending to Shaky, all I could do was stand there in shock.

Hodgie called the doctor and had Shaky rushed to the hospital. He was taken to one of large public hospitals in St. Louis. I don't know how many stitches he had, but he still has the scars on his neck. He had to have blood transfusions, and he was out of action for two months. Most of the hospital's patients were black, and so afterwards we gave Shaky the nickname "Mercury," after Mercury Morris, the Miami Dolphins' star running back. We call him Mercury to this day.

We kept it pretty quiet. It was reported only that Shaky had had an accident. In those days the reporters were pretty good about things like that. Leo Monahan of the *Herald* and Tommy Fitzgerald of the *Globe* would cover for you.

Shaky came back and he was fine, and he helped take us to victory in the Stanley Cup.

Shaky was such a crazy bastard. He couldn't fight worth a damn, but he has the distinction of having fought with Gordie Howe in an All-Star game. He was married to the granddaughter of Conn Smythe, who owned the Toronto Maple Leafs. Shaky played in Toronto and married her. But she took off with another guy and left him with the kids.

———

Carol Vadnais was acquired in a trade with the California Golden Seals late in the 1971-72 season. We were skating around the Boston Garden during the warm-up before a game, and in the stands behind the net was this huge man with a gigantic head and an afro haircut. I had never seen anyone like him in my life.

I said, "Who the hell is that? Look at that guy!"

Vad said, "That's my buddy, André the Giant."

"The wrestler?" I asked.

"Yeah," he said.

After the game André came into the dressing room. I used to have a picture of André holding me up in one arm and Bobby Orr in the other.

We knew this girl who was gorgeous, but who loved the Bruins so much she would do absolutely anything for us, and we fixed her up with André. We all went out after the game to have drinks. We were in a place on Commonwealth Avenue that had a bar and a swimming pool inside. I'll tell you how big André was. He ordered a beer, and when he held it, he only needed two fingers to cover that can of beer.

At one o'clock the manager came and asked us all the leave. We were all together, and Bobby Orr said something to André, and André picked the guy up and threw him into the swimming pool! The cops came, and we left.

Afterward we drove to the old Madison Hotel, where Vad, André, and I had rented a suite. Vad and I had one room, and André had the adjacent room. André was in his room with this girl, and Vad and I were wondering how this eight-foot-tall, 450-pound guy could make love to this petite woman. So we snuck into André's room to watch. She was on top of him – he'd have crushed her – and he was pounding away. He was grabbing her and whapping her down on top of him. I thought she was going to die.

Vad and I started giggling, and we had to sneak out of there before he saw us. Turned out that the only normal things about André were his teeth and his dick. Everything else was huge!

———

We were playing in Oakland in November 1971 when Derek Sanderson asked me if I wanted to go out with his date's twin sister. His date was a girl named Jo Anne, who had worked as a secretary for player agent Bob Wolff in Boston, but then she and her sister had moved to San Francisco. Her sister Donna was working for the Aetna Insurance Company as an executive secretary to one of the big shots and was making good money.

"I have a couple of broads after the game, this girl Jo Anne Flynn and her sister. Will you come with me?" Derek asked.

"I don't know, Derek," I said. I was married to Linda at the time, but it didn't matter because we guys screwed around whenever we could. "If we win the game, I'll come with you."

He said, "Whaaaat?"

"Derek, first we have to win," I said. "Then I play. But we're not going to lose to these pieces of shit," meaning California, and of course we kicked the crap out of them.

We went to Flankers, which was owned by Oakland Raiders wide receiver Fred Biletnikoff. It had a bar and a beautiful dance floor. We were there because it was the custom of the whole Boston team to have one beer together after every game on the road. After that, you could do whatever you wanted.

We were all sitting around, and some of the guys were trying to hustle chicks, and others were dancing, and some of the guys were leaving to go someplace else.

I said to Derek, "Where are these broads of yours?"

"I don't know," Derek said.

"The heck with it," I said. "There are lots of them here."

When Jo Anne came in, I said to Derek, "Man, look at her. My God, she's good-looking."

"That's Jo Anne," Derek said.

Then Donna came in. She was sporting an afro two feet high. She sat down next to her sister, and Derek whispered to me, "This is my chick," pointing to Jo Anne, "and that one is yours."

"What's with the hair?" I said to Derek.

"I don't know," he said.

Donna sat down. She looked nice. My first question to her was, "What do you do?"

"What kind of question is that?" she said.

"I was just trying to make conversation, girl," I said. "I'm sorry."

"Don't talk like that in front of me," she said.

"Okay," I said.

I whispered to Derek, "What's with this chick?"

We had a couple of beers and we talked, and I said, "Look, I'm sorry. I was just trying to make conversation."

Then Donna told me that she had been sick, and that it was her first night out in a long time.

Ellen, a blonde who was a girlfriend of Donna and Jo Anne's, joined us, and Don Awrey started getting into her. Derek was trying to hustle Jo Anne, though you could see there was nothing going on there, and other guys were trying to get Jo Anne to dance. Finally, after an hour of conversation, I asked Donna to dance. It was a slow song, because there was no way you were going to get me to dance fast.

We were staying in Oakland the next two nights, and I asked Donna if she wanted to have dinner with me the next night. She said, "I don't know. We'll see." I came to learn that that was a typical answer for both Donna and Jo Anne. They could never give you a yes or a no. It was always maybe. It frustrated me. Make a decision, damn it. Finally she said, "If I'm here, I'm here. If I come, I'll be here at seven-thirty."

She didn't arrive until eight, but she arrived. Jo Anne and Ellen were with her, and Donnie Awrey took Ellen to dinner. Shaky Walton took Jo Anne. Shaky was a smooth operator, and he snowballed Jo Anne – they had a little bit of a fling.

That night I said, "Donna, you don't want to drive home. Why don't you stay with me?" I was rooming with Wayne Cashman at the Edgewater Hotel in Oakland, and Wayne let me know that he didn't want any extra guests because we had a game the next day. I said, "Cash, you're right," and I went and got another room.

I got into bed, and she went into the bathroom. She was in there for ten or fifteen minutes.

I said, "Is everything all right?" I found out later she was nervous. She came out and turned the lights off, and she was pretty well naked, and when I got a good look at her, I said, "Oh, my God."

She said, "What?"

"You are beautiful," I said. And she was – beautiful.

I fell in love with that woman that night. We had a tremendous evening, a great time, and the next day on the bus I told Wayne Cashman, "This is the woman for me."

He said, "Phil, come on. What about Linda?"

"I can't stand being with Linda any more," I said. "She doesn't even like me. I don't like her. I'm in love with this woman. You don't understand."

When we got to San Francisco Airport, I called Donna and left a message saying that we were going to Los Angeles. I called her again and again, and I kept calling.

One time in the middle of the 1971-72 season I told Harry Sinden I wasn't feeling well, got the practice off, flew from Boston to San Francisco, saw Donna, and came back. Nobody ever knew. I played in the game, and I played great.

We won the Stanley Cup again that season. The day after we won, I left for San Francisco. It was May 1972, and I spent a week out there having perhaps the most fun I have ever had. I was with Donna, Jo Anne, and Ellen, and they were packing up because they were moving back to Boston. Donna was leaving her job, and I told her I'd help her, that I'd get her a car and a job.

"My wife and I are going to split," I said. I didn't know how I was going to do that yet. God forbid. I'm a Catholic, and I knew my father would go crazy. I had two kids. How could I do this? But I knew I had to be with this woman. I was in love with her, totally, head over heels, right from the get-go. She was everything I wanted in a woman. Or so I thought at the time. As years go by, things happen, but at that moment, that's absolutely how I felt.

The first night I was out there, Donna and I slept in the back bedroom. Sheer curtains were draped over the canopy of the bed, and I'll never forget, we started to make love, and her dog, Allie, a standard poodle, jumped on the bed, and the bed collapsed. There I was upside down, and we were laughing. The next morning I got up, and we sent out for pizza, and all day we drank beer, ate pizza, and packed boxes.

Our last night in San Francisco, I took Donna, Jo Anne, and Ellen to dinner at the Mayfair up on Nob Hill. I felt like King Farouk escorting these three good-looking women. It was really fun.

I rented the truck, bought the boxes, and paid for four first-class tickets to fly back from San Francisco on the top deck of a United

Airlines 747. Throughout the flight we sat in the dome drinking champagne, eating caviar, and having a great time.

They rented a house in Centerville, on the Cape, where Donna and Jo Anne's parents had moved. I bought Donna a blue Plymouth Duster. All I wanted was to be with her.

During this time I called Linda once or twice but I didn't tell her where I was. When she asked, I just said, "I'm just out. I'm gone. I'll be back at the end of the week."

I didn't leave Linda until 1973.

———

The Bruins finished the 1971-72 season with the best regular-season record, and we made it to the finals of the Stanley Cup, a six-game series in which we beat the Rangers four games to two. It was a great series.

Our team was at its best, but I have to tell you I was not mentally sharp for that series. I had 8 assists, which isn't bad, but I didn't score any goals, and I have to give credit to Eddie Giacomin, who made a lot of good saves for the Rangers, and I thought that Walt Tkaczuk, Billy Fairbairn, and Steve Vickers did a great job against our line.

But I was a mess because of the trouble in my marriage. I was totally in love with Donna, no doubt about that, and I wasn't sure what I was going to do. I kept telling myself, You're Catholic. I knew what my Dad was going to say: "Phil, you have two kids. The woman doesn't deserve to be treated like that." All these emotions swirled around me. I had screwed around on Linda before, but I had never fallen in love with another woman. I had to pull every ounce of energy I had to get ready mentally before a game.

The only other person who knew what I was going through was Wayne Cashman, my roomie. We'd talk in the room. I'd say, "Cash, I can't take this any more. I gotta get out of this."

Cash would say, "We've got a goddamn game. Come on. Get focused." And he was right.

Kenny Hodge knew a little of what was going on because he and I were also close. The other guys really didn't know how I felt about Donna. They just thought I was catting around.

I really don't remember much about that Bruins-Rangers series except for the celebration after the last game. We won, and Johnny Bucyk, our captain, carried the Stanley Cup around the ice, and we skated over and kissed it. The Rangers fans threw garbage at us when we skated around the rink, and I remember thinking how much I couldn't wait to get out of there. I had so much on my mind. I just wasn't into it. It was sad. The last thing I remember was that as we got onto the bus to leave Madison Square Garden some Rangers fans tried to push our bus over.

We finally got away, and we took an Eastern Airlines charter flight home to Boston, and even though it was almost midnight, there were thousands and thousands of people waiting at the airport to see us. Derek Sanderson paid one of the baggage handlers forty bucks to swap clothes with him. He put on the baggage-handler uniform and escaped the crowd.

It was an hour's flight, but I really wasn't into partying. I was such a mess I can't even remember what we did after we came home. Did I go out with the guys that night? Did I go home? I don't remember.

12

IN JULY 1972 I got a call from Alan Eagleson asking me if I'd be interested in playing against the Russians. "We're putting Team Canada together to play them," he said.

"Is Bobby Hull going to play?" I asked him. Bobby had signed with the World Hockey Association.

"We're not sure yet," he said.

I wanted to know some of the details. "How much money do we get? Where's the money going? Who's going to get it if we play?" I asked.

"We're not even sure we're going to play," he said. "I wanted to let you know we'd really like you and your brother to play on the team."

I talked to Tony about it. At first he didn't want to play. "Who wants to do that?" he said. Tony and I had a hockey school in the Soo with Gene Ubriaco and Matt Ravlich. If we went to Russia, we'd have had to close the school.

When Eagleson called back, he said the series was on, but that no WHA players would be invited. I got pissed off. I thought that if Bobby Hull and Gerry Cheevers couldn't play, then it ought to be called Team NHL, not Team Canada. Bobby was with Winnipeg and Gerry with New England. To me not letting the WHA guys play was totally wrong.

"This is Team Canada, and they're not playing?" I said. "Then I'm not playing."

"We're just inviting NHL guys because all the money is going to the NHL players' pension fund," Eagleson said.

Eagleson ended up talking Tony and me into playing.

Alan Eagleson did some very good things, and he did a lot of very bad things. I had respect for what he did setting up the collective bargaining agreement with the league, but I also felt that he couldn't be trusted, because not only was he head of the NHL Players' Association, he was also an agent for several of the players, including Bobby Orr. I felt strongly that he was in a conflict of interest, because if any promotional or financial opportunities came along as a result of his being head of the Players' Association, his clients stood to gain from them.

I later found out that Eagleson, Bobby Orr, and a guy named Frank Harnett owned the television rights to the Canada-Russia series. As a result, the guys who played didn't get any money from the television deal and Bobby Orr got a ton of money, even though Bobby was hurt and didn't play. I didn't think it was right.

Ultimately, Eagleson ended up cheating Bobby as well. In 1994 Bobby went after him full bore with the FBI. I went to the trial to testify in front of a judge and jury on how the guy was a crook. He was found guilty of extortion, was disbarred, and fled to London, England. He can never return to the United States. So it wasn't until later in life that Bobby found out I was right, and after that we became much closer.

On August 14, 1972, my daughter Laurie's birthday, we went to Toronto for training camp for Team Canada. Tony and I had to give all our hockey-school money back. Eagleson promised we'd be reimbursed, but we never were. Our hockey school was never the same afterward. We never could get it back again.

They wanted thirty-six players so they could have two teams to play intrasquad games in practice. Harry Sinden was chosen to coach the team, and he told us, "If you're invited and you come, you're going to play." Getting thirty-six players into the games is going to be a neat trick, I thought to myself. Of course, some guys didn't get to play, and they left the team before the series was over. I can't say I blamed them.

We all reported for physicals. We stayed at a hotel called Sutton Place, and we started practicing the morning after we arrived. We thought it was going to be like an All-Star game, serious but fun. We had two weeks to get ready.

Early on the players had a meeting with Alan Eagleson about the arrangements. I asked him, "Aren't the owners supposed to pay for our pension?"

"Yes," he said. "They are allowing you to play, so the money from the games will contribute to the pension fund."

"That doesn't make any sense."

He said, "It's going to be supplemental. The players are going to get more."

"How much more?"

"We don't know."

I was asking the questions all the guys had been asking each other, and it was right there during that meeting that I became the leader of the team. No team captain had been named but I was the guy asking the hard questions for all the guys.

"Will we be paid?" I wanted to know.

"No, you will not be paid."

"Not a penny?"

"You're going to get twenty-five hundred dollars' expense money."

"Where is all the money going?"

Eagleson tried hard to explain everything.

The first four games of the series were played in Canada. The final four were in Moscow. The opening game was played at the Montreal Forum, with Prime Minister Pierre Trudeau in attendance.

Donna came up to Montreal for that first game. The team was staying at the Château Champlain, which is now owned by Serge Savard, and I got Donna a room in another hotel. I snuck out of the hotel where we were staying to see her. I told my brother, "I'm going to see Donna."

Tony said, "You're nuts."

"I know, but I want to see her," I said.

I went downstairs and Donna and I made love all afternoon before I went to the game.

Pierre Trudeau dropped the first puck, and even though it was just ceremonial, I was determined to win the faceoff. I was excited. I wouldn't let that Red bastard win it.

I had never seen the Russians play. I hadn't even heard of any of them. The goalie, Vladislav Tretiak, was the star of the Russian team, but to me he was not a good goaltender. I didn't know the rest of them, and I didn't want to know them. They were Commies, and that's all I needed to know. I wasn't interested in their lifestyle, but I found out they wanted mine. When they got over to Canada, they were treated royally. They ate like kings, and they shopped and bought jeans. Tretiak was the worst offender. I figured, if you're a Communist, what do you need money and clothes and material things for? So I didn't respect them, because you should be what you say you are.

I was out there on the first shift with Frank Mahovlich and Yvan Cournoyer, and I scored the first goal in thirty seconds. There was a shot, and a rebound, and the puck was out in front of the net, and I whacked it in. Foster Hewitt, the legendary *Hockey Night in Canada* broadcaster, shouted, "Mahovlich scores the goal. No, no, Esposito scored the goal!"

About three or four minutes later Paul Henderson scored from a faceoff.

And then we were hit with a couple of penalties.

We knew the Russians could skate. After we got a penalty, they put their power play on, and they passed the puck, and they could really move it. They started scoring with ease, and we were shocked. It scared the shit out of us.

It was 92 degrees outside in Montreal, and there was no air conditioning in the Forum. We hadn't trained very much or very hard. We were at it less than two weeks. The Soviet team had trained for two years. We ran out of gas. Totally. And they beat us, 7-3. To tell the truth, our goalie, Kenny Dryden, wasn't very good against the Russians, because they could move the puck from side to side. Straight on, Kenny or Bernie Parent were terrific. But if you could get them moving side to side, you had them.

Harry Sinden came in after the game, and he said to us, "Gentlemen, we are in for a long, tough series. And we better get our act together. We have another game two nights from now in Toronto. Please start taking better care of yourselves."

I remember being asked to speak to the press after the game. It was hot, and I couldn't stop sweating. Someone asked if I was surprised. "Hell, yes, I'm surprised," I said. "I didn't know those guys could skate like that. Nobody told us." Nobody had told us anything. We had no idea who they were.

The next morning we got on the plane and flew to Toronto. We got off, practiced, and it was all serious business after that. Harry changed the starting lineup at the morning skate, and he put my brother Tony in the net. He took out the line of Rod Gilbert, Vic Hadfield, and Jean Ratelle. He put Stan Mikita in, and Stan played with Frank Mahovlich and Yvan Cournoyer. He put Wayne Cashman and Jean-Paul Parise on a line with me. He took out Donnie Awrey and Rod Seiling, which I thought was a huge move, and he put in three gritty players, Serge Savard, Billy White, and Patty Stapleton.

It was 0-0 after the first period of the second game, and Tony was incredible. I have never witnessed that much sustained goal-tending excellence in a period.

In the second period, Wayne Cashman took Vladimir Lutchenko down – there should have been a penalty on Cash – and Cash took the puck and passed it in front of the net. I grabbed it, brought it in, and I shot to the outside of Tretiak just as Kuzkin, number 4, hit me over the back of the head with a stick. I scored, so I didn't feel the hit very much.

In period three Brad Park made one of the greatest passes I've ever seen in my life, right onto the stick of Yvan Cournoyer in full flight. He went around the defenseman like he was a telephone pole, and he beat Tretiak easily.

Peter Mahovlich then scored a short-handed goal that was one of the most beautiful goals I've ever seen. I banked the puck off the boards trying to kill the penalty, and Pete picked it up at full stride, faked a slapshot, went around Gusev, number 2, skated in, faked out Tretiak, and put the puck in the net. I skated over to Pete and tried to pick him up, but he was too heavy. What a goal!

Frank Mahovlich then finished the scoring on a pass from Stan Mikita. We let the Soviets know we could skate too. We won the game 4-1.

Game three was played in Winnipeg, and Harry Sinden started Tony again. What I remember most about Winnipeg was that at the end of the rink they had the biggest picture of the Queen I have ever seen.

We went ahead early when Parise beat Tretiak, and then Russia scored a short-handed goal, which killed us. Jean Ratelle scored, and then I scored, but then Valeri Kharlamov scored another short-handed goal, and then they scored two more goals to tie us 4-4.

After the tie, our record was 1-1-1. We flew to Vancouver, and Harry changed the line combinations again. Billy Goldsworthy got into the game, and Ken Dryden went back into the net. The Soviets outplayed us, and they won the game 5-3, and what I'll never forget is how that crowd booed us. They were yelling obscenities at us. It was brutal. And we didn't deserve that.

I was picked as the star of the game for Canada. When I got out there afterwards, the television commentator Johnny Esaw asked me a question, and I don't even remember what it was because I was so angry. My anger just came pouring out. I never really knew what I said until ten years later when I saw a tape of it. And now, every time I see it, I get embarrassed by it.

I said, "If the Russian fans boo their players in Moscow like you people are booing us, I'll come back and apologize personally to each and every one of you, but I don't think that's going to happen. I really don't.

"We're doing our best. They're a good hockey team, and we don't know what we can do better, but we're going to have to figure it out. But to be booed like this is ridiculous." I gave the whole country a tongue-lashing on national television.

Before we played the Russians in Russia, we played two games in Sweden against the Swedish national team. The Swedes were dirty players. They speared us and spit at us. And it seemed we couldn't do much about it because fighting wasn't allowed in international competition so we couldn't punch their lights out. Besides, the Swedes weren't fighters. They wouldn't fight back. But they sure would spear us with their sticks.

Ulf Sterner, who had played for the Rangers in 1964-65, filed his stick down almost to a point. It looked like a steak knife. In the first game against the Swedes, Wayne Cashman came in to check him, and Sterner stuck out his stick and hit Wayne right in the mouth and split his tongue wide open. Cash looked like a snake.

After Sterner got thrown out of the game, he headed for the dressing room, and Cash went after him. I followed him along with five or six others. Cash was looking for Sterner, wanting to kill him. We were trying to restrain him. Blood streamed out of his mouth. He couldn't talk.

One time when I was playing football I bit my tongue and split it, and doctors tried to put stitches in. I had to eat through a straw for a week. This was much worse than that. Wayne was in terrible, terrible pain. That night his tongue started to swell. He was choking to death when we got him to the hospital. The doctors took care of it, but he couldn't play again that whole series. Cash didn't leave though. To his credit he stayed with the guys to the end.

We tied that first game in Sweden. Afterward someone called and said there was a bomb in our hotel, and we had to evacuate. Someone also phoned in a couple of death threats, saying that I was going to be killed. I didn't tell my brother about them because I didn't want to upset him. I remember walking down the street in Stockholm with Tony and Cash, and all the time I tried to position myself right between them. I figured that if someone was going to try to shoot me, they would have to go through Cashman or my brother first. When they moved, I moved too so I would be back in the middle. When they asked what I was doing, I'd say, "I like to be in the middle. I'm a centerman." It was hilarious and crazy, crazy, crazy.

Back home, everyone thought the Swedes were going to be pushovers, but they tied us, and we continued to get terrible press.

The headlines in Canada were just unbelievable. We got nasty notes and terrible mail. We couldn't believe it.

We needed those two exhibition games against the Swedes to become a team. After that first game a big group of us bought two cases of beer, and we sat in one of Stockholm's parks across from the Grand Hotel. Guy Lapointe's wife had given birth back home in Canada, and we drank beer and celebrated the birth of Guy's baby. We were alone in a foreign land, reviled in our own country, but we were together, and it helped make us into a team. "Okay, guys, all for one, and one for all," we said. "We're all by ourselves. We've got to band together."

Other guys spoke up. They said, "We're only us. Not even the coaches are with us. We're just us. Fuck Eagleson. Fuck the Swedes. Fuck the Russians. Fuck the Canadian government. Fuck the newspapers."

We didn't care about anybody but ourselves, and we became a very close bunch of guys. We cared for one another big time. To this day I have a special feeling for everyone who played on that team. When the series was over and I resumed playing for the Bruins, if I was up against Peter Mahovlich, Bobby Clarke, Paul Henderson, Rod Gilbert, Brad Park – whoever, it didn't matter – I just felt a special bond with them. September 2002 was the thirtieth anniversary of the series, and we tried to get every living guy who played there to come to a reunion. Gary Bergman and Bill Goldsworthy had died, but everyone else is still alive, and I really enjoyed seeing them again.

One of the players who let the series affect him was Frank Mahovlich. In the game against the Russians in Vancouver, Tretiak came out of the net, and Frank lay on him and wouldn't let him get back in position, and the fans booed him. I thought it was a great play. But the booing affected Frank a lot, and by the time he arrived in Europe to play the Swedes, he was acting very weird. Frank had heard that the Russians had bugging devices in the rooms. He said, "We should sleep in tents. The tents won't be bugged. We'll have kerosene lanterns, and we'll be by ourselves." We looked at him like, Are you serious? The rooms were so bad we'd have been better off in tents. And they were bugged.

We won the second game in Sweden, and we really played them mean. The Swedish press called us hooligans and "The Canadian mafia," and to tell you the truth, we played as dirty as they did and maybe dirtier. But they had started it by spearing, and even though it was an exhibition game, boy, we went after them with both barrels. Beating them up was more important to us than winning.

Right before we were scheduled to leave Stockholm and fly to Russia, Alan Eagleson, Harry Sinden, and John Ferguson called a meeting of the players in the cafeteria of the skating rink where we practiced. They told us that the Russians were changing the deal, that they didn't want our wives and girlfriends to come with us. They were also reneging on a couple of other promises they had made to us.

Since I was the unofficial captain of the team, I got up and asked Eagleson and the coaches to leave. We talked about the situation, how they were changing the deal. I said, "I play in Boston, so it's not me who's going to get killed if we don't play well against the Russians, it's you guys who play for the Canadian teams. It's Paul Henderson in Toronto and you guys from Montreal and you, Josh Guevremont and Dale Tallon, from Vancouver. I'm of a belief that if they stick to the deal, we should play, but if they change the deal, we're gone. The hell with them." The guys agreed.

We called Eagleson, Harry Sinden, and John Ferguson back into the room and told them what we had decided.

Harry said, "Fine, I'm with you guys." Eagleson said he was with us too. Whether he meant it or not was immaterial. The next day we were told that everything would be as originally agreed. We were flying to Russia, and our wives or girlfriends were meeting us there.

13

THE RUSSIANS were always trying to pull something. They always had to get an edge, no matter what. When we arrived in Russia, they confiscated our equipment bags. They made us wait in the airport for two hours while they checked everything. Who knows what they were checking for? We had brought over 350 cases of beer, 350 cases of milk, 350 cases of soda, and boxes of steaks and other food. When we arrived in our hotel rooms, we ended up with half, though there were rumors that the Canadian embassy had taken a lot of it. But I can't believe that. I believe the Russians stole it. They had nothing over there. And besides, what could we do about it? Nothing.

We took two buses from the airport to our hotel. From the bus I could see that Russia was barren. The hotel rooms were shabby, and there was little for our wives to do, because there was no shopping to speak of.

No one had any food. People would wait in long lines for hours in front of a grocery store. When the store ran out of food, they would close the door, leaving the rest of the people in line with nothing.

Any one of us could have gotten laid for a chocolate bar. The girls were all over us. A couple of the guys took advantage of the opportunity.

We could sightsee, but there were no restaurants. We ate at the hotel. We never knew what they were going to feed us. One time they served us crow. Blackbird, they called it. Linda was thin and couldn't afford to lose weight, but she had trouble eating it. Another time they served us bear steaks. They were tough but they weren't bad. We ate horse steaks. Wasn't bad. It was lean. We didn't tell the girls what we were eating.

One night we went on a food raid. I bribed the girl at the front desk to give me the key to Alan Eagleson's room. He had a little suite, and we went and raided his refrigerator. I opened the fridge door, and staring at me was a cooked turkey with only one drumstick eaten. I grabbed the turkey and took it back to my room. I told the other guys of my prize, and they and their wives came in, and we ate that turkey down to the bare bones.

When Eagleson found out, he asked, "Which one of you guys stole my turkey? Come on. I know it has to be one of you."

Nobody squealed, but Alan, it was me. Eagleson was eating turkey and drinking beer and we were eating blackbird. That SOB. He would tell us that everything he was doing he was doing for the team, but we could see that wasn't always true.

One day Whitey Stapleton, the Chicago Blackhawks defenseman, announced that he had found a Chinese restaurant! We were overjoyed. We asked Whitey to go with us, to show us where the restaurant was. He said, "I had my fill last night. I can't eat Chinese two days in a row."

He gave us general directions to the restaurant, and the rest of us got into a bus and off we went. We drove around for hours and when we got back to the hotel Whitey was laughing his head off. There had been no Chinese restaurant. Whitey had made it up. We called him a lot of names.

The Russian food was so bad I thought I was having a heart attack. I went to a Russian hospital, and they did a fluoroscope, and the doctor said, "There is nothing wrong with your heart. You have heartburn." It was causing the muscles of my heart to contract.

Boy, were we paranoid in Russia! You could lock your room from the inside, but once you left, they didn't let you take the key and lock your door.

Once we got into our hotel rooms, we were afraid to talk. Like I said, we were told before we arrived that the rooms were bugged. When we ran out of beer, we would drink rotgut vodka, and one night after a lot of vodka drinking, we decided to conduct a search of our room for bugging devices. As we looked for microphones we made comments like, "You fucking Commie bastards." We inspected the chairs, looked under the rugs. Didn't find a thing.

In one of the other rooms a couple of the guys – and I never did learn who they were, though Wayne Cashman and I got the blame for it – found a little lump on the floor under a throw rug, pulled back the rug, and found a little metal box and five screws. Thinking it was a listening device, the guys unscrewed it, and beneath it was another little box with four screws. They unscrewed them too, and then they heard a huge crash below. When they looked through the hole, they could see the floor of the hotel's ballroom where the chandelier had fallen and smashed into a million pieces. They had unscrewed the chandelier from the ceiling of the ballroom!

We all had to chip in $3,850 to replace the chandelier. Thank God it was at two-thirty in the morning or the chandelier would have killed people. Everyone ate in that ballroom. I really think our airline pilots might have done it, because no player confessed to it. At banquets I tell the story as though Cash and I did it, though this time it really was someone else.

The Russians really tried to mess with our heads. They tried to take every advantage. In the middle of the night the phone would ring, and when I picked up the receiver, no one would be at the other end. They were trying to keep us awake. This happened to other guys as well. Anything to throw us off our game.

One night the phone rang, and Linda said, "My God, who is that?" I said, "It's nobody. They're just trying to keep us awake," and I grabbed the phone cord and yanked it out of the wall.

A few minutes later there was a knock at the door. They asked me to plug the phone back in. After I told them that I couldn't because I had yanked the cord out and broken it, at four in the morning they sent a repairman to fix it.

I really hated the Communist system of government. I didn't have animosity toward the Russian players, only their society, their life. In Red Square you could only walk on one side of the street. Soldiers with guns kept you from the other side. We were not allowed to travel outside Moscow without an escort. We were told they had nuclear weapons and missiles all over the countryside, and they didn't want us to see that.

It was a society ruled by soldiers. Once when I was walking through a big park, a whistle blew and men in suits and women in little skirts went and picked up shovels from the soldiers and started to dig and plant flowers. Fifteen minutes later another whistle blew, and they put down the shovels and grabbed their briefcases or purses and continued on their way.

Another time a little kid who was about eleven came up to me and said, "Chew gum. Chew gum." I had a five-stick packet of Doublemint. As I was handing it to him, the sticks fell out of the packet onto the ground. When he went down to pick them up, from out of nowhere a soldier carrying a machine gun appeared and stepped on the kid's hand.

"What's this all about?" I said.

My interpreter, Gary Smith, said, "Don't get involved, Phil." And he grabbed me.

"This is wrong, Gary," I said.

The kid meanwhile glared at the soldier, bent down, and picked up the gum. The soldier grabbed him by the scruff of the neck and put him in a paddy wagon and carted him off.

I could not rest until I found out what happened to that kid. Gary told me he had to spend eight hours in jail for fraternizing. I had Gary send the kid an autographed hockey stick and a puck. Whether he got it, who knows?

When we rode on the bus from the hotel to practice or to the games, two Russian "interpreters" always rode with us. We were sure they were KGB spies. On one trip Peter Mahovlich tried to kick them off the bus, and we almost had a fist fight. It's a good thing the guy he was arguing with didn't try to fight back, or he'd have been dead. It was war. That's how crazy it got.

I often wondered if I could kill someone, to actually get a gun, get someone in my sights, and shoot. I've been in a few hockey fights, but I never wanted to kill anyone. But I hated Russian society, with its tapped phones and secrecy and spies and long lines, so much, I would have killed those sons of bitches on the bus. And when I think about it, if I had had to kill the players to beat them, I'd have done that too. That's how much we wanted to beat them. It wasn't just two teams. It was two ways of life battling to prove which was superior.

By the time the games in Russia rolled around, we were very nervous. The first game in Moscow was played in their main arena, Luzhniki Ice Palace, and before they introduced us, little girls came over and handed us flowers. When I was given mine, I squeezed them so hard that I broke the stems and my flowers fell to the ice. When they announced, "Number 7, Phil Esposito," I skated two strides forward, raised my arm to wave, but my skates caught on the flowers and I fell on my ass on the ice. When I looked up from where I was sitting, the Russians were actually smiling.

I got up and took a bow, and people started to laugh, and as I was waving, I looked around and saw Soviet leader Leonid Brezhnev. Remember his eyebrows? I made perfect eye contact with him. The man sitting beside him smiled a little, and when I made eye contact with Brezhnev, I blew him a kiss, and when the guy sitting next to him started to smile, Brezhnev growled at him, and the smile disappeared.

Most people would have been embarrassed at falling like that, but I wasn't. I waved. Tretiak and a couple of the other Russians commented on how gracious I was to get up and bow. And my fall loosened everyone up. When the game began, we were all fine.

The Russian arena was different from ours, and they used that to their advantage. They had a rope screen instead of glass. The rope was very tightly woven, and when the puck hit it, it would bounce off, and the Russians knew just what it would do.

We played great for two periods. Jean-Paul Parise, Bobby Clarke, and Paul Henderson scored, and we led 4-1 with just eleven minutes left in the game. We were hitting them, dominating them, though for most of the time we would have at least one player in the penalty box. The referees were from the Soviet bloc – except one who was from West Germany – and they were bad. They were cheating. Sure, they were. The referees were under orders from the Russian officials. The refs called penalties that never happened: awful, awful refereeing. We played two men short, one man short the whole time. We got penalty after penalty, and they had power play after power play.

My brother Tony played goal, and we lost the game 5-4. I could see his frustration afterwards. The emotion was so great none of the goalies was able to play two games in a row.

After the game we were in the dressing room, and some of the Canadian players were down. I said, "Guys, we're not going to lose another game to these bastards. We got 'em. We'll win the next three in a row. We're going to win this series." My heart and soul told me that those guys couldn't beat us again. I was determined not to let them do it and so was Paul Henderson, who was also very vocal about it.

Between each game we had a day off, but there was nowhere to go, so we practiced.

Ken Dryden was in the net for the second game, and we won 3-2. We killed a lot of penalties again, and Pauly was unbelievable. He scored one of the prettiest goals I had seen in a long, long time. He split the defensemen, went right through them, and beat Tretiak from far out.

Alexander Yakushev scored on Dryden when the puck hit the rope, slingshotted out in front of the net, and he put it in. Except for that play, Dryden was awesome.

We won the third game in Moscow too. The game was a blur. We won it 4-3 on a Paul Henderson goal, the second night in a row Paul put in the game winner. Now the series was tied 3-3-1. The final game would decide everything.

The coaches put Ken Dryden in net the last game of the series. In the first period J.P. Parise was thrown out of the game. The referee who was closest to him didn't call a penalty, but the other one did. J.P. complained and they gave him a ten-minute misconduct. He then approached the ref holding up his stick, threatening to hit him with it, but he controlled himself and didn't swing. For a second there I thought he was going to kill him.

Midway through the second period Russia was ahead 5-3. I was on a line with Frank Mahovlich and I told Harry Sinden, "Get Frank away from me. The man is losing it. This guy is killing me, and he's killing everyone, to tell you the truth. Put Peter with me." Peter Mahovlich was his younger brother.

After the second period ended, the score was still 5-3. In the locker room Paul Henderson told the rest of the guys, "We're not going to lose. If we win the first five minutes, then we've got them."

We went out there, and I scored a goal that was set up by Peter Mahovlich. I can see this play in absolute slow motion in my head. Peter picked up the puck behind our own net and came steaming up the right boards. I circled and started to cross from the blue line toward the red line. I wanted him to have access to a pass or to use me as a pick. As I saw him get to the red line, I knew he was going to shoot it in, so I cut toward him, then veered to the left. Peter got to the blue line, shot it in, and then I zigged back in toward the front of their net, threw the puck into the corner and then Peter turned on the jets and went after it with the Russian defenseman Lutchenko on his heels.

I saw Peter fighting with the guy, and I knew he was going to get it, so I stopped and went back to the hash-mark area in front of the net.

Peter was big, and he knocked Lutchenko off the puck and passed it out front. The puck deflected up in the air right in front of the net, and I caught it, dropped it down, and then swiped at it and missed. Tretiak went down, and then I swung again, and this time I beat him and scored to cut their lead to 5-4. When that puck went in, I couldn't curtail my excitement.

I couldn't understand how they could have left me alone in the slot at the hash marks. How could they not have checked me? But early in the series I had established my ground there. If anyone came near me, I'd throw elbows. Every part of my body would be moving except my ears. If anyone got close, they got an elbow in the face. And that backed them off.

With the score 5-4, I made what was perhaps the biggest play I ever made in my life, and it was not a goal. I was on the ice and Ken Dryden was out of position on the right side of the net when a Russian came from the corner behind the net and shot. I dove, and with my left skate I stopped the puck from going into the net. It happened so quick that a lot of fans never saw it, but some people say it was one of the best plays I ever made.

So the Russians were still up by a goal when I got everybody into a huddle on the ice. I said to Cournoyer, "Yvan, I want you to skate as hard as you can to the red line and cut straight across. I'm going to win the draw, and Parkie, you put it on his stick. Corney, you're going to score."

I won the draw and it was deflected, and Brad Park shot and missed and Cournoyer put in the rebound to tie it at 5-5. But the light didn't go on! The Russians were cheating again. The goal judge didn't put the light on!

From his seat in the stands Alan Eagleson saw what happened and went crazy. He was carrying on so angrily that Russian soldiers came in to arrest him and drag him away. All of a sudden Peter Mahovlich saw what was going on, and he left the bench, jumped over the boards, and started swinging his stick at the soldiers, who had guns. Our whole team started to climb over there.

Peter grabbed Eagleson. We were all shouting, "Get over here. Get on the ice. Come with us." Whitey Stapleton, Pete, and myself were swinging our sticks at the soldiers, and everyone was acting like a lunatic until Eagleson finally made it onto the ice.

As Eagleson was walking across the ice, he and trainer Frosty Forristall were giving everybody the finger. Eagleson turned to the goal judge and gave him the fist.

In the end the goal did count. The referee had seen it go in, and he overruled the goal judge. In that game we had two referees, this guy, who we liked, and another guy, an asshole, who they had promised would never ref in the games again. But they put him in anyway. It was surreal, very bizarre.

The game was still tied with two minutes left. I made up my mind that I wasn't going to come out of the game until we scored.

I was on a line with Peter Mahovlich and Yvan Cournoyer. Paul Henderson jumped over the boards and called for Peter to come off, and after he hit the ice, Yvan got the puck, and Paul raced down the left boards and called for it. Yvan passed it across ice and put it right on Paul's stick.

Henderson took the puck behind the net, and as the two Russian defensemen, Liapkin and Vasiliev, skated over to him, I circled in the front of the net. He fell down, and the puck squirted out to me by the faceoff dot.

I had the puck as I skated away from the net, and I still was able to wrist the puck toward the goal. Tretiak made the save, and the rebound came out. Henderson, who had gotten himself back up, was standing right there, and he put the puck in underneath him. For the third game in a row Pauly scored the game winner.

"That was as close as I ever came to kissing another man on the lips," I said to Paul.

Paul was never as good before the Russian series, and he was never as good afterwards. During that series he was possessed. That one winning goal made him famous for life in Canada, like the goal Mike Eruzioni scored for the United States in the 1980 Olympics.

After Pauly scored, we were ahead for the first time with only thirty-four seconds left in the game. I figured Harry Sinden wanted me to come out, but I looked at him like, Don't you dare take me out. I was determined not to let them score.

I never left the ice. I was not going off until the whistle blew. I was bad that way, but I could not help myself. I felt I *had* to stay out there.

The puck came around the back of our net, and I got it, and I looked up to see that the time was running out, and when the horn blew, I looked up and cheered, and all the Team Canada players on the ice went crazy. The trumpeter from the Montreal Forum was sitting in the stands blowing loudly, and the Canadian fans in the stands – three thousand of them – were going crazy.

When the game ended I found myself right beside Ken Dryden, and I grabbed him. All the guys came over. The emotion we all felt more than anything else was relief.

I skated past the Russian coach, Kulagin, a big fat guy with a fat face who we nicknamed "Chuckles." I said, "Too fucking bad, you fucking Commie prick."

Afterwards Kulagin told the reporters, "The one thing we couldn't match the Canadians with was emotion." No, they couldn't, because they were robots. If they didn't do exactly as they were told, they were penalized or ostracized. Ironically, over the years the Canadian game has become more like the game the Russians used to play, and the Russian game has become more the way we used to play. Because of the big salaries today, it's rare to see NHL players score a goal and show their joy and excitement. Every once in a while I still see a player consumed with the emotion of winning. Does it matter whether you win or lose if you're making three million a year? A lot of guys don't care as much. Man, I cared. I hated to lose. I learned that you can't win every game, that in hockey the team that makes the most mistakes will always lose. But even though it's a game of mistakes, not a game of positives, you constantly have to think about the positives and never dwell on the negatives. And that's true in whatever sport you play.

After that last game, we wanted to get out of Russia in the worst way. But when the game was over, Eagleson reminded us that we still had to play a final exhibition game in Czechoslovakia. We didn't give a shit about playing the Czechs. The Czechs hated the Russians because they incarcerated them and forced them into a Communist system. As far as I was concerned, we and the Czechs were on the same team.

Our wives flew home while we took a charter flight to Prague. I don't remember much about that game except that I got my nose broken and Serge Savard scored with forty seconds left in the game to give us a tie.

Air Canada sent a Boeing 747 to fly us home. Had we lost the series to the Russians, they wouldn't have sent a Piper Cub. But we won, and Air Canada flew us home in style. On that flight we ate anything we wanted: lobster, steak, french fries, and plenty of booze.

We landed in Montreal. Alan Eagleson was a member of the Conservative Party who had been a politician and was still politically involved. Pierre Trudeau, the prime minister, was a Liberal.

Trudeau drove up to the back of the plane, and we were supposed to walk down the ramp in the back to greet him, but Eagleson decided to snub him, and for fifteen minutes there was an argument about which end of the plane the players should exit from.

Wayne Cashman, my brother, and I decided, "Fuck them. We're not getting off the plane at all." My brother and Cashman were too drunk to get up anyway, so the three of us just sat there while Eagleson made the rest of the players leave by the front door.

Prime Minister Trudeau came into the plane to see us. I said, "I'm sorry, Mr. Trudeau, but they want us to go out the front because you're a Liberal and they're Conservatives, and I just decided, the heck with it."

"I understand," he said. "But I just wanted to shake your hand. Thank you."

When the players and Eagleson came back on the plane, he said to us, "Why didn't you guys get off with the rest of us?"

I was sickened by his using us to advance his political agenda. I said to him, "Fuck off. Get away from me, you piece of shit."

Our next stop was Toronto. We landed in a fine, misty rain. The premier of Ontario was a Conservative, so Eagleson allowed him right on to shake hands with everybody. We got into cars and took part in a parade from the airport to downtown. I made a speech. My nose hurt from being broken, and my tie was undone, and I had my Team Canada blazer on. Everyone must have been happy with what I said, because they applauded.

Eagleson wanted us to go to a party, but I went back to the hotel. I didn't want to be used as a political football. The mayor of Sault Ste. Marie wanted to throw a parade for Tony and me, but Tony wanted to go home to Chicago, and I didn't want to make Tony look bad, so I told the mayor we were both going home after four weeks on the road, that I wanted to get back to Boston. He said he understood.

The next morning I was in Boston, training with the Bruins for the upcoming season. Two days later I played in a pre-season exhibition game. Wayne Cashman had returned, though he still was having serious problems with his tongue.

It was good to be back with the guys on the Bruins, good to be home in Boston. Prime Minister Trudeau called and asked if I would come to Ottawa for an award ceremony. I said, "No, thank you, I don't want to. I've done what I've done, and that's all."

Paul Henderson took advantage of his fame from playing in that series, and he has made a living out of his celebrity from playing and beating the Russians. I guess if I had lived and played in Canada I'd have done the same thing.

Looking back, it was one hell of a series. It was the toughest thing I ever had to do in my life as a hockey player. The mental anguish we all went through was overwhelming. And I never was able to play at that level again.

From that moment on, for me as a player, it was all downhill.

14

LINDA HAD COME TO RUSSIA with us, and I treated her very badly. I wasn't in love with her any more. I didn't want to be with her. We were under a lot of pressure during that series, and I took it out on her. I was not a good person, and I'm ashamed of what I did.

I left home one weekend and went to visit Donna in Centerville on the Cape. Her old man, Dick Flynn, an Irish guy who liked his brandy, took me down to the basement, and said, "So, what are your plans for my daughter?"

"Dick," I said, "I'm thirty-one years old. Your daughter is twenty-five. I don't think I have to tell you what my plans are."

"You're a married man," he said. "What are you doing fooling around with my daughter? That's not right."

"My wife and I are going to split."

He said, "You're not split yet."

"I know I can't stay married to her, and I love your daughter very much, and I plan on marrying her and being with her the rest of my life," I said.

"I don't know about this, but this is wrong," he said. Then he asked me, "Do you drink brandy?"

I said, "I'm more of a beer drinker."

"Here, have a brandy with me," and he gave me one, then two, then three, and I had a beer chaser, even though I had to drive back to Boston.

As I was leaving I said to him, "Listen, don't you worry about what I'm going to be doing with your daughter. We love each other, and I'm going to be with her. I know I'm married, but I'm going to get a divorce, and if we get married, we do, and if we can't, I'm going to ask her to live with me."

"That's not right," he said. "I won't let her."

"I don't think you can stop her."

I went upstairs and told Donna I had to go, and then I left. As I was driving back to Boston, I fell asleep at the wheel. I had a Lincoln Town Car, and as I drifted off, I hit the steel barrier on the side of the road. The noise woke me up, and it saved me from going over the edge and getting killed.

I pulled over and went to sleep for about a half-hour. When I got home, Linda was all over me. "Where were you?" It was then that I made up my mind – sooner or later I would tell her.

It was sooner. Linda kept accusing me of fooling around. She said, "I'm tired of it."

I got my balls up, and I said, "I'm not going to lie to you," and I told her the truth.

122 THUNDER AND LIGHTNING

"Get out," she said.

"Linda," I said, "if I leave, I'm never coming back."

"I don't care," she said. "Get out."

Then, when I started to leave, she grabbed my leg and began pleading with me, "Don't go," and at the top of the stairs my two daughters, Carrie and Laurie, were watching, and they were saying, "Daddy, Daddy, don't go." That was very tough.

Whenever I hear Wayne Newton sing the song "Daddy, Don't You Walk So Fast" on the radio I have to change stations.

"I'm sorry, Phil," she said. "Don't go."

"You have nothing to be sorry for, Linda," I said. "You're right. I gotta go. I'm outta here." And I never went back to her.

I called Donna and told her I had left, and she was in shock. After that we saw each other constantly. For about five weeks I lived in the Howard Johnson Hotel down from Bachelors Three in downtown Boston. I then leased a forty-two-foot Chris Craft with a captain that I kept in Quincy on the Neponset River, and I lived on it for about eight months. Then I rented an apartment, and I invited Donna to move in with me.

15

WHEN THE 1972-73 SEASON BEGAN, we were missing a group of guys who had left for the World Hockey Association. The big three were Teddy Green, Gerry Cheevers, and Derek Sanderson. We still had a hell of a team, though, and we still thought we had another shot at the Stanley Cup championship.

We were playing the Rangers in the first playoff game when I got hurt. I can still see it so vividly. I went to my right across the red line. I got to the blue line and started to veer back as Ron Harris came charging toward me along with three other Rangers, Steve Vickers, Jimmy Neilson, and Walt Tkaczuk. I saw they were trying to check me, and I went to make a cut, and my skate gave out. Ron Harris was down low and he hit my knee, and I heard it pop. I went down.

Bobby Orr was the first to reach me. I said, "Bobby, Jesus Christ, he got me good."

He said, "Take it easy, Phil. Take it easy. Danny will be right out." Danny Canney was our trainer.

I was helped to the Zamboni entrance. I hobbled to the dressing room, and I walked into the medical room by myself. I said, "Leave me alone." I shut the door. I tried to do a deep knee bend. I was wearing full equipment, and I figured if I could do a deep knee bend, I was okay.

I got down all right, but I couldn't get up. And the pain was excruciating. I shouted, "Danny. I can't get up." He and the doctor and the assistant trainer came in. They picked me up, put me on the training table, cut my socks and equipment off, and took my shin pads and skates off. The doctor said, "We've got to get him to the hospital."

They called an ambulance, and I was taken to Mass General. I had medial-collateral ligament damage. The next morning they operated on me, transplanting some ligaments from my elbow.

That's when Bobby Orr and the other guys came and took me to Bobby's bar for the night.

While I was in the hospital recuperating, fans came to my room to see me. I'd say hi, and they'd leave pretty quick. I didn't mind. It was nice to know they cared. Two days after my injury an Italian guy came to visit me. He was young, and the way he talked, with a heavy accent, I figured he had come right off the boat from Italy. He looked at me, and he started crying. He said, "Look what the goddamn Irish guys did to you. Those fucking Irish pigs." I guess he was talking about Harris and Neilson. He went on and on.

"Take it easy," I said to him.

"Just give me the word," he said, "just tell me, and I'll kill the son of a bitch." Meaning Ron Harris. He said, "They wouldn't do that to Bobby Orr."

"What are you talking about?" I said.

He said, "I'm going to go up to New York, and I'm gonna shoot three or four of those sons of bitches!" He showed me he had a gun.

I gave Donna the sign, and she went and got security. I said to him, "Listen, it's part of the game. Don't worry about it. Ronnie didn't do it intentionally." I was trying to calm him down. I said, "I think you should leave. I need to rest."

The guy was crying when the security guard came in and handcuffed him and got him out of there. I don't know what happened to him. After that, the hospital staff locked me in my room. They wouldn't let anyone else in.

The nurse said to me, "We've had John Wayne stay here, President Kennedy, and Katharine Hepburn, and I can't tell you how many other people, but no one has ever been locked in his room before. But you – you have been locked in your room."

It was winter, and the heat was on full blast so that room was always hot. I couldn't stand it, so I kept the window wide open. I was not far from the window, and I had a net, like a fishing net, and I hung it outside to keep my beer and wine cold. It took them two or three days to catch me. Then I had Donna bring me a cooler, because I couldn't stand the hospital food. My favorite little Italian pizza joint was called Salvie's, and Salvie would make macaroni, lasagna, pizza, or sub sandwiches for me, and he'd bring them up. I ate well while I was in the hospital.

Dr. Carter Rowe came to see me before I was discharged. I said, "When can I play again, Doc?"

"We'll see how it comes."

"I want to know when I can play."

"That depends on a lot of things," He said. "The truth is you'll be lucky if you're playing in January. You had a very serious knee operation."

"Like hell," I said. "I'm going to be back for the opening game," which was in September.

"God bless you if you can," he said, "but you had a very serious operation. However, it turned out so well, I'd like you to be a guinea pig with my students. I may call on you." And he'd bring medical students to see me, and he'd show them pictures of my knee before and after.

I really liked Dr. Rowe. He would say to me, "My prize patient! You gave us a lot of problems." And then he'd always say, "But man, did it turn out well!"

I was living with Donna in a one-bedroom apartment on Boylston Street near the Prudential Center. About ten days after I got out, I was lying in bed, and I started having terrible chest pains. I thought I was having a heart attack.

We got in the car, and Donna took me to the emergency room. I was on crutches with a cast up to my waist, and they took me in right away. I was sweating, and I really felt like I was having a heart attack. They did a procedure on me to see how much gas was in my system, and it was the most painful thing I have ever been through in my life. They held my one leg, because I couldn't move my other one, and two orderlies held my arms, and they stuck a needle in my wrists to get into that big vein. When they went through the cartilage, I could hear a *crrrreeekkk*. I started swearing like a woman giving birth.

"You sons of bitches," I said. "I'll get you, you bastards." I was screaming like crazy.

I wasn't having a heart attack. I had a very high level of gas that had formed in one of my arteries, and they took care of it.

I also developed phlebitis in my leg. For quite a while I had my blood tested every day, and I had to take Cumedin.

One night during that time Donna and I had an argument. I said, "Screw you. I don't need you. I'm outta here."

"Where are you going?" she said.

"I don't know, but I'm out of here."

I had my cast and crutches, and I was wearing a pair of shorts. It was still April, freezing cold. I hobbled to the elevator, pressed the down button, and left.

When I got to the lobby I said to myself, Where am I going? Where the frick am I going? I have no nowhere to go. If anybody should leave, it should be her.

So I got back into the elevator, went back up to our apartment, knocked on the door, and when Donna opened it, I said, "I have nowhere to go."

"Get your ass in here," she said. "Don't be stupid."

And everything was okay after that.

We went to Wellfleet on the Cape, a beautiful place with sand dunes. The doctors had told me that walking in the sand and the shallow water was the best thing for my leg. I was still on crutches so I bought myself an all-terrain vehicle that could go up and down the dunes. I would ride down to the beach, and before long I was able to walk the dunes, and then I was walking the whole length of the beach and back.

I still had a hard cast on my bum leg. I would tie a plastic garbage bag around it, and I'd go down to the ocean and walk in the surf. Of course, I got it wet, stupid bastard that I am.

That summer, even though I suffered through a lot of pain from my leg, was fantastic. It was one of the best summers I ever spent in my life. My dad came down. He had never met Donna, and he was okay with it. Tony and his wife came down and visited. They were okay with her as well. We spent a lot of time down by the ocean swimming. It was a time of relaxation. Once a week Donna and I would drive back to Boston so I could get tested and get a week's supply of Cumedin, because I was still experiencing blood clots.

Every night in bed Donna would take her foot and brace my toes, which were sticking out of the cast, and I'd push against her foot for half an hour to forty minutes while we were watching TV.

I got my cast off in mid-June. I was skating again in August. I really believe I recovered as quickly as I did because of all the time I spent running in the surf and sand. I'm convinced there is something medicinal in salt water. When I was running the Tampa Bay Lightning, I wanted to get salt water from the bay and have it pumped into our dressing room, but I couldn't get it done. The doctors said that if you pour salt into the water it will have the same effect. But I don't believe it. To me there is nothing like natural salt water. I'm convinced that's what enabled me to heal as quickly as I did.

I skated for the first time in late August on a rink in Stoneham, Massachusetts. It scared me because my leg was flopping all over the place. It felt like there was nothing attached. But I skated. Kenny Hodge was watching me. I said, "Hodgie, I'm just sort of pushing off my left leg and coasting."

I went to training camp in September. I had a big brace on my leg. I did drills but I didn't participate in a lot of scrimmages. But the leg was getting stronger, and I knew it. On September 28, we had an exhibition game against the Chicago Blackhawks, and I played. I scored a hat trick.

As I told the doctor I would, I opened the 1973-74 season. I had 68 goals and 77 assists for 145 points that season and for the fifth time won the scoring championship. I was also named the league's MVP. We got all the way to the finals of the Stanley Cup before losing to the Philadelphia Flyers in the sixth game 1-0.

That year Kate Smith became famous as Philadelphia's good-luck charm. Every time she sang "God Bless America" before the game, the Flyers won. Kate was a big woman, and I believe she was the "fat lady" they were referring to with the saying, "It ain't over until the fat lady sings."

And so, before the sixth game in Philadelphia, I went over to Kate Smith and handed her a flower to try to change the jinx. Boy, did that piss off the Philadelphia people. Not that I cared. They were the crudest, rudest fans in all of hockey. One of them said to me, "I hope your mother gets cancer and dies." Is that sick?

We lost that game anyway. We probably lost the series in the second game, when they beat us in overtime in Boston. We were totally in control. Gilles Gilbert, who came from the Minnesota North Stars, was our goalie, and he didn't have a good series.

Then in game six we lost 1-0. I had seven or eight shots on goal, but Bernie Parent was perfect that day. Rick MacLeish got credit for the win, because he scored the game winner, but Bernie was the catalyst. He was unbelievable in net. He had never played that well before, and I don't think he was ever that good again. It wasn't like me not to score, and I was very disappointed.

But that 1973-74 season was very satisfying for me after coming back from knee surgery. Some of the reporters wrote that I had made a comeback, but I had never been away. I told them, "Comeback from what?" I had problems with the press when they said things like that.

The next year, 1974-75, our Bruins team and my line were at the top of our game. I was in a position to be the first player to score 50 goals in the first 50 games since Rocket Richard in 1944-45, but I just missed doing that by one, and I ended up with 55 goals in 52 games. At the end of the year I had 61 goals and 66 assists for 127 points, my fifth goal-scoring championship. I figured I would be a Boston Bruin forever.

16

I WAS TRADED to the New York Rangers on November 7, 1975, in my mind a day that lives in infamy.

We – the Bruins – had played in Buffalo. In the last dozen games I had scored 6 goals and had 10 assists. We arrived in Vancouver, and we weren't going to play for two days, so that night I went out with Hodgie, Cash, and Carol Vadnais to a restaurant, Hy's Steak House.

In the corner of the place sat Jim Pattison, a huge car dealer up in Canada. He owned the Vancouver Blazers in the World Hockey Association.

I knew Pattison because about two months earlier he had courted me to jump from the Bruins and join his team. Donna and I flew out there, and he offered us a million dollars cash signing bonus plus four hundred thousand a year to play for six years. I was to get a front-office job after I retired, the salary to be negotiated. It was a hell of a lot of money, and Vancouver is a beautiful city. Naturally, I told him I'd consider it.

On the plane back to Boston, I asked Donna, "What do you think?"

"It's gorgeous out there, and it's an awful lot of money. What do *you* think, Phil?"

"You know what?" I said. "I really love Boston. I don't want to leave."

"Maybe you'd better talk to Harry Sinden," she said.

Harry and I had been talking contract, and he hadn't offered me very much. I went back to see him. I didn't have an agent. I never brought up the Vancouver offer. I didn't want to use that. I just told him, "I don't want to leave Boston. Come on, let's have something here." He offered me a six-year deal at four hundred thousand dollars a year. I felt it was fair, considering what I had done.

"You want a no-trade clause, Phil?" he asked me.

"Harry," I said, "you and I have been through so much together, I don't need a no-trade clause. If you tell me you're not going to trade me, that's good enough for me."

As we shook hands he said, "Phil, you will be here as long as I'm here."

That was in October, just before the 1975-76 season began on the fourth, and I was happier than a pig in shit. Donna wanted a place where she could raise horses, so I bought a sixty-six-acre estate in North Hampton, New Hampshire. I didn't care about living in New Hampshire, but the taxes were low. She wanted it, so I bought it. In the end she didn't like living there because it was isolated and she was lonely.

We were on the road, and I was playing well even though I didn't particularly like Don Cherry's coaching style. We called him "rap-it-around-the-board-and-get-it-in-deep Don." That wasn't my style of play, and it wasn't Bobby Orr's either. Bobby could do whatever he wanted, and I suppose I could too, but the rest of the guys were told, "Throw it in deep and go in and forecheck."

Our players were used to carrying the puck in and making plays. But Don would say, "Don't even look for the pass down the middle." God forbid you did that. "Just rap it around the fucking boards. And you better be there."

It was very difficult to make plays, but that's what Don wanted, so that's what we did.

When I ran into Jim Pattison at the steak house that November, he said to me, "You should have taken my offer, Phil. You're going to get traded."

I had had a few glasses of wine. I said, "Traded? You're full of shit. Get out of here, Jimmy, what are you trying to start?"

"I'm telling you, the scuttlebutt is that you are going to get traded," he said.

"I think we're going to make a trade," I said, "but I don't think I'm going to be part of it. I've won five scoring championships. Come on! I've won two MVP awards. We've won two Stanley Cups. I'm a first-team All-Star every year. I'm going to be traded?"

"That's the scuttlebutt," he said. Even though he was in the other league, Jimmy knew what was going on. In hockey there are *no* secrets. Hockey is like being in a hairdresser's salon. There's a bunch of gossipy coaches, general managers, and owners. The players don't gossip nearly as much as management does. Management is always yapping about things.

I went back to the hotel. For the first time I wasn't rooming with Cash. I was with a player by the name of Hank Nowak. And that night for some reason I took from my neck a medal of Jesus blessed by the Pope I had bought when I first made the NHL. I guess I had gotten a little intoxicated – in truth I was drunker than a hoot owl – and somehow I had misplaced it.

The next morning the phone rang, and Hank picked it up. Hank said, "Phil, it's Grapes." "Grapes" was our nickname for Don Cherry. We also called him "Sour Grapes." I wondered, It's seven-thirty in the morning. We don't play until tomorrow. Why is he waking me up?

Hank handed me the phone.

Cherry said, "I've got to talk to you." I thought to myself, Oh, Jesus. I said, "If you want to talk to me, you're going to have to come up and see me." I hung up on him.

Hank said, "What's up?"

I said, "I think I've been traded."

There was a knock on the door, and in came Don Cherry and Bobby Orr. Don was wearing the ugliest pajamas I ever saw in my life. Don's made a lot of money in Canada by wearing really ugly clothes. Bobby Orr was in a T-shirt and a pair of slacks.

I was sitting at the end of my bed in my underwear, hungover, and I had my head in my hands.

"What the fuck is going on, Grapes?"

He said, "Phil, I . . . well, I . . ."

"Come on. Tell me. I've been traded, haven't I?"

He said, "Yeah."

"Fuck me," I said. "For who? And where?" He looked at me, and I looked at Bobby, who was standing by the window. I said, "If you tell me New York, I'm going to jump out that window."

The New York Rangers were our arch-rivals. I hated New York. Whenever we went to play at Madison Square Garden, all we got to see was the dingy block between 7th and 8th Avenues and 33rd and 34th streets. We never saw the hot spots. We would fly in on Eastern Airlines the day of the game, play, stay in the Statler Hilton, a rundown hotel right across the street, and fly out the next day. New York was filthy. It was the last place I wanted to go.

"Bobby, open the window," Grapes said.

That how I learned I was going to New York.

Bobby couldn't believe I had been traded. Bobby and Don were close. Bobby could do no wrong in Don's eyes, and let's face it, Bobby was the greatest defenseman ever to play this game.

Don said, "Vad got traded too."

"Vad has a no-trade clause," I said.

He said, "You're kidding me?"

"No, I was talking about it with him last night."

Don said, "Fuck it, maybe you guys shouldn't go. Fuck Harry in his ass. Don't go."

My reaction was, "I gotta go. That's the game."

All I could think of was the million-dollar cash bonus I had turned down to go to Vancouver because I had wanted to stay in Boston. Some of the other guys like Derek Sanderson, Gerry Cheevers, and Teddy Green took tons of cash to jump leagues, and four years later, when the WHA folded, many of them came back to the NHL and were welcomed with open arms. Me, I was more loyal than anyone, including Bobby Orr, only to have the fuckers fuck me like that.

I was really upset. It's twenty-eight years later, and I'm still not over it. I still haven't forgiven Harry Sinden. We've talked, and I've tried to be friends and I've laughed with him and had a few drinks, but I treat him like anybody else. There isn't that special feeling any more.

Harry never did call me to say I had been traded. That angered me too. He had Don Cherry do it for him. After all we had been through. Harry would not have kept his job in the National Hockey League if we had lost the series against the Russians in 1972, and I was as responsible as anyone, maybe more than most, for our winning that series. I thought he owed me. I *still* think he owes me.

He told me later that he made the trade because he knew Bobby Orr was leaving. He and Alan Eagleson couldn't come to a contract agreement. Harry likes to have the best defenseman available in the game – it's the way he builds his teams – and at that point Brad Park of the Rangers was the next-best defenseman to Bobby. Harry called Emile Francis, the general manager of the Rangers, and asked if he could get Park, and Emile asked for me. At first Harry said no, but then he said, "Okay, but I need someone to replace Esposito." Emile offered Pete Stemkowski, and Harry said, "I want Jean Ratelle." Ratty was second in the league in scoring to me. He was a pretty good player and a pretty good guy, one of the better people you'll meet in this game, a real gentleman. Emile said, "I need a defenseman to replace Park. I know I can't get Orr, so I want your next-best." Carol Vadnais was considered next-best on the Bruins, although Dallas Smith was there too. But Vad had more personality. He was meaner. According to Harry and Emile, who I talked to later, that's how it went down.

I called Donna on the phone back in New Hampshire. It was ten-thirty in the morning back east. She said, "Phil, it's all over the radio that you've been traded. I've been hearing it for the last hour."

"I just found out about it."

"Oh my God," she said, "what are we going to do?"

"We're going to New York."

Donna and I weren't married then, just living together. I said, "I'm taking a plane today. I'm flying to Oakland to play for the Rangers. I can't believe this has happened." I went on about "Harry, that dirty double-crossing bastard, how could he screw me like this?"

The Bruins practice was at eleven at the Vancouver rink. The guys were there when I went in to get my equipment. I walked into the dressing room, and I walked over to each player, and we were all crying. Bobby Schmautz, who I hadn't been that close to but liked a lot, was there, and we had a lot of tears. Hodgie and I cried. Cash couldn't believe it. I also remember Johnny Bucyk saying, "I can't believe this is happening."

Don Cherry kept saying to me, "Don't go." Vad, who had the no-trade clause, said, "I'm not going."

I said, "I am going. I got traded, and I'm going."

"Tell them you're not going to go, Phil," Cherry said. "Fuck them. What are they going to do? Suspend you? What are they going to do, Phil?'

"Nope," I said. "That's the way it is. I'm going."

I got on the airplane, flew first-class, and I had four or five vodkas before I landed in San Francisco. The Rangers had a car waiting for me. At four in the afternoon I was taken to the Oakland arena. Nobody was in the Rangers dressing room.

I went in there and met Frank Pace, the trainer, and a guy named Jimmy Young. Frank Pace and I never got along. I was used to the Bruins' trainers, Frosty Forristall and Danny Canney, who were absolutely perfect except for their drinking. They drank a lot. In fact, they were drunk all the time. But it didn't matter to us, because the equipment was clean, the stuff was always nice, and the underwear clean.

I went to my stall. They had given me uniform number 5. The guys began to drift in, and they were happy and friendly. Pete Stemkowski was cracking jokes. Then I found out from the guys that the equipment I was wearing belonged to Larry Sacharuk, who wasn't even hurt. He was there, they just didn't dress him. They gave me his stuff and his uniform number.

I complained. "What's this? This belongs to Larry Sacharuk."

Frank Pace said, "He's not going to play tonight, and we don't have an extra sweater."

"Is Cat here?"

He said, "No, Cat is in New York."

"I don't think I should wear number 5," I said. "That's another player's sweater. I just don't think it's right. Why give me another guy's sweater?"

But they didn't have a choice, because the cheapskate Rangers didn't even have an extra set of sweaters. The Bruins always carried an extra two or three, in case one got stolen or ripped.

Pace said, "What are you, a prima donna?"

"Fuck you, this is not right," I said.

I noticed that on the sweater was the letter C. For captain. I couldn't believe it. I was coming to a new team, and they were making me captain?

"I can't be the captain of this team," I said. "I just got here. What the fuck is going on here?" I couldn't believe how stupid they were. Rod Gilbert should have been the team captain, or Walt Tkaczuk, not me. Years later I asked Emile Francis why, and he said, "I wouldn't have made Rod Gilbert captain if he was the only player on the team." Cat said Rod just wasn't the captain type. I disagreed with him totally.

We played the game against California, and we lost to the pitiful Golden Seals 7-5. I got two goals and two assists, but a Seal named Gary Sabourin scored four goals against the Rangers goalie, Johnny Davidson, three from the blue line. I couldn't believe it. I also couldn't believe it when after the game these guys went back to the dressing room and they were laughing, joking, having a good time. I was thinking, What the fuck is this? I was in the shower with Pete Stemkowski, Walt Tkaczuk, Ron Greschner, and a couple of other guys, and the only one who seemed upset was Ronnie. Right away, I knew Ronnie was a guy I needed to get close to.

In Boston, if we lost a game, everybody was pissed. Especially if we lost to a team we never should have lost to, like California. Our philosophy was to always beat the teams you're supposed to beat. Especially the teams that are worse than you – you *have* to beat them.

I said to the other Rangers players, "I can't fucking believe you guys. We just got beat by a shitty team. And you don't care?"

Stemmer said, "Hey, we got another one tomorrow night in Los Angeles. You can't win them all."

"Why not? Why can't you win them all?" I said. I couldn't believe it. I was devastated. I was appalled by the situation.

I went to the coach, Ronnie Stewart, and said to him, "Listen, first off, I don't want to wear Larry Sacharuk's sweater any more. And secondly, I don't want to be the captain."

Ronnie said he would give me my own sweater. But he said, "Emile wants you to be the captain. You're going to be the captain."

The next day we went to Los Angeles to play against the Kings. I was skating along the boards of the old Forum, and there was a little rut by the penalty box, and as my foot got caught in that rut I got hit hard, and my ankle twisted. I thought I had broken it.

I got carted off. Frank Pace tried to tape the ankle, but he couldn't do it right. The doctor had to come in and do it. I couldn't skate on it, so I just sat in the dressing room the whole game. We lost that one too. Imagine, losing to the shitty Kings!

The team was going to Vancouver, but I couldn't play, and they sent me back to New York for X-rays. I got on the plane and flew back to New York, where I met Donna. We needed to find a place to live. The Rangers suggested we live at the Southgate, which was kitty-corner from the Garden on 31st Street and 8th Avenue. At the time it was a worse dump than the Statler Hilton. They've remodeled it since.

I walked in there with my lady, hobbling on crutches. I opened the door to the room they wanted to give us, and I said, "I'm not staying here. No way."

I checked out and went to the Drake Hotel. The Drake was nice. I had a little suite. I called Emile Francis, and I told him, "I'm not staying at that fleabag."

He said, "That's where all the players stay the day of the game."

"That's ridiculous."

The next day I saw the doctor, and he told me I had a real bad sprain, and they put a plaster cast on it. He said, "It would have been better if there had been a break, because we'd know that in four weeks it would heal. But I can't tell you how long this is going to take."

I missed six games, every one a loss, and in the papers they were saying, "This is the worst trade in the history of New York hockey. Esposito is old and finished and can't play any more." To make it worse, Carol Vadnais still had not reported. Eventually, he got them to give him more money and joined the team.

They had to give me a little more as well. Emile Francis hadn't read my contract before he traded for me. My Bruins contract called for my getting $400,000 a year, $125,000 as salary and $275,000 in an irrevocable trust for when I retired. The Bruins ownership didn't like the arrangement, because they couldn't deduct the full amount from their taxes as depreciation. That turned out to be another reason I got traded. Jerry Jacobs, who owned the Bruins, the cheap bastard that he was, complained, "What if he doesn't retire until he's forty-five?" Jacobs told Harry Sinden, "You've got to get him to change his contract." But I wouldn't.

When I got to New York, Bill Jennings, who was the president of the Rangers, saw the arrangement and hit the ceiling. Emile called

me on the phone at the hotel. "What is this irrevocable trust?" he
wanted to know. I explained it to him. He said, "You have to change
it." I didn't want to, but I said to myself, This isn't worth the aggravation. For a little more money, I changed the contract and took my
full salary.

When the Rangers came back from the road, I still wasn't able to
skate. I missed eight or nine games before I was able to freeze my
ankle with Novocaine and go out and skate. I still had trouble,
couldn't do the things I wanted to do, and that only pissed the fans
off more.

I tried. God, I tried. I was devastated. I had never been booed
like that in my entire career, not by the home-team fans. I had been
booed on the road, but I loved that. The more they booed and yelled
at me, the better I played. But booed by the home-town fans? The
Rangers fans were relentless.

The ankle eventually got better, and I began to score again. Had
I not sprained my ankle, I probably would have scored 60 goals that
year. My linemates, Rod Gilbert and Steve Vickers, were fine players,
and they were also goal scorers, so they weren't as conducive to my
game as Hodgie and Cash had been. Steve liked to be around the
net, and Rod wasn't a corner man. He had a great shot, was a good
scorer and a smart hockey player. I was a guy who liked to camp out
in front of the net and have the wings pass me the puck. It was
wrong for Ronnie Stewart to put me on a line with Rod and Steve.
But you don't say anything to the coach. You do as you're told.

━━━━━━

In the middle of that 1975-76 season Emile Francis called me on the
phone and said, "Phil, I think I'm going to make a coaching change.
What do you know about John Ferguson?"

"I think he's terrific," I said. Emile didn't know it but he was
getting fired too.

Once Fergie came in, I felt I had an ally. He was a guy I had gone through torture with in the 1972 series against the Russians – he was the assistant coach – and having played against him I knew he was one tough son of a bitch. Now Fergie was coming to New York, coaching for the first time, and he was going for it. I felt better about things.

Fergie was a tough competitor. We were playing the Bruins, and I was standing on the ice near the Rangers bench when Wayne Cashman skated by. I said hello to Cash and Ferguson punched me hard right in the back. He said, "Talk to him after the game. You don't talk to him before or during the game. Once the game has started, he's not your friend."

"Jesus Christ, Fergie," I said. "You took my breath away."

"I'll take more than that away," he said.

I said, "Relax, for Christ's sake."

Another time John threw a water bottle at the linesman and hit him right in the head.

I really liked John Ferguson. He tried hard. He wanted to do the right thing.

When he arrived, I told him about my injury. "My ankle is really bad," I told him. I was unable to practice with the team, because it was too painful to skate without the Novocaine, and so I couldn't do the drills.

I was trying my best, but the team had serious problems. A lot of the Rangers were drinking. Most of the Rangers players lived on Long Island, and we practiced on Long Island. Every day after practice the guys would go to lunch at a place called the Digs in Long Beach. They would spend the whole afternoon drinking beer and then go home at four or five in the afternoon for supper. Then we had to schlep into the city for our games, which was stupid.

A few of the guys on the Rangers also were doing drugs. The only guy on the Bruins who had done anything like that that we knew of was Derek Sanderson. I remember one time I went to a Rangers team party, and the wife of one of the players, who I thought was a lunatic, put grass in the brownies and never told us. I ate the brownies, and I was totally spaced out. My wife was sitting beside me. John Davidson was across the room. We were looking at each other, waving at each other, grinning goofily. We didn't know what had hit us.

Donnie Murdoch, who was a rookie in 1976-77, was a talented kid, but he had a wicked problem with alcohol and drugs. At first I thought it was just a drinking problem. You could smell the booze on him every morning. He'd go out on the ice half in the bag, and even in games. Once with the Rangers he skated into the goalpost and they had to get him out of there.

We were living out on the beach in Long Island, and one time we had a tremendous snowstorm, and he came out and couldn't find his car. He had been so drunk when he parked it he couldn't remember where he had left it. We had to wait two days until the snow melted. I had to pick him up and take him to practice.

It was when I went to a party with Donnie early in the season, at one of the United Nations apartments, that I found out the problem wasn't just with alcohol.

Donna and I walked in, and I couldn't believe what I was seeing: girls were walking around topless! They had been hired by a guy they called the "Snow King." At the time I didn't know who he was or even what that meant.

One of the girls came over to me and said, "Would you like something to drink, or would you like something?"

"I'll have a beer," I said.

"That's not what I mean," she said.

I wondered what she was talking about.

"Okay, then," I said, "I'll have a Coke." She must have thought I said, "I'll have coke," because she brought over a little container that looked like an ashtray, and it was filled with a white powder that I assumed was cocaine.

I said to Donna, "Let's get out of here – *now!*" I told her, "I have nothing left but my name." Not that I was any angel, but if the cops had raided the place and I had been arrested, how could I have explained what I was doing there?

Later that season Donnie was caught at the Canadian border with drugs and was suspended for forty games. I'm not sure he wasn't set up by a girl. He was quite a lunatic when it came to his women.

This Rangers team had the worst attitude of any team I played on. I was the captain, so I called a team meeting. I called them together and said, "We have to talk about this. Come over to my house at Atlantic Beach, and I'll get some beer." Half the guys didn't show up. Pete Stemkowski didn't come, and neither did Walter Tkaczuk, Steve Vickers, or Rod Gilbert, which really hurt me, because I thought Rod would come for sure. But I think Rod was stung that they made me captain. I think he felt he deserved it, which he did. Plus Rod and Ferguson didn't get along, and I was "Fergie's boy," as the guys used to say.

I was so devastated that some of them didn't show for the meeting that I said to the ones who came, "Guys, this is why we're in trouble. We can't win a hockey game, and I'm not used to losing. I don't like losing."

Gilles Marotte said, "Hey, Phil, this is the New York Rangers, not the Boston Bruins. Get over it. Fuck the Boston Bruins."

"Gilles, you're right," I said. I had been comparing everything to my experience in Boston. And at that moment the realization hit me that I would never be a Boston Bruin again.

I had been used to the way we did it in Boston, but now I was in New York, and this was the way they did it. I said, "Now I know why you guys could never beat us. You're not dedicated. Nobody gives a shit. Believe me, on the Bruins we cared. Nobody here cared that we lost to the lowly Seals. Come on." It was an attitude I couldn't stomach. I know I made some enemies on the team because of it. I told the players I wanted them to be more dedicated.

When Fergie came in, things got better, because Fergie also hated to lose, and Fergie didn't like the attitude either, and he started to change it.

Fergie was merciless with Rod Gilbert. He called him "that fucking little frog bastard, that piece of shit." He'd say, "He's such a chickenshit."

"Ferg, I don't want to hear that," I'd say.

Hey, look, if the French guys had a dime for every time they got called "frogs" or if I had a dime for every time I was called a "wop" on the ice, I'd never have needed the Japanese to buy the Lightning.

And God forbid, if you were Jewish, we called them every name in the book including "hebes" and "kikes." There were only two in the league: Larry Zeidel, who was a lunatic, and my teammate in Boston, Teddy Green, who wasn't really Jewish. We'd drive Greenie crazy. We'd say to him, "The fucking Jews don't play hockey. They own the teams. Are you kidding me, Greenburg? Let's go."

Fergie did what he could to make the Rangers better. One day Fergie called to tell me, "I just traded for your friend Kenny Hodge."

I said, "Terrific, fantastic. Who did you have to give up to get him?"

He said, "Ricky Middleton."

There was a silence from me. Middleton was young, and he was a hell of a hockey player. I said, "Really? Rick is a pretty good player, Ferg."

He said, "I had to get him out of town. If I didn't, he would have ended up in trouble."

"What do you mean?"

"It's not important," he said, "but he's in real trouble and I had to get him out of town."

Trust me, it happens. When I was running Tampa Bay, I had to get a player out of town or else the cops were going to send him to jail.

Ricky went to Boston, straightened himself out, and he became a terrific player for the Bruins. And do you know who straightened him out? The Boston Bruins. All of a sudden Ricky Middleton knew what it was like to have teammates who cared whether he played well or not. In New York they didn't care.

Once in 1977 I threw Walter Tkaczuk's wife out of my house. For two hours she sat there, and the gist of the conversation was, "Why do you care so much? Sometimes you're going to win. Sometimes you're going to lose. Who cares? You're just collecting your money, aren't you? That's all it is."

"That's *not* all it is," I said.

Obviously, it was what her husband believed, though Walt didn't play like that once he got out on the ice. But that must have been what he believed in his mind.

Finally, I just said, "I think you better leave, cause I have had enough of you and your fucking husband and the rest of these guys. If this team is ever going to win, we're going to have to get rid of people like you."

She got up and left. The next day Walter came up to me, and he was laughing. "You threw my wife out," he said.

"I absolutely did," I said. "Waldo, do you believe what she was saying? Do you not give a fuck?"

"I want to win," he said, "but fuck it, if you don't win, what are you going to do? Are you going to die?"

"No, you aren't going to die," I said, "but you have to have some pride. Don't you want to win the Stanley Cup? Don't you want to wear a ring? I have two of them. I want another one. I'd like one from New York more than anything."

He laughed at me, and other guys also laughed at me. It was as though nobody cared.

I often wondered what might have been had I not been traded to the Rangers. I had scored 60 goals five years in a row, and if I hadn't gotten traded, I'd have scored 60 goals in 1975 as well. After I got traded to the Rangers I must have played 35 games on a bad ankle. I ended up with only 38 goals. The Rangers finished dead last in the Patrick Division.

17

I PLAYED IN THE CANADA CUP in 1976. In the first game I scored two goals against Finland. We went to play the second game in Toronto against the Russians, and I dressed, but Scotty Bowman used me sparingly. I sat on the bench almost the entire game. I was thirty-four years old. As I sat there, I was so furious I could barely see straight.

After the game reporters asked me about it, and I told them, "Don't ask me. Ask the brains over there." I was doing this for my country. I wasn't doing it for Scotty Bowman. "Phil can't skate well enough to play against the Russians," Scotty said.

When we got back to Montreal, I was walking into the Forum with Gerry Cheevers, my roommate, when we saw Scotty, who said good morning to us.

"Don't you fucking say good morning to me," I said. "I don't like you. You don't like me. Let's be honest, for Christ's sake. We have a job to do for our country, and I'll do it. I'll be here for that, but don't you dare be a hypocrite and try to be nice to me."

Bowman didn't talk to me the rest of the series. I scored four goals and three assists in the seven games I played in, but that series didn't mean nearly as much as the one in 1972. We didn't even face the Russians in the finals. The Czechs knocked them out.

After Scotty benched me, I had no use for him. You don't embarrass me like that. Come on. Don't give me that stuff about the Russians being too fast. I played against them too often.

In 1976 Donna and I got married and bought a house on Long Island by Atlantic Beach on Tioga Street, right across from the water. Many times when I was depressed about hockey, I'd walk with my two dogs on the beach. Nobody else would be there. It was winter, and the wind would be blowing. I would throw a ball, and the dogs would chase it, and I'd sit and think about things. I may not look like a pensive guy, but I can walk for miles by myself, or go to the movies by myself and not even watch the movie.

On the beach, my mind became free. It was like being out on a boat, drinking a beer and relaxing and listening to the water and thinking about things you need to make decisions about.

It wasn't long after we moved into that house that Donna's twin sister, Jo Anne, came to visit. She lived with us for the next seventeen years.

The next year Paramount fired Bill Jennings and hired Sonny Werblin to run the Rangers, the Knicks, and Madison Square Garden. I liked Sonny a lot. He was an incredible human being. Sonny'd call and say, "What are you and Donna doing?" "Nothing." He'd say, "Lee and I want to take you out to dinner."

I'd always think, What if the other players find out? They would call me a brown-nosing bastard. But I could accomplish a thing or two talking to Sonny. I convinced him that we needed our own practice facility closer to the city; that's why we began practicing in Rye. And that's why we could then live in New York City rather than way out of town on Long Island.

We'd go with the Werblins to the 21 Club. He'd make sure I was in the public eye. He wanted our names on page 6 of the *Post*. He told Ron Duguay, "Go down to Studio 54. Go party. Get your name in the paper."

One time Sonny took us to 21 with Howard Cosell, who made a pass at Donna. I told Howard to take his hands off her, and he'd laugh. His wife, Emmy, would laugh and say, "Howard, you're such a bad guy." It wasn't at all funny to me. I'd say, "I don't want you touching her like that. I've had enough of you." And he'd laugh.

But Donna didn't like it, and neither did I. He was a sleazy old geezer. Like I am now – a sleazy old geezer. We all get there.

Howard was a shit stirrer if I ever saw one. One time Rod Gilbert, Donna, and I were in Las Vegas with Howard, and he almost got me killed. We were sitting around the pool when George Foreman, who had just become the heavyweight champion of the world, walked by with his entourage. George was wearing a pair of farmer's overalls with nothing underneath. I remember thinking that this was one of the biggest men I had ever seen.

Cosell yelled over to Foreman, "Hey, champ. Come over here."

"Hi, Howard," Foreman said.

Howard said, "I got a goddamn hockey player here who says he can kick the shit out of any black man any time."

Foreman looked at me, and I said, "I didn't say a word, man. I didn't say a fucking word."

"I know," Foreman said. "Ah, Cosell, one of these days I am going to nail you but good." And Howard started laughing.

When Foreman left, I said to Howard, "What are you trying to do, get me killed?"

"Phil, you can handle him," he said, laughing.

One of the first things Sonny Werblin did was make the Rangers players move into the city. We moved to 59th Street and 2nd Avenue, the thirty-third floor of the Landmark Building. We moved into a one-bedroom apartment, and my sister-in-law Jo Anne slept on the pullout couch. It was a new lease on life. That was when I had the most fun in New York.

Donna, Jo Anne, and I would go out to dinner along restaurant row on 58th Street between 2nd and 3rd avenues. There were Italian restaurants, Dewey Wong's, and Mr. Laff's. I'd be with the two of them – both were gorgeous women, you could see they were twins – and we'd hit every restaurant. I don't know what people thought when they saw me with them. I used to say to Donna about her sister, "This pisses me off. I take care of her, but I don't get any fringe benefits. You'd think once in a while she'd give me a fringe benefit." Which never happened. I figured I must have spent fifty thousand dollars a year on Jo Anne, and that was after-tax dollars because I couldn't claim her as a dependent.

I was making four hundred thousand dollars a year. I was living a great life. The Rangers were getting better. People were starting to like me in New York, because I was playing well. I had no injuries. I felt great and I still looked great. It's only after fifty when everything starts to sag. Then you start sitting on your balls and you can't wear boxer shorts any more.

———

To get to practice we travelled over the Tappan Zee Bridge to drive to Orange County. A lot of times I'd pick up Donnie Murdoch, Ron Duguay, and Ron Greschner, and we'd drive together.

Ron Duguay was tall, good-looking, soft-spoken, and tried hard on the ice. Ronnie liked the game too much to get in trouble with booze and drugs. Ronnie is sharp as a tack, and today he is straight as an arrow and married to the model Kim Alexis, a wonderful woman.

The guys would fight for the back seat so they could sleep.

"Okay, boys, tell me what happened last night?" I'd say.

Murdoch would say, "Phil, man, you should have seen this chick. I'll tell you what, we did everything, and I mean everything. She was nuts out of her mind. We had a blast."

I'd be so envious. I'd say, "Tell me more. You guys are keeping me young."

Those guys used to keep me in stitches. I really enjoyed their company.

There were times when Donnie Murdoch was out of it. During one practice, he was skating, but he was falling, and he was holding his stick up high. We were afraid he'd spear someone or slice someone with his skate. I told John Ferguson, "Get him off before he gets hurt or he kills somebody."

One time Fergie took Murdoch in the back room and smacked him. I also did that once. I told him, "Straighten up, you son of a bitch," and I slapped him across the face. He was numb.

When he was clear-headed, Murdoch was a heck of a hockey player. He pissed away what could have been a great, great career.

After he was caught with drugs and suspended, he returned for the end of the season. He and Donnie Maloney played with me on a line they called the Godfather Line. Two Dons and a Godfather. I loved that. That was cool.

Several years earlier I had had the opportunity to test for the part of Gino, Talia Shire's husband, in the movie *The Godfather*. Gino is the guy who sets up Sonny Corleone, played by James Caan, and gets him killed.

I was supposed to go with Tony Conigliaro of the Red Sox and test for the part. But then I found out I would have to miss half the hockey season to make the movie. It was 1971, and I was at the top of my career.

I said, "If you give me a couple hundred thousand dollars, I'll do it."

"It's a low-budget film," they said.

"Then I can't do it," I told them.

The Godfather was the greatest movie of all time. There is one line in that movie that I have lived by ever since I heard it: "Keep your friends close but your enemies closer." I wait for the scene where Marlon Brando says that to Al Pacino. And I have tried hard to do that, especially in the hockey business. You watch your enemies and try to figure them out, because you can't fight them.

My final appearance for Canada came in 1977 in the World Championship. The Rangers had missed the playoffs for the second year in a row since I arrived. I had never missed being in the playoffs in my life before coming to New York, and it killed me, absolutely killed me. That year the Canadian team was made up of guys who were not involved in the NHL playoffs. They called us the Scrubs. A lot of guys decided not to go. I went. After the Blackhawks lost in the first round, my brother came with us. Walt McKechnie was there, and so was Wilf Paiement. We were not a very good team.

I got into a couple of scraps during the series. We were playing an exhibition game against Sweden, and in the middle of the game Stig Salming, Borje's brother, speared me right in the balls. I wanted to get him back, but I didn't get the chance until after the game, when I had an altercation with him in the hotel.

We were staying at the Park Schroenberg in Vienna, across the street from Schroenberg Park and Palace. I went into the hotel elevator and Stig was in there with a couple of his teammates. I popped him right in the mouth and got him good.

They kicked us out of the hotel, and I went to the Hilton. The night before we were scheduled to play the Swedes in the tournament game, I went to their training table while they were eating, and I said, "If you fucking guys think you're going to beat us, you're crazy! We're gonna hurt you. We are going to *hurt* you."

I was crazy. I was a nut there, because we had a bad team, and we didn't have a chance of winning. I thought maybe I could scare them. And we beat the Swedes. And we beat the Czechs. But we lost to the Russians. They killed us, 8-1. It was like it was back in 1972: we were in the penalty box the entire game. I felt so sorry for my brother. If it weren't for him, we'd have lost 16-1.

They made us wear helmets for the series. While we were skating before the first game, Alan Eagleson, who had set up the series, came over to us and said, "Everyone has to wear a helmet."

"I'm not wearing a helmet," I said. I had never worn a helmet in my whole life.

"They are not going to let you play if you don't wear a helmet."

"Then we'll go home," I said.

"You can't do that."

The money was supposed to go to the pension fund, so we wore the helmets and played. After the final game Gunther Sebetski, president of the International Ice Hockey Federation, came over to me. I grabbed my helmet and threw it at him. He thought I was giving it to him as a gift. After the game he brought it down to the dressing room for me to sign.

"I wasn't giving it to you, you asshole," I said. "I was throwing it at you. You can stick it up your ass. I'm not signing that piece of shit."

Phil!" Eagleson said.

"Get away from me, Al," I said. "Just leave me alone." I was so pissed. I felt that we had been thrown to the wolves so that the NHL and Hockey Canada, which was Eagleson, could make some money. They kept saying, "It's for the Players' Association," but the Players' Association didn't make any money. After nineteen years as a player, I get a pension of thirty-two thousand dollars Canadian. Years later we found out that Eagleson had screwed us on the supplemental pension from the 1972 series against the Russians. Eagleson was a thief. He stole money from Bobby Orr. He stole from me. He stole from the Players' Association. In plain English, he stole. And he finally ended up in jail because of it.

John Davidson, myself, and a couple of the other guys got a small measure of revenge on Eagleson during that series. A group of us were in Eagleson's suite when he said, "Why don't you guys go down to the bar and help yourself. Get all the wine and beer you want."

We looked at each other, and we went down to the bar, and we began ordering wine by the case. Some bottles cost two hundred dollars. We stacked up the bottles of wine on John Davidson's strong arms like a stack of wood. It was piled so high he couldn't see where he was going.

We went upstairs to one of the players' rooms and, man, did we drink some wine that night! When Eagleson got the bill, he went nuts. "Are you guys crazy?" he said. "Do you know how much the wine you drank cost me?" We were not sympathetic. He should never, ever have said to us, "The drinks are on me."

In 1978 Ron Duguay, Ron Greschner, myself, and a friend of Greschner's opened a club called Styx on 79th Street. We operated it from 1978 through 1981, when all the money disappeared, and it went under. But while it was going strong, we were hot, hot, hot.

Ronnie Duguay was a heartthrob. The girls loved him. Cher, Morgan Fairchild, and Farrah Fawcett all came in to see him. Morgan Fairchild was very pleasant, a nice lady. Cher seemed shy to me. She came in, sat down, and had dinner. Farrah came in too. I remember her legs. They were the most gorgeous legs. Once I flew the Concorde to London, and she and Ryan O'Neal were on the plane, and whenever she got up, every guy in that plane turned his head. She had a short skirt on, too and, God, did she have great legs. *Whooooooo.*

Every night the place was jammed. People lined up around the block to get in. It was packed for three years, and yet I lost over $250,000. I was playing hockey, and I couldn't watch the cash registers or the books. I couldn't be there at three in the morning to close.

I noticed that Greschner's friend did a lot of traveling. He went to the Super Bowl. He went to Hawaii. I wondered, "Who's watching the store?"

One time while I was there I watched a bartender go into the cash register, put money in, give a customer change, and slip a bill into his own pocket.

The second time he went to do it, I slammed the register door on his hand, broke the tips of his fingers, and threw him out, fired him on the spot. What are you going to do?

I hired Jo Anne, Donna's twin sister, as the maitre d', and she noticed that a lot of stealing was going on.

In the end I accused Greschner's friend of stealing the money, though I couldn't prove it.

"I'll have you killed, you son of a bitch," he told me.

"You will, huh?" I said. "Try it."

For a couple of weeks I looked over my shoulder.

The bar was a serious bone of contention between Donna and me, especially after Jo Anne saw what was going on. Jo Anne would go back and report to Donna.

Donna hadn't wanted me to open a club in the first place. But other players had invested in restaurants and had been coming away with five, six, seven hundred dollars a week in spending money. I wanted to be in on this. Unfortunately, it didn't work out for us. As soon as Duguay, Gresch, and I said we were refusing to put in another penny, the place went under. The place went bankrupt and we closed it up.

I was stupid. I told Donna, "This isn't the first mistake I ever made, and it won't be the last."

18

IT BECAME TOO DIFFICULT for John Ferguson to act as both general manager and coach. I don't know how Emile Francis did it all those years. He must have run everything from his office in Long Beach. You could do both in other cities, but not in New York. Beginning in 1978-79, Fergie concentrated on being the general manager and he hired Jean-Guy Talbot to be the coach.

After we failed to make the playoffs the second year in a row, Sonny Werblin fired Fergie and Talbot and brought in Freddie Shero to be general manager and coach. Shero could do both because he had lackeys do much of the work for him. He had Mike Nykoluk coaching the team and another of his buddies doing his GM work. Freddie really didn't do shit. But Freddie knew how to delegate.

To tell you the truth, when Freddie was sober he was a good coach. He studied the game. He knew all the techniques of coaching and playing. But boy, there were times . . .

One time Steve Vickers got a penalty, and he went into the penalty box, and Freddie kept calling for "Tkaczuk and Vickers, Tkaczuk and Vickers."

"Fred," I said, "Steve is in the penalty box."

He kept hollering, "Tkaczuk and Vickers."

"Fred," I said again, "Steve is in the fucking penalty box."

"Oh, okay." After he said it again, I finally jumped onto the ice and killed the penalty myself. Sometimes I wondered whether Fred did that to see if we were in the game or whether he was doing it because he was half in the bag. I really never knew.

Freddie the Fog was a great nickname for him.

In 1978-79, Fred's first year with the Rangers, he tried to bury me. Every day he would come in, and he would have to walk through our dressing room to get to his office where he had his beer on the radiators, and he'd say to me, "Espo, if you keep playing, you're going to be too old for the Old-Timers' games." Fred had lived in England quite a while and had developed a taste for warm beer.

He'd turn around and walk away. He did this almost every day. At first it really hurt my feelings. After about the twelfth time, I said to him, "Fuck you, Freddie," and he just kept on walking. All the guys started laughing. I didn't know why he was treating me like that.

Later that season he traded me to the Chicago Blackhawks for Jimmy Harrison.

Shero really liked Harrison. He had Ulf Nilsson playing center on the first line and Walt Tkaczuk on the second line, and I was on the third line. Freddie figured that since I was on the third line, they might as well get a guy who didn't make as much money as I was.

I was taken off the bus headed for the practice rink in Denver and told I had been traded. I took a cab back to the hotel. I was packing my stuff when they told me, "The trade is off. You're not going anywhere." The medical report had come in on Harrison, and his back was so bad that the Rangers killed the trade.

That also really hurt my feelings. I didn't deserve that. They wouldn't have done that to Bobby Orr or Gretzky or Lemieux. And I was more of a company man than they were. I was loyal to my team. Very loyal, though I guess I was kind of outspoken.

I survived the first half of the season and was put on a line with Donnie Murdoch and Dave Maloney. After getting only three or four goals in the first half, in the second half I began scoring like a maniac, and finished the season with 42 goals. I was scoring almost a goal a game at thirty-seven years of age. That year I played in my last All-Star game. Freddie wasn't happy about that because it cost the Rangers ten thousand dollars, which is what my contract called for if I made the game. My brother Tony had a broken finger, but he also played in the game.

We played the Los Angeles Kings in the opening round of the playoffs, beat them two out of three, and I scored the winning goal in overtime. I was skating down the middle of the ice. Murdoch had the puck on the right wing and centered it. Maloney was on the left, and when Darrell Edestrand came up to meet me, I overpowered him, beat him to the puck in front of the net, and jammed it home.

The next round was against the Flyers. That was a tough series. Shero had coached the Flyers, and he knew them. We carried out his game plan to perfection. We forechecked the defensemen all game long, and we kept up the traffic in front of their goal. And we beat them. We had to wait for the end of the Montreal-Boston series to see who we were going to play for the Stanley Cup.

Sonny Werblin invited Donna and me to watch the final game with Howard Cosell and Howard's wife, Emmy. I was pulling for the Boston Bruins like you wouldn't believe. Dave Maloney wanted to play Montreal.

Howard Cosell had a few drinks too many and once again he started putting his hands all over Donna. Again I told him, "I want you to keep your hands to yourself."

"Take it easy, Phil," Sonny said.

"Well I just don't like it," I said.

Howard laughed, and Emmy said, "Howard, behave yourself." He stopped immediately.

That was the game that Montreal tied after the Bruins were penalized for too many men on the ice, then won in overtime. Things like that happen. It's part of the game. Don Cherry got the blame, but that wasn't fair. Look how far the Bruins went that year.

When the game ended and Montreal won, I said, "Too bad. I'm going to tell you, we could have beaten the Boston Bruins."

Howard said, "A lot of the guys want to play those Canadiens."

"I don't know why," I said. "They are too good in the finals."

We went up to Montreal, and in the first game we beat them 6-2. Our goalie, John Davidson, was excellent, awesome.

After the game, I said to Fred Shero, "Let's get out of town. We have too many young guys. They're going to want to party."

"We'll be fine, Phil," Fred said. I was rooming alone, because I was the oldest player. I'll never forget, it was about five in the morning, and I heard a ruckus. I opened my door, and four or five of the guys were in the hallway wrestling stark naked with four girls. They just looked at me. I didn't say a word. They giggled and went back into their room. Donnie Murdoch was one of them. The other three are still married to the same women, and I don't want to get them in trouble.

We went out there for the second game, and Scotty Bowman decided to pull Kenny Dryden and start Bunny Larocque in goal. I was so happy because, as bad as Dryden may have been in that first game, he could turn it on. I felt we could beat Bunny Larocque.

The Canadiens were warming up with Larocque in goal when Doug Risebrough wound up and hit a slapshot that caromed off Larocque's head. He went down like a ton of bricks. Bowman had to put Dryden back in.

We scored two quick goals, but after that Kenny stopped everything we fired his way. Their defense tightened up. Their defensemen included Larry Robinson, Serge Savard, and Guy Lapointe, three Hall of Famers, so you can imagine how difficult it was to score on them.

They kept pecking away, and at our end John Davidson had a bad knee. It began to act up on him, and we lost that game.

We came back to New York and lost the third game 4-1. Johnny wasn't very good in that game either. Montreal won game four in overtime to go up 3-1. We should have won that game. We had them on the ropes. But J.D. couldn't move. Then Montreal won game five 4-1 to win the Cup. That was just about the closest the Rangers had come to winning the Stanley Cup since 1940. We should have won it that year. We should have, really.

I remember taking a faceoff during overtime in game four. Dougie Risebrough said to me, "Phil, you don't want to do this. You're too old for this." He was trash-talking.

I looked at him and said, "Oh, yes I do. Because I'm old and I might not get another chance. I want this."

"Well, I can't let you get it," he said.

I smiled at him.

The game winner was scored in overtime by Serge Savard. Serge was steady, not flashy. God, he was good. He twirled at the blue line. He came in and blasted one over J.D.'s left shoulder.

I wanted to retire after that season, but quite frankly I didn't want to give up the four hundred thousand dollars a year I was making. I had never made money like that. Two years later, the Rangers hired Craig Patrick as general manager, and when Craig came, my days were numbered.

19

WAYNE GRETZKY first joined the Edmonton Oilers in the WHA in 1978-79. He was eighteen years old, a baby. I remember Wayne as a fifteen-year-old playing in Sault Ste. Marie as a junior for the Greyhounds, a team that my dad owned a share in. Wayne came from Brantford, Ontario. I used to call my dad three or four times a week. I'd say, "How are the Greyhounds doing?"

One time he said, "Phil, we have a skinny little Polock kid here who's going to break every goddamn record you ever set."

"What are you talking about?" I said.

"The kid's name is Wayne Gretzky," he said.

"Yeah, Dad," I said. "Right."

I went to see Gretzky play the Russians in a junior tournament, and I didn't think he was anything special. I called my dad, and I said, "Gretzky's okay, Dad, but you're making mountains out of molehills."

"No, Phil," Dad said. "He's that good."

The next year he went to the World Hockey Association as a seventeen-year-old. When Wayne came into the National Hockey League in 1979-80, it was basically my last year, and I only played against him a couple of times. He wasn't good on faceoffs, but I had never seen a player who saw the ice like he did. He had eyes in the back of his head. He always knew where the puck was going to be. When you went to check him, he knew it before you did, and he knew what he was going to do with the puck before you ever had a clue. Wayne also knew what you were going to do with it before you did. He was just the smartest player I've ever seen, and he had the best vision on the ice. Gretzky could just see things. People would say to me, "Why can't you hit him?" "You can't hit what you can't catch," I'd say. Wayne was too smart for the defenders.

Later in his career, he was playing against the Rangers, and I was broadcasting. We were in Edmonton. Kevin Lowe, who was behind the blue line, flipped the puck up in the air. Wayne was skating toward the red line, and he knew if the puck got past the red line and he touched it, he would be offside. Wayne timed it – he leaped up in the air inside the red line and waited for the puck to come down, watched it come over his head like a wide receiver, got it, and continued. He leaped in the air so he wouldn't lose momentum, suspended himself as the puck came toward him, waited for the puck to come down, and then kept going! Amazing! No one else could have done that! He was incredible! Who else would have thought of that? And he did it effortlessly.

In 1979-80, my last full season, I had 34 goals and 44 assists. On February 2, 1980, I became the second player in NHL history to score 700 goals. Gordie Howe finished his career with 801. He was fifty-one years old and still playing for Hartford. Gordie gave us all hope.

We were playing Philadelphia. Donnie Maloney gave me a great pass up the middle. I closed in on Wayne Stephenson, and I gave him a little fake and beat him on the stick side for my 700th goal.

Then on March 12, I scored my 30th goal of the season, the thirteenth year in a row I scored 30 goals, tying Bobby Hull's record.

After the 1979-80 season Sonny Werblin hired Craig Patrick to be the Rangers general manager. Sonny wanted Freddie Shero to concentrate on coaching, to spend more time on the ice, and he ordered him to cut down on his drinking.

We had a bad team in 1980-81. I don't know what happened. It was a blur to me. When Craig replaced Freddie as general manager, Freddie stayed on as coach, but I think he just quit. He was just playing out the string.

We started the season badly. There was no camaraderie. You could smell beer on Freddie's breath. It wasn't any secret. Freddie was a great guy. I really liked him. He was an excellent coach, a technical student of the game who was able to get his players to do what he wanted them to do. But when he was drinking, as he did in the latter part of his career, there was no way he could function and he became a very strange person. Freddie had a piece of paper he'd write on. He would then look at it. Players would ask me, "What is he looking at?" I would say, "When the red light goes on, it means goal."

In late November 1980 Sonny Werblin fired Fred Shero and had Craig Patrick take over as coach as well as remain the general manager. Craig was supposed to be the interim coach until Herb Brooks could get out of his contract in Europe.

Once Craig took over as coach, our chemistry got a lot better. But every time a new coach comes in, the cards get shuffled. After Craig traded Donnie Murdoch to Edmonton, I was still relegated to the third line.

Craig and I got along, but I saw the handwriting on the wall. John Davidson had a knee operation. Wayne Thomas and Eddie Mio played goal, and our goaltending was terrible, and that was pretty much it for the team. The Rangers weren't going anywhere. We weren't any good, and I wasn't having a whole lot of fun playing any more.

I had been playing for eighteen and a half years. In December 1980, I woke up on Christmas eve and I said to Donna, "I've had it."

"What's the matter?" she asked.

"I think I'm going to tell Craig Patrick that I'm going to retire."

"That's nice," she said, and she rolled over and went back to sleep.

It was time. One reason was the NHL rash. It's a form of eczema. They don't know what causes it, but I think you get it from the equipment you wear. I'd put my equipment on, and I'd start to itch. Today if I skate eight times in two weeks, I get the rash on my ankles and my back.

One theory is that you get it from the fiberglass wrapped around hockey sticks. When the sticks come from the factory, they are all the same. But some players like a stick that lies flatter than they make them, and some players like a stick that is higher. If you skate low, like Gretzky, you want the blade flatter on the ice. I preferred to have as much blade as possible on the ice.

Stanley makes a rasp – a file – that you use to cut off the heel or the toe of the stick. I would file down the stick to my specifications. I would work on my sticks with the rasp, and then I would get this rash on my hips and elbows and on my back where the shoulder pads sit. The theory is that the fiberglass gets in the air and into the underwear and the pads, and it would feel like little needles sticking into you. Some guys like Tommy Reid itched so badly they had to retire. Guy Lapointe spent time in the hospital because of it. It's a very bad thing.

I was playing in Edmonton just before I decided to retire. It was windy and cold and miserable, and I had to ask Donnie Maloney to apply Vaseline to the affected areas on my back. I had Donnie do it for me, because the trainers in New York were terrible. I would then put cotton on the rash areas to alleviate the itching. I also put Vaseline on my ankles and knee caps. After the game it took forever to get the Vaseline off.

After the Edmonton game I scratched myself so badly that I began bleeding. I said to Donnie, "This isn't worth it any more. I'm suffering, man."

I went to practice. I said to Craig Patrick, "Craig, I have to talk to you. I think it's time for me to hit the road. You're playing me with the third or fourth line. I'm not playing a lot."

"We're not a real good team," he said, "and I'm playing the kids."

I understood. I said, "I don't want to go out sitting on the bench."

"You sure you want to retire?" he asked.

"No, I'm not," I said.

"Maybe you ought to talk to Mr. Werblin."

I had lunch with Sonny Werblin at the Pan-Am building, which is now the Met Life building, on the top floor and told him how I was feeling.

He wanted to know if I was sure, and I told him I wasn't sure at all.

"Let me tell you about Joe Namath," he said. Joe had played for Sonny when Sonny owned the New York Jets. "I used to tell Joe, 'Never, never overstay your welcome in this league.'" Sonny said to me, "That's the one thing you ought to be cognizant of." He used that word. "I'm not telling you you should retire," he said. "That has to be your decision."

"But I'm not sure," I said.

"Nobody is ever really sure," he said. "But if you don't want to quit, don't." He asked me, "Do you think you can still play?"

"No doubt," I said, "and if the team was better, I'd probably be contributing a lot more. But the team is bad and Craig is playing the kids."

"Craig Patrick will never, ever do anything to hurt you," Sonny said.

I said, "But Craig might have to, because he has to do his job, and if I'm not contributing, it's time for someone else to play."

"That's your decision, Phil," he said.

"I think I've had it. I think it's time."

"We'll meet tomorrow," he said.

It was December 28, 1980. I left Sonny and went to see Craig Patrick. "It's definite," I told Craig, "It's over for me." And then I told him that I had always wanted to go out like Ted Williams, announcing my retirement and playing in my final game. "God, I'd love to do that," I said.

"Why don't you?" Craig said. "We'll announce your final game, and you'll play in it. You can do that."

The next day I went with Sonny and a few of my teammates to the 21 Club to announce my plans. Don Maloney, Doug Sulliman, and I were all teary-eyed.

The team had several days off. We decided I would play my last game on January 7, 1981. My mom wasn't feeling well, so my dad came down by himself for the game. My kids also came.

We played the Buffalo Sabres, and I played as good a game as I could play. I had a couple of assists and was productive. The difference between this game and earlier ones was that Craig Patrick played me on a regular shift and the power play, and I played on a line with Donnie Maloney and Doug Sulliman, the Rangers' best players.

In the third period, Ronnie Hoggarth, the referee, called a penalty on me.

"You've got to be kidding," I said.

"I let you get away with it twice before," he said.

"Give me a break," I said. "I hardly touched the guy."

"You think I *want* to give you a penalty?" he said. "I have to call it."

Later, with the score 3-3 and only seconds left in the game, I got the puck in the slot. Donnie Edwards was the Sabres goalie. I took a split second longer than I used to, and I took a snapshot, and Mike Ramsey, who had played on the U.S. Olympic team, went to block the shot, and he hit it with his glove and stopped it from going into the net. That puck should have been in the net. That was proof to me that it was time to retire. Two years earlier no one would have stopped that shot.

When the game ended, one of the Buffalo players, a kid whose name I can't remember, asked for my stick, and I gave it to him. That's a lot different from what Wayne Gretzky did in his last game. Every shift he wore a different jersey and used a different stick and kept them to keep or sell as memorabilia.

After the game, I came onto the ice for an encore. I took the puck and skated toward the other end, acknowledging the cheers and the clapping of the fans. When I flipped the puck into the empty net, there was a roar. I bent over, got the puck, and threw it into the crowd. Then I waved and skated off the ice.

Afterward Donna threw me a party at Oren and Aretsky's, on 3rd Avenue and 85th Street. My dad, my brother Tony, and Joe Bucchino, who worked for the Rangers, were the only ones who said I was crazy to retire. My dad left the party at one-thirty in the morning. I left a little bit later.

I woke up the next morning, and I was sitting in my chair in front of the TV not knowing what to do with myself.

Donna said, "Why don't you walk the dogs in the park?"

And that's what I did that morning.

At the time a reporter asked me if I was dreading my retirement. I said, "Your life isn't over. It's like reading a book. You are enjoying that book, but you know sooner or later that book is going to end. And now you have to search for another book. You have to search for something that is going to give you as much pleasure and enjoyment as the last book."

I had played organized hockey since I was twelve years old, and ever since then I was focused on that book, and every day I couldn't wait to get to the next page. And then suddenly the book was over. So when my career was over, I just closed the book and said, "Wow! That was good!" And that was exactly how I felt. It's like sex. Sometimes you have great sex and say, "Wow! That was good." And then sometimes you go, "Yeah, okay, I think I'll go to sleep now." So for the idiots who don't read books, I know they've had sex, so that's the way I can explain it to them.

20

AFTER MY RETIREMENT Craig Patrick called and asked me if I wanted to be his assistant coach. "You can go to practice and go on the ice with the guys," he said. I accepted the offer.

During games Craig and I stood side by side. On the bench he was very quiet. I was always the opposite: I liked to yell at the referees, because it helped me get into the game.

But Craig kept saying, "Keep quiet, Phil. Don't yell at them. I don't want my coaches yelling at the refs. It just makes them go against us."

"I disagree," I said. "When you yell at them and tell them they made a bad call, they think twice before making the next call."

"You are not supposed to talk to them," he said, "and I don't want you to."

I said, "Fine."

One afternoon I was sitting in my chair in my apartment on 67th Street watching television. Donna was out, riding or walking the dogs, and I was just sitting there. I had no ambition to do anything. I guess I was depressed. I knew my being an assistant coach wasn't going to work. And Craig knew it too. What fun was it if I couldn't even yell at the referees?

I wasn't happy. I was too close to the guys. I had just played with them. A few days later I said to Craig, "This isn't working out. I can't do this. When I'm at the game I feel I can still play, and I know I don't want to, because I can't, so it would just be better for me to get away." He agreed. I was still being paid. The Rangers paid me until the end of the season.

For the rest of my life I would have to satisfy myself by playing in Old-Timers games. The first Old-Timers game I played in was in Stamford, Connecticut, at the Dorothy Hamill Arena. Gordie Howe, Bobby Hull, and I all played. Gordie was fifty-two and Hull forty-two. We were playing against college guys who could skate pretty well, young guys, lawyers and stockbrokers in their twenties and thirties.

I mean, these guys were flying. Gordie and I were sitting on the bench, and Gordie said, "Jesus, these guys can skate."

"I know," I said. "Goddamn, they are getting a little too serious."

Gordie said, "Yeah, they are. We've got to talk to them."

Gordie and I went out onto the ice, and I heard him say to one of the young guys, "Hey, take it easy, son. Slow down. You don't want to embarrass us old guys."

The guy said, "What's the matter, old-timer? Can't keep up?"

The puck dropped, and I sent it over to Bobby, and out of the corner of my eye I could see Gordie whacking the guy who had taunted him.

Whack! Smack! Boom! Bang! The guy went down, and he started moaning, "Oh Jesus. Oh Jesus."

Gordie said, "Get up, you fucking suck. Get up. I didn't hit you that hard."

I skated over and said, "Gordie, what happened?"

"I speared him in the balls," Gordie said.

"You're kidding me," I said.

"No," Gordie said. "That will slow him down."

Gordie skated over to their bench, and he said, "Does anybody else here want to try to embarrass me?" He then repeated the question to drive home the point.

No one said a word.

I said, "Gordie, you are fucking nuts."

"No way they are going to embarrass me," he said. "I won't let them."

I love Gordie. Gordie is one tough son of a bitch.

———

Two months after I quit as Rangers assistant coach, Sonny Werblin and then one of the Garden executives, Jack Krumpe, asked me if I'd be interested in the TV broadcasting job. I said I would be, but I told them that I didn't want to take long-time announcer Bill Chadwick's job from him. It wasn't my style to do that. Bill "The Big Whistle" Chadwick – they called him that because he had once been a referee – had been there for a thousand years. Jack said that Bill was going to retire and that they were going to replace him whether I took the job or not.

"In that case, yeah, I'd like to do that," I said. I figured it would be fun. I always thought I could do it. As a player I had been a guest commentator during the playoffs for NBC. I had announced during the Stanley Cup final. So I knew what it was all about.

In August 1982 I signed a four-year two-hundred-thousand-dollar-a-year contract to broadcast the Rangers' games. The first year my partner was Jimmy Gordon. Jim and Bill Chadwick had been really close. I was sure Jimmy thought I had bumped Chadwick from his job, and I knew I had better do something fast or he would resent me. Before my first broadcast, I said, "Jimmy, listen, you're the boss up here. You're the play-by-play guy. I'm the color guy. I don't want to overstep my bounds with you, and if I do, I apologize in advance. You lead me. You set the tone. You set the pace. When you want me to talk, make me talk. You are totally in control here."

I knew I had to do that, because if you don't get along with your play-by-play man, you're in trouble. Look at Howard Cosell and those other guys on *Monday Night Football*. In the beginning they all got along, but then egos got in the way. And the broadcasts suffered.

Jimmy and I were absolutely fine from the beginning. I think one of the reasons he lost his job at the end of the year was that he was a hard-nosed union man. One time I came in early before a game to get in the booth and do my homework. It was pitch-black, and I turned on the light switch.

Out of the corner came a deep voice: "What are you doing? You can't do that."

"What's the matter? I said. "What did I do?"

Jimmy said, "You turned the lights on."

"So what?" I said.

"You can't turn the lights on," the voice said. "That's my job."

"You gotta be shitting me. I just turned them on."

"It's against union rules," he said.

I said, "Get the fuck out of here," and I held the switch, and I flipped it on and off fifty times.

He reported me to the union, and they threatened to go on strike right then. Sonny Werblin told me if I didn't apologize, there wouldn't be a hockey game. All because I had turned the lights on in the booth.

So before the game I apologized, and the game went on. Jimmy Gordon said to me, "Phil, you were wrong. You shouldn't have done that."

"Aw, come on, Jim. This is a joke," I said. But it wasn't a joke. Jimmy and all the electricians were really pissed at me.

After the game Jimmy and I usually went our separate ways. He might or might not have a drink or two, but then he'd go up to his room and read. I was used to going to a bar with the players and sitting there shooting the shit about the game, but I couldn't do that any more because the players considered the announcers part of the media. It became very lonely for me on the road.

The next year they replaced Jimmy with Sam Rosen, and Sam and I had a lot more laughs. We really clicked. One year we were sponsored by Minolta cameras, and their slogan was "The magic eye of Minolta." Sam would do the commercial each game live on camera, and while he was talking they would switch to a picture of the camera, and he'd talk over it.

When they switched to the shot of the camera, I'd be making faces at Sam, trying to get him to crack up. He would giggle, and after doing the commercial, he'd say, "Phil, you have to stop doing that." But he'd go on the next day, and once again I'd make faces and try to get him to laugh. We would kill each other.

Sam Rosen and I had so much fun broadcasting the games. I absolutely loved it, except that the general manager, the coaches, and especially the players made us feel that we weren't part of the team, and that really bothered me.

It was like I wasn't part of them. Management didn't want me to talk to the players, and I couldn't talk to the press, because if I said something derogatory the reporter would use it against me and it would end up in the papers, and the players would only become more alienated.

Later, when I became general manager of the Rangers, I tried hard to make the press, especially the reporters who traveled every single day with the team and the broadcasters, a part of the team. And to this day they aren't, and that's why you don't have the loyalty from the radio and TV guys. I guess management doesn't want them to know the inner workings of the team, what's going on behind the scenes. Maybe they're afraid you might say something on the air they didn't want the public to know.

―――

While I was broadcasting, I began the Phil Esposito Foundation to help retired and indigent players who couldn't cope with having their careers end. I knew there were a lot of players like that. I was a so-called superstar, and if I hadn't had the broadcasting job I wouldn't have had any money. Most of the guys had made less money than I had, and when they retired, they had little or nothing left. Once you retired, you were gone, and nobody gave a darn about you.

I wanted to give something back, and I felt that this was the best way for me to do that. We raised money by promoting the Masters of Hockey games. I hired Warren Breinin, who was a specialist in career orientation, and I paid him out of my own pocket. I just felt I had to do it.

I went to the Players' Association and said, "I want a dollar a game from each player," which amounted to eighty dollars per player a year. Alan Eagleson threw me out, and I will never, ever forgive him for that. I went to the membership board of the Players' Association, told them what I was doing, and asked each player for just eighty bucks a year. They voted no. And it really bothered me. I went to the NHL. They said no.

I called all the former players I knew, and I got a few sponsors, and we put on these Masters of Hockey games. Over a period of four years we held one in Detroit, one in Boston, and two in New York. We raised a couple of hundred thousand dollars each game.

We didn't give all the money directly to the guys. If a guy was drugging, we put him in Hazelton. We put other guys in Betty Ford to get them off their drugs or alcohol. Then we found jobs for them. Roger Crozier never had a drug or alcohol problem, but he was having a hard time finding work. We found a job in the insurance business in Washington, D.C., for him. I mention Roger's name because he would be glad for me to do so. We helped other guys pay for college.

The program helped eighty-two players. We helped a couple of football players as well and an actor who was a friend of Michael J. Fox. Michael and I met on the corner of Columbus Avenue and 76th Street, in a restaurant there. He was starring in the *Family Ties* TV show with Meredith Baxter Birney and Justine Bateman. In the show he was conservative, and his parents were hippies. We talked, and I told him what I was doing. Michael played in a couple of the games.

During one spring training season I traveled to Fort Lauderdale and talked to about forty New York Yankees players and minor-leaguers about planning for their future after baseball. We were making an impact. We knew we were doing a good thing.

After a while the organization grew too big. The demand for our services kept growing, and no one was getting paid for their time. A lot of players start foundations and get money for running them, but I couldn't do that, and so four years after I started the program, I decided I couldn't do it any more. I had become general manager of the Rangers, and I had no time to spend on it. The Players' Association took it over, and they are doing it now. That's fine, as long as someone's doing it.

━━━━

Around this time my daughter Cherise was born, and Donna decided that we should move out of the city because she didn't want Cherise to grow up there. I loved living in the city. I would have lived there forever. It was a perfect lifestyle for me. But as in Boston, Donna wanted to have horses, and we built a beautiful home in Bedford, New York, an hour and a half north in Westchester County, on four acres. There were trails and a barn just down the street. Donna was happy – she could ride her horses.

━━━

On June 5, 1984, I was elected into the Hockey Hall of Fame along with Jacques Lemaire and Bernie Parent. It wasn't that big a deal to me because I feel there are some players in the hall who shouldn't be there, and as a result it sort of cheapens it for everyone. I don't know how Tretiak, the Russian goalie, got in there. I don't get it. But it's a nice honor, because you can write "Hall of Fame" after your name when you're signing autographs. I was awarded the Order of Canada, and I have the right to put "O.C." after my name, but I've never done that. Awards and trophies just don't mean all that much to me. I know getting into the hall was important, but some guys make such a big deal out of it, and I'm just not that way. I have kept one MVP trophy and one scoring trophy. I have my MVP from the Players' Association, and that was important to me because the players voted for it. As far as my scoring champion trophies, I have five or six of them, and I'm very proud of that, but you don't see them on my mantle. The one memento up on my wall that means a lot to me is my retired jersey from the Boston Bruins. That may have been the greatest thing ever to happen to me.

That occurred on January 17, 1985. It was almost to the day – January 16, 1962 – that I was called up from the minors and joined the Chicago Blackhawks, so you know how many years it was for my number to be retired. It was really important to me.

My first reaction was, "It's about time," because they could have done it much earlier. They never should have given my number to any other player after me.

The season after I was traded to the Rangers, we played the Bruins in Providence in an exhibition game. I was skating around, and I noticed that Tommy Songin of the Bruins was wearing number 7, and my heart went down to my toes. I hated Harry Sinden for that. I hated the man!

Songin skated over and said to me, "I didn't ask for it, Phil. They just gave it to me." You can bet that Sinden did that just to make me mad. And it really, really bothered me.

At the time they were retiring my number, Ray Bourque was wearing it, and Harry said to Ray, "You'll still wear number 7. When you retire, we'll put your name up there with his." Harry called and told me that was what the Bruins were going to do, and that was fine with me. It's not bad company to be with a guy like Ray Bourque, who played twenty-one years with the Bruins.

When they held the ceremony Ray skated over to me wearing number 7, and he took his jersey off and handed it to me, and much to my surprise, underneath he was wearing 77. I had no clue he was going to do that.

Around Christmas Bourque apparently had gone to Sinden and said, "I want Phil to have 7. I'll wear 77."

"Are you sure?" Harry said.

Bourque said yes.

If you look at the tape of the ceremony, you can see Bourque come over and start to take off his sweater, and you can see me saying to him, "What are you doing?" When he took it off and I saw that he was wearing 77 so that 7 would never be worn again in Boston, I was flabbergasted.

"That's the first time Phil Esposito has ever been at a loss for words," Bourque said.

I was close to tears. It was very emotional for me to see Wayne Cashman and Kenny Hodge pulling my number 7 uniform up to the top of the rafters of the Boston Garden along with those of Bobby Orr and the other guys there.

I'll never forget what Bourque did for me. I don't know if I would have been as generous if I had been in his shoes. Maybe I would have. I don't know.

I did the color commentary for the Rangers all through 1984-85 and 1985-86, a year in which coach Ted Sator led the Rangers into the playoffs past Philadelphia and Washington and into the conference finals against Montreal. During that Montreal series I got a call from Jack Krumpe asking me if I'd be interested in being the general manager of the Rangers the following year.

"You've got Craig Patrick, Jack," I said. "Craig's a good guy. I'm not so sure about that." And to tell the truth, I wasn't keen on doing it. I liked broadcasting. I didn't like that the coaches and players treated me like a reporter, a complete outsider, but other than that I loved the job. And I liked Craig a lot. I still do.

"We're going to replace Craig," Krumpe said. "There are other reasons, personal reasons."

When someone says that to me, I don't ask them why. I just let it go.

In June 1986 Krumpe called me up. "I want to talk to you about something," he said. "Would you come over?"

When I arrived at his office in Madison Square Garden, he said, "We'd like you to take over as general manager. We're going to let Craig go. Even though I love Craig."

Everybody loved Craig. I don't know if he was having marital problems, but it wasn't long after that that he got a divorce. But what they told me was that Craig was not paying attention to his job and they were going to replace him.

"I'm not sure I want this," I said. "I really enjoy broadcasting. It's something I do well. No doubt I'd like to make more money . . ."

Five days later he called me again. Once again we left it open. Later that week I got a call from Joe Cohen, who ran the TV operation for the Rangers. He told me the Rangers were going to replace Craig and he let me know that Art Baron, the head of Paramount, which owned Madison Square Garden, wanted to talk to me about the job.

Joe said, "I strongly suggest you take it."

Joe had good information. Not long after that Jack Krumpe invited me out to meet with him and Art Baron at Baron's apartment at the Hampshire House. We were sitting around his dining-room table, and Baron said, "We'd like you to take over as general manager. We're going to replace Craig. We want you to be the guy."

My ego got to me. I was sure I could do a great job. And they offered to double my pay back to the four hundred thousand dollars I had made as a player. The money got my attention because the house in Bedford was costing me a fortune, and with that added money I could do the things I wanted to do, like join a country club to play golf. One other thing I knew: taking this job was risky. If I stayed in television, I could be there forever. It didn't matter whether the team won or lost.

I repeated what I had been saying all along. "I'm not sure I want to do this."

Art Baron replied, "Phil, you don't understand. You either take the job or you don't work for Madison Square Garden."

I'd like to think he was joking. I thought to myself, Come on, he can't be serious. He has to be joking with me.

Art was a nice man, but he was tough. I liked Art Baron a lot. I said to him, "Come on, Art, you're kidding." And he laughed. Which is why I'm not sure whether he was serious or not.

"Come on, Phil," Art said. "Jeez, why would you not want to do this?"

Art put it in my head, and I called Jack Krumpe and told him I'd take it if he also gave me a $1,000-a-month car allowance. That's what the general manager of the Knicks told me he was getting. I ended up getting $750, which was pretty good, and with that money I leased a Mercedes. I never liked the car, but Donna wanted one. She drove it, and I drove a Ford Thunderbird, which I loved. What the hell did I need a fancy car for? I don't. Still don't. So on July 14, 1986, I accepted the job of general manager of the New York Rangers.

After I got the job, Emile Francis, who was running the Hartford Whalers, called me up and offered his congratulations. He said, "Now, expect to be fired."

"What?" I said.

"You've been hired," he said, "and from this point on, they are going to try to fire you."

I never forget that, and he was absolutely right. New York was a tough, tough gig. I didn't realize what I was getting into.

21

WHEN I TOOK OVER as Rangers general manager, there were a lot of people there, including some of the players, who made me feel uncomfortable and unwelcome. Rod Gilbert, Steve Vickers, and Walt Tkaczuk had been Rangers their whole lives, and all of a sudden I was their boss, and they seemed to resent it. I know for a fact that Rod would have killed to get that job.

Though they weren't playing any more, Gilbert, Tkaczuk, and Vickers were always around the Garden. Gilbert worked for the Rangers. He still does. They weren't supportive when I was playing with them. Why would they support me as general manager?

The first person I hired was Eddie Giacomin. Eddie for years was the Rangers' goalie. I liked Eddie, and I wanted him to teach the goalies. And I thought, why not have an ex-Ranger as an assistant coach? Also, my plan then, though it didn't happen in the end, was to bring in Wayne Cashman, my former Boston Bruins linemate, as the next head coach. I figured that hiring Eddie as an assistant coach would ease the pain of Wayne being in charge.

The first day I had the job I was ready to roll up my sleeves and go to work. What people didn't understand was that for three years I had been a broadcaster, and I had watched every game the Rangers had played during that time. In my job as analyst I probably could see more than the general manager, coach, or players.

I felt I was a pretty darn good judge of talent, toughness, and effort, and when I took over I knew there were four or five guys I wanted to get rid of immediately, including Willie Huber, a large guy who didn't hustle. It took me over a year to get rid of Willie, because everyone else also knew what he was.

One time in Philadelphia, when I had taken over coaching duties, Willie skated off the ice.

"Where are you going?" I asked.

"I'm coming off. I'm tired."

"You are not," I said. "You're staying out there."

I made him stay out there for four shifts – seven minutes – until he was dropping dead. And the more he stayed on, the better he played.

"Willie," I said, "it's all in that big head of yours."

Another player I wanted to get rid of was Reijo Ruotsalainen, who to me was not a team player. He got wind of the fact I wanted to trade him, and so he left the Rangers and stayed home in Finland. When he tried to play in Switzerland, I stopped him, cold. "You have a contract," I told him. "I'm not letting you play." Eventually he came back and played for Edmonton. We had another player, Mark Pavelich, who quit the team and wanted to play in Europe, and I fought him tooth and nail, and he didn't get to play either.

When I was a broadcaster, I caught one guy snorting cocaine before we got on a plane. If I had been a player, I would have whacked that son of a bitch. But since I was a broadcaster, I minded my own business. Well, as soon as I became the general manager, I traded him as fast as I could to get him out of there.

I knew that we needed some scoring and we also needed a goalie to go along with John Vanbiesbrouck. I wasn't satisfied with Glen Hanlon, so the first thing I did was go out and get free agent goalie Doug Soetaert. Soapy had lost his job in Montreal to Patrick Roy. After I went and signed him, I traded Hanlon to the Detroit Red Wings for center Kelly Kisio and winger Lane Lambert. I liked Kisio's grit and attitude, and he eventually became our captain. Lane Lambert never did play a lot, and I ended up trading him to Quebec.

My next move was to trade Mike Allison, a twenty-five-year-old kid with a bum knee, for Walt Poddubny of Toronto. The Rangers' doctor told me that Mike's knee was really bad. "It might go next year or next month or next week," he said. "But sooner or later Mike is going to have to quit because of his knee." Poddubny was a very fluid skater and he was in perfect health. He was playing left wing for Toronto, and only five minutes a game at that, but I really thought he had a lot of potential as a centerman, because he could shoot. God, could he snap the puck. That's where I put him, and Walt ended up scoring 35 or 40 goals a year for us.

Let me explain how I made my trades. I analyzed it in baseball terms. If I could trade a .250 hitter and get a .255 or .260 hitter, I did it. I also considered whether the player had character and whether he was a good guy to have in the dressing room.

The guy I was looking for more than any other was a player like Gary Carter of the Mets. I didn't know Gary from Adam at the time, but I thought Gary Carter was the stone, the glue, of the New York Mets, and I badly wanted to acquire a player like him for the Rangers.

Unfortunately, the Rangers' management prevented me from accomplishing that goal. In September 1986 I acquired Mark Messier from the Edmonton Oilers. Peter Pocklington was in deep financial trouble. His meat-packing business was going down the tubes. His oil investments were too. It was public knowledge he was trying to dump his most expensive players, including Messier and Wayne Gretzky, because he couldn't afford to keep them any more.

I called Glen Sather, the general manager and coach of the Oilers. We worked out a deal. I was going to send Kisio, Vanbiesbrouck, Tomas Sandstrom, and a second-round draft pick for Messier and five million in cash.

Glen and I were set to go, but the owners had to get involved because of the money. Pocklington agreed.

Dick Evans, president and CEO of Madison Square Garden, and Jack Diller, president of the Rangers, said, "No, we're not going to spend five million dollars for Messier. We don't need to put people in the seats."

"We can win the Stanley Cup with this guy," I said.

"You're giving up three good players."

"Yeah," I said. "Kisio scored about twenty goals, we'll never win in this town with Vanbiesbrouck, and as far as Sandstrom is concerned, I don't like giving him up, but I'm getting fucking Messier." Mark Messier was an unbelievable hockey player.

They said no. "Work the deal without the money," they said, but the Oilers wouldn't do it without the money, so we never traded for Messier.

I was back having to make small trades, building the team slowly. In mid-November 1986 I traded Bob Brooke to Minnesota for Tony McKegney, Curt Giles, and a second-round pick in 1988. The primary reason I traded Brooke was that Rangers coach Teddy Sator played him too much, and I couldn't stand it any more. Brooke played more than the better players on the team! He was okay, but he was a college player, and I doubt he'd have even made the team if it hadn't been that Herb Brooks, who had gained his reputation coaching college players in the Olympics, was coaching the Rangers when Brooke first came up. In addition to McKegney, who was intense, tough, and could score, I got Curt Giles, a good little defenseman, plus I got that second-round pick.

Teddy Sator wasn't happy about the deal, but I didn't care. I just didn't like his coaching philosophy. The team was going nowhere.

He had his system, and he wanted the players to fit into it. A lot of coaches nowadays do the same thing. They don't let a player be himself. They don't let him do what he does best. Now if you're Wayne Gretzky, Mario Lemieux, or Mark Messier, you can play your game within that system. Anyone else, you'd better play using his system, or you don't play. I don't agree with that.

I also didn't like Teddy's two assistants. "You should get yourself a couple of other guys," I told him, "because these guys are hurting you."

Looking back, Teddy wasn't a bad coach, but he was Craig Patrick's coach, and I wanted my own man.

After the Rangers lost a couple games in a row, I flew out to Vancouver to fire him. I had no coach in mind who I wanted, so I decided I'd coach myself until I could hire a new coach. I had never coached before in my life. I told Teddy and his two assistants, "I'm making a change. I'm going to coach. I want to coach for a while."

Teddy just said, "Okay, if that's what you want . . ." And they were gone.

The first game I ever coached was against the Vancouver Canucks. We were down by three goals after the first period. I came into the dressing room, and I guess they thought I was going to rip ass and throw things. "Whoa, boy, my nerves," I said. "I'm glad that's over with. I don't know about you guys, but it seems to me that that fucking team is embarrassing us."

I made eye contact with each player. I remember Tony McKegney. He was very intense looking at me.

"Look," I said, "why don't we just go out there and have some fun? Come on, just play your game."

We went out, and Tony scored four goals, and we won the game 6-4.

The other thing I remember about the game was that I put Jan Erixon on a guy who had scored twice for the Canucks. "Erixon," I said, "I don't give a shit if he goes to the toilet. You stay with him. If he goes to the bench, skate to the bench with him. I don't care if you never touch the puck, understand? This guy doesn't touch the puck the rest of the night and he doesn't get another goal." And Jan did a hell of a job, and we ended up winning the game.

After the game Tony McKegney came up to me and said, "Wow, I wouldn't believe we could come back like that."

"Yeah, we did, didn't we?" I said. "You guys are a good team. You have to have fun at this game, and you haven't been having any fun. None of you."

The next day at practice we fooled around. I made them turn their sticks upside down and scrimmage.

"Screw the drills!" I said. "Let's play hockey! Let's have some fun."

I bought a tanning bed for our practice facility in Rye. The guys wanted to know why. "I don't know about you guys," I said, "but when I played I used to look at myself in the mirror in January and February, and I looked like chalk and felt sick. But if I had color, I felt good. Here's a Jacuzzi and a tanning bed."

If you look at yourself in the mirror during the gray days of January, you're halfway through the season and you're tired, you can't say, "Take five days off and go to the Bahamas." So instead of sitting in the tropical sun, they were able to get some sun using the tanning bed, and it made them feel good. The guys thought I was nuts, but they enjoyed it.

McKegney, one of the few black players in the league, wrote on it, "McKeg's Lounge."

In the meantime I interviewed candidates for permanent coach. One was Tommy Webster, who had coached the Windsor Spitfires in Junior A for several years and had been an assistant coach for the Hartford Whalers. I knew Tommy from playing with him a couple years in Boston.

Tommy impressed me. He had studied the game, and I liked his philosophy. During our conversation, I told him, "I want our team to be entertaining. You've got to go forward and score. Defense is fine, but I want a coach whose philosophy is going to be on the same wavelength as mine." Every coach I ever interviewed said the same thing: "Absolutely." And then they did what they wanted. But Tommy was different. He and I really did agree.

I asked him, "Webbie, why do you want to coach in the NHL? Is it because you're going to make a lot more money than you do in Junior A?"

"That's part of it," he said. "But coaching is my career, and I want to coach in the NHL. Though I have to admit that coaching in New York scares me a little bit."

"Why would New York scare you?" I asked.

"It's big, and there's a lot of media attention."

Coaching in New York turned out to be extremely difficult for Tommy.

"I demand loyalty," I told him. "If you're not loyal to me, I won't tolerate it. You'll be gone. Fired. I'll fire your ass as fast as I can."

Tommy said he understood, and Tom Webster turned out to be the most loyal coach I ever had. Wayne Cashman was another coach who always was loyal to me. There wasn't anything Wayne wouldn't do if I asked him. Webbie was in the same mold.

In late November 1986 I hired Tom Webster to be my permanent coach for the Rangers.

The players really liked him. He was soft-spoken, though he could be tough if he had to be. Tommy's philosophy was defense and pinch, to play offensively, and to have a great power play. He wanted our power play to be the best in the league, and I loved that, though our power play never did turn out to be what we wanted.

And if I asked Tommy a question during a meeting, he would give me an answer. He wasn't one of those political coaches who spends half the time covering his ass. He'd tell you how he felt about something.

And whatever I did, Tommy backed me 100 per cent. He didn't second-guess me in the papers. We may have disagreed, but we did it privately, and that was fine. He didn't stab me in the back, like some of my subsequent coaches.

The Rangers' biggest problem, Tommy and I agreed, continued to be our goaltending. We still had John Vanbiesbrouck, and on December 18, 1986, I acquired Bobby Froese from Philadelphia for Kjell Samuelsson, who went on to have a great career with the Flyers. Froese played great for us. He was great in the dressing room. He was a good guy, and everybody liked him.

We also had a kid goaltender I liked a lot who Craig Patrick had drafted: Mike Richter. I always said that if the Rangers ever won a Stanley Cup, Mike Richter would be the goalie. And I was right.

When Tommy took over, everything went smoothly for about a month. We had a great win over the Washington Capitals in Washington. But before the game Webbie wasn't feeling too well.

"Are you okay to go?" I asked.

"Yeah, I'm fine."

In the middle of the second period, I could see from my seat in the press box that Tom wasn't on the bench.

The PR man came over to me and said, "Tommy is really sick. He can't go back out there."

I went down to the dressing room, and he was really dying. He was throwing up and crapping back in the locker room. He couldn't even lift up his head.

Wayne Cashman, who was his assistant coach, took over for him the second half of the period. I went behind the bench in the third period with Wayne. With little time left in the game, we were a goal down. Tomas Sandstrom came off, and I put Pierre Larouche out there. Pierre had quick hands, great hands! He was on the right side, and Tomas Sandstrom looked at me. It was the same look I had given coaches a thousand times, that look that said, Put me back out there. I'm going to score.

"Tomas," I yelled.

Someone said, "He just came off."

On a cruise
to Italy in 1979.

Bridget.

The Boston Bruins retire my number.

My retirement party in Sault Ste. Marie in 1981. From left to right: Wayne Gretzky, me, Tony, and Bobby Orr. Wanna challenge us?

GM of the Tampa Bay Lightning.

Me and Bridget with Rosella and Henry Paul in New Orleans.
We brought the Lightning to Tampa Bay.

From left to right, Carrie, me,
Cherise, and Laurie.

My grandsons Dakoda and Dylan
(on my knees), baby Rocco, and
Niko in front.

Me and Niko grab a smoke.

Laurie, Dakoda, and Chris Rapp.

From top: Carrie, grandson Dylan, son-in-law Alex, and grandson Niko.

Bottom: The Esposito gang. Sitting from left to right: my nephew Jason, my daughter Carrie, me, and Tony. Standing: Carrie's husband Alex Selivanov, Bridget, my daughter Laurie Rapp, my grandson Dakoda, and son-in-law Chris Rapp.

Daughter Cherise.

Bridget and me.

"I don't give a shit," I said. "Tomas, go on out there. Get in the high slot. Tell Pierre to come here a second."

Pierre skated over. I said, "Pete, you have to win the faceoff and get the puck to Tomas."

I loved Pierre Larouche. He said, "No problem, boss."

Pierre did exactly what I told him to do, and Sandstrom scored, and after we won the game I was asked, "Why did you put Sandstrom back in?"

"I don't know," I said. "He looked at me. The same look I used to give Harry Sinden all the time."

It was a huge win for us. But Webbie was really sick. He had an ear condition that made it impossible for him to fly. He needed surgery to get the problem fixed.

We needed to improve on faceoffs, so on New Years Day 1987, I acquired Bobby Carpenter from Washington. I got him for Mike Ridley, a good player who was a free agent; Kelly Miller, a struggling skater; and Bobby Crawford, who I didn't want. I didn't want to give up both Ridley and Miller, because Kelly was a great penalty killer, but Carpenter had just scored 50 goals for Washington, and he could win faceoffs, so I made the deal. Ridley went on to have a tremendous career in Washington. I can relate to that: it happened to me when I left Chicago and went to Boston. They always say that Tommy Ivan's worst deal was trading Hodgie, Stanfield, and me to Boston. Boston was a struggling team, hadn't made the playoffs eight years in a row, and we went there and all of a sudden, bingo, we clicked. You just don't know.

That's the thing about a trade: I don't give a crap what anybody says, you don't know about a trade because different teams have different players, and on one team a guy can fit in, and on another team he won't. I made a lot of trades. They called me "Trader Phil," but if you check the records Neil Smith made more trades than I did. Glen Sather made more trades than I did. But I knew who had to go.

Webbie came back after his operation and I went back upstairs, but on a flight to Vancouver he suffered a relapse, and in late January I could see he couldn't do it any more.

I talked to his doctor, who told me that pressure and tension brought it on. Tommy seemed relaxed, but it was just a facade. Coaching the Rangers in New York was eating him up inside.

New York is pressure-packed. That's why if you're playing there or coaching there, you better get compensated well, because the minute you get hired in New York, they're trying to bury you. And it doesn't matter whether you're a coach for a baseball, football, basketball, or hockey team. When you think about it, the only venues in sport that don't have corporate names are in Manhattan. It's still Madison Square Garden. It's still Yankee Stadium, still Shea Stadium. Madison Square Garden has been in that same spot since 1968, and the mystique of New York and the Garden adds a lot of pressure. It does for every coach, every general manager, anyone who works in sports there. And the media is on your ass constantly. There are the newspapers and now vicious talk radio, and there's nothing you can do to blunt the stream of criticism. In New York, when people said derogatory things about me, it hurt me bad. I remember saying to my brother on the phone, "Why do they do that? Tony, I can't do anything right here. Diller's on my case. The fans are on my case. The coach is going crazy. The players don't like me. The agents don't like me." Christ, I was searching for someone – anyone – who liked me.

At the same time you're always trying to please them. When they cheered for you, you felt good. Then they'd boo you. And the fans at the Garden could boo you like nobody else. You felt like crawling under a rock. I reacted differently. My back would get up, and I'd put my feet down like an entrenched cat. I got stubborn in a way that I didn't want to get, and it became very difficult. This was the pressure Tom Webster was feeling, and it made him so ill that he couldn't coach any more.

He told me, "I just can't do this, Phil. This is not fair to the organization, not fair to the players."

"Okay, Tom," I said, "Here's what I'm going to do: you'll step down and get yourself healthy and come back next year." That was the loyalty I showed Tom Webster. I named myself the coach for the rest of the 1986-87 season.

I coached the Rangers the rest of the season, but I still did it the way Tommy Webster wanted to do it. Sure I had leeway behind the bench, but it was his forechecking system, his backchecking system, his power play, his penalty killing. If a player was dogging it, I made personnel changes, but I did things exactly the way Tommy wanted me to do them.

I moved Walt Poddubny to center. Tommy didn't really like him and neither did the scouts. Walt was a terrible faceoff man, but he could skate. He didn't like the traffic, the tough going, but he could shoot as well as anybody, and so I put him at center, and he scored 40 goals for us that year. Some of my other moves didn't work out, but that one did.

By February 1987, the team was on a roll. We were in second place. With the help of Eddie Giacomin, I was alternating Vanbiesbrouck and Froese, and they were terrific. I also had great help from Wayne Cashman. Wayne and Eddie ran practices. I had to be in the office.

I was making as much money as I made as a player. I commuted to Bedford, which was a pain in the ass, but some nights I would stay in the city and go out and have a great time. At this point in my life, things could not have been better.

22

IN THE MIDDLE OF THE 1986-87 SEASON, the NHL scheduled a series of exhibition games against the Russian Red Army team, which travelled from arena to arena. The schedule included a game against the Rangers at Madison Square Garden, and I was dead set against it. First, I didn't want any of my players getting hurt, and the other consideration was that a Russian MiG had just shot down Pan-Am flight 007 over Russia. Harold Ballard (owner of the Maple Leafs), Eddie Snider (owner of the Flyers), and I all felt we didn't want the Russians playing in Canada and the United States and getting our money. I also knew our team didn't have a chance against them. Why were we making the Russian players into folk heroes? For money? And where was the money going? Alan Eagleson, Billy Wirtz, owner of the Blackhawks, and John Ziegler all were involved.

I voted against it, but John Ziegler, who was the league president and who I thought was a good guy, ruled that we had to play.

We were sitting at a meeting in Palm Beach at the Breakers, and Ziegler was going around the room. He came to Ed Snider, who said, "We're Jewish, and we don't like it that the Russians went after the Jews, but we'll do it for the league's sake. We'll let them play, because it will help the league."

Then they came to Harold Ballard, who was about eighty years old. Harold was beautiful. He said, "Mr. Ziegler, you little shit. And Eagleson, you fucking crook! As long as I have a hole in my ass, they're not coming into my building." Harold got up and shuffled off to the bathroom. Well, I died. I couldn't believe he said that. The whole place broke out laughing.

I was next. I said, "I think Harold put it perfectly! But I have been authorized to vote yes, and we will play, though I am personally against it."

When Harold came back into the room and was told he had no choice, he told Ziegler, "Okay, we'll play at two o'clock in the morning!"

After the meeting, Harold, who was sitting with his girlfriend Yolanda, called me over and asked me to join him for lunch. He started ranting all over again. "That goddamn Ziegler. That fucking Eagleson. Them guys are the biggest crooks. These fucking guys don't care about this. I don't want the damn Russians in my building."

I just sat there and listened.

━━━

Though the Rangers were playing well, I thought our team needed a superstar, a guy who could score goals and bring some excitement to the offense. Minutes before the trade deadline, on March 10, 1987, I traded Bobby Carpenter and Tommy Laidlaw to the Los Angeles Kings for Marcel Dionne, who had starred for many years with the Red Wings and the Kings.

Carpenter had lost his scoring touch, big time. He was still pretty good on faceoffs, but he just couldn't put the puck in the net. He had scored only two goals in his last thirty games. And I played him a lot. So I moved him, along with Laidlaw, who I really didn't want to trade. Tommy was a pretty darn good defenseman, but this was New York – the press desired a superstar, and we needed some zing. Marcel was closing in on 700 goals, and he could really score. He was thirty-five years old, but he also was a good guy, a great team guy, and I wanted him. The Kings wanted to rebuild, and I felt we were going to make the playoffs and he would help us get past the first round.

The Rangers had done the same thing when they got me. I turned thirty-four just after I came to New York, and I scored 42 goals. I had helped take the team to the finals in 1979. I thought Marcel could do the same thing. He always kept himself in terrific shape. He had those big, thick legs. He could dart around, was very good with the puck, and he could score.

Even after Marcel arrived, our biggest problem was our inconsistency. We'd win three in a row and then lose four in a row. Consistency has always been a problem with the teams I've managed. Obviously, I blamed the coaches. I figured that sometimes the players weren't properly prepared or weren't motivated, but in this case I was the coach, and I wasn't motivating them, because I wasn't at the practices. How many times can you come in and give a pre-game pep talk? It gets old.

In order to make the playoffs, we needed to beat the Blackhawks in the final game, and we won 5-3. (After I took over from Tom Webster my record for the season was 24-19. Not bad!)

We met the Flyers in the opening round of the playoffs, and John Vanbiesbrouck shut them out in the first game, but Philadelphia won three of the next four. The final loss was a 5-0 shutout. I was upset. I felt the players had quit during that game because they didn't want to have to go back to Philadelphia for a seventh game.

We didn't have a bad team. Philadelphia went to the finals that year. I was determined to improve the team for the next season. That's the goal of every general manager – to make your team better.

Everybody thought the Rangers had an unlimited budget – that I had an unlimited budget – but that wasn't the case. In fact, I never knew what my budget was. I kept asking, and Dick Evans or Jack Diller would say, "You do what you have to do." But then I'd get a memo from one of them saying, "You're over your budget." I'd call them up on the phone and say, "What are you talking about? You told me I didn't have a budget." They'd say, "We don't want you spending all this money you've just spent." I'd say, "Well, okay." I couldn't figure out what to do. It was so confusing with the Rangers.

I had grand plans for the Rangers in 1988-89, but they were derailed when Vanbiesbrouck put his hand through a glass coffee table in June 1988. He said he tripped and fell, and I believed him. What was I supposed to do? Accidents happen. He hurt himself badly and worked hard at rehabilitation to get the feeling back in his hand. I had Bobby Froese, and Mike Richter was coming, and I felt they could do the job. My intention had been to trade Vanbiesbrouck for an impact player, a scorer, but when he got hurt it limited my options.

Nothing, however, disappointed me as much as what happened next: Glen Sather of Edmonton and I were talking trade at the NHL meetings at the Breakers Hotel in Palm Beach when he said to me, "Would you like to have Wayne Gretzky?"

I had continued to hear rumblings that Peter Pocklington, the Edmonton owner, had financial problems. This was proof of it.

Would I like to have Wayne Gretzky? Who wouldn't want Wayne Gretzky? He may have been the best scorer in the history of the game. All I could think about was how Gretzky would transform the Rangers into a powerhouse and a dynasty.

"What do you want for him?" I asked.

"You can have him for fifteen million," he said.

Glen and I made a deal. For Gretzky I was to give up Kisio, Vanbiesbrouck, Sandstrom, a second-round pick, and fifteen million dollars.

I went back to Diller and Evans and told them, "This is the deal. We're getting Wayne Gretzky. I need fifteen million."

For as long as I live I'll never forget what Dick Evans said: "Why do we need Wayne Gretzky to put people in the building?"

"Well, we can win the Stanley Cup," I said. The Rangers had not won the Cup since 1940. I pleaded with him. I said, "Come on. You turned me down with Messier. Don't turn me down for Gretzky. Wayne is going somewhere. Pocklington needs the friggin' money."

"The seats are full, Phil," Evans said. "Frankly, we don't care if you ever win the Stanley Cup. What we want you to do is make the playoffs and go to the finals."

"You know what, Dick," I said, "I don't think you have the right guy running your hockey team." Meaning me. "I want to win. I took this job to win. I didn't take it just to get to the finals."

Evans said, "There is no way in the world we are going to pay fifteen million dollars. We can't justify that on our books because the Garden is packed every night."

In that respect he was right. But if we wanted to win, we needed a Gary Carter. The Oilers ended up trading Wayne Gretzky to the Los Angeles Kings. Bruce McNall paid the fifteen million dollars and put Los Angeles on the NHL map.

The fact is that New York Knicks basketball was more important to the Paramount people. If they could have gotten Michael Jordan for fifteen million dollars, they would have done it in a heartbeat.

Can you imagine if I had gotten Wayne Gretzky? What was fifteen million dollars? What the fuck is money? You make it back. If we had had Gretzky, we might have won four or five Stanley Cups.

Was I a little aggressive pushing Evans and Diller to make the deal? Absolutely. Did I piss them off? Absolutely. And from the moment they turned me down on Gretzky and I let them know what I thought of them doing that, I was on the downslide. I had said to them, "You got the wrong guy. I want to win. You should get a guy who doesn't care about winning."

I was devastated. Four days later the Oilers traded the Great Gretzky to Los Angeles. On that day I traded Walt Poddubny and two others to Quebec for defenseman Normand Rochefort and center Jason Lafreniere. Rochefort had played in the 1987 Canada Cup and, boy, was he good! He hit people. I knew the fans at Madison Square Garden would love him because he could body-check and he loved to hit people. But no one noticed, because the Gretzky trade got all the headlines.

In June 1988, Tom Webster let me know that he still wasn't healthy enough to return as coach for the upcoming season. Rather than go through another year as both general manager and coach, I told Evans and Diller that I wanted Wayne Cashman to be my coach. But because Cashman had no prior experience, they said no. And Eddie Giacomin didn't have any coaching experience either, so they turned him down as well. They had gone through that with Webster, and so they said to me, "No matter what, you have to get someone with experience."

I submitted a list of names of coaches I liked. Pat Quinn was number one on my list. I loved Pat. I thought he'd make a great coach, and he has. Pat was coaching in Philadelphia, and the Flyers wouldn't let him out of his contract. The next choice, picked by Evans and Diller, was Michel Bergeron, who was the coach of the Quebec Nordiques. I had no opinion about him, but once I was told by my bosses to do something, I did it.

Michel was a fiery little guy, who was very animated behind the bench. I soon found out he had a short man's Napoleonic complex, no doubt about it. He smoked like a chimney and drank coffee like no one I had ever seen. It's no wonder he later had a heart attack.

To get Bergeron, I had to deal with Quebec team president Marcel Aubut. In my talks with Aubut, he agreed to take a hundred thousand dollars or a first- or second-round draft pick for his coach.

Evans or Diller, I can't remember which, called to tell me that they had completed the deal for Bergeron. I was told to go over to the Queen Elizabeth Hotel – this was in Montreal – and sign the papers. I went with Kevin Billets, the Rangers' lawyer, and when I read the contract, I saw that the deal had been changed to a hundred thousand *and* a first-round pick.

"I didn't agree to this," I said.

"This is what Evans agreed to."

"Are you kidding me?" I said.

I called Evans on the phone.

"Giving them both is crazy," I said.

"You want him," he said. "We want him. Give it to them. Do it."

So I did it, and the next day in the papers all I read was that I had given Quebec too much for Michel Bergeron.

The first thing I said to our new coach was, "I'm thinking of asking Guy Lafleur to come out of retirement and play for us."

He said, "Oh great! Guy would be perfect." Right away I was impressed that he and I were on the same page.

I went to see Guy. I said, "Do you want to play again? Come on. Don't you want to play in Madison Square Garden?" Bergy also called him, and he talked to him even more than I did. They probably talked in French.

I liked Guy. He was on Montreal's voluntary-retirement list, and I had to get permission from the Canadiens, and I gave them an eighth- or ninth-round draft choice. I was criticized for signing a guy who was thirty-seven years old.

I also picked up a kid by the name of Craig Redmond, who was put on waivers by Edmonton. He was their first-round pick, a hell of a skater, but Glen Sather told me his father was difficult. "The guy drives his kid crazy," he said. Glen said he hated to lose him, but the trouble his father gave him was too great.

After I signed him, Redmond's father would call me on the phone, "My kid's not playing enough. You're using him wrong. The kid should be . . ." He drove me crazy too. I said to myself, Who needs the aggravation? Even though Craig was talented and only twenty-three, I put him on waivers, and the Los Angeles Kings picked him up.

———

I was in the final year of my contract, and after the 1987-88 season I asked Evans and Diller for a two-year extension, and they said no.

I knew then I was history. A team should never let a general manager or coach go into the season with just one year left on his contract; they're lame ducks, and the players and the fans sense it, and it makes the job even more difficult.

Despite how I felt about my contract situation, I was thrilled because the team was playing great. In mid-November 1988 the Rangers were leading the Patrick Division, and Michel Bergeron was doing a great job. I wasn't going on the road with them. I was leaving them alone. I wasn't keeping an eye on my coach, the way some general managers do to protect themselves. I believe the coach has to have the authority on the road. If the general manager travels with the team, he's the one with authority, not the coach.

For a short while the press stopped calling me the "Mad Trader," and started calling me a genius. Isn't it funny how your reputation can go up and down like a toilet seat at a mixed party? Take Bill Barber of the Flyers. One year he was coach of the year. The next year they fired him saying he was horseshit. He didn't change his coaching philosophy. The players wouldn't believe in him any more.

It wasn't long before I had turmoil again. This time my trouble was with Michel. He informed the press he wasn't going to play John Ogrodnick any more. I couldn't understand why he would say that in the papers. If he wasn't going to play him, then it was up to me to trade him. But how could I get anything for him if everyone knew my coach wasn't going to play him? His value went to nothing.

I went to Michel and said to him, "Look, you play who you want, but what are we going to do with this guy now? He's making three hundred thousand dollars. The guy scored 50 goals one year with the Detroit Red Wings. You're telling me you can't get 20 goals out of him?"

"I had him in Quebec," he said, "and I don't like him."

A reporter from the *New York Post* asked me about Michel's not playing him, and I said, "Michel and I are a team. If he says he's not going to use a player, that's fine, as long as we win. If we lose, it's on him." When Michel read that, he was furious with me. That was too bad he felt that way, but it was the truth.

When he came to see me, he brought his agent with him. I said, "Are you kidding me? I got to deal with an agent – for a coach?" I threw the agent out.

"Listen," I told Michel, "coach the team and shut the fuck up!" Those were my exact words. I said, "You make me laugh. I let you pick the players and decide who you're going to play. I don't tell you who to play. But if you're wrong, you're responsible for our not winning."

It didn't take long for everything to be smoothed over. The Rangers gave me a one-year extension, Ogrodnick came back and played very well, and the Rangers kept winning. Maybe it was Bergy's way to motivate him. I don't know. Maybe it shook Ogrodnick up.

But I could feel the tension between Bergeron and me growing. Part of it was that he kept pushing me to get French-Canadian players. Remember, there were very few Czech and Russian players in the league back then. The French-Canadian coaches liked to play French-Canadian players. There was a bond between them. If he could have gotten all French-Canadian players, he would have. And that didn't bother me one bit, if they could play hockey. I didn't care where the players came from. Who cares, as long as a player does his job? One time I told him, "These guys you want aren't better than anyone else."

There was one player in particular, Michel Goulet, whom he had coached in Quebec. Bergeron said to me, "He could take the place of everybody on this goddamn team." Bergeron kept on me to get him. I told him, "I like Goulet, but he's making a million dollars a year. We ain't gonna do that. Goulet isn't worth that kind of money, and I'm not doing it, because to get him in a trade, I'd have to trade players I don't want to trade."

Meanwhile, the last time the Rangers were in first place for this long was the 1971-72 season. We really had something going. If only I could stop Bergy from going over my head. The press had a big role in causing the friction between us. If Michel said something about me, the reporters would call me up and try to get something going. Like the time in early December 1988 when the Rangers were on the road in Calgary, and Bergeron announced to reporters he wanted a five-year extension.

A reporter called me. I said, "So do I! And if I got one, maybe he'd get one. But I haven't got it, and he ain't getting it."

I called Joey Bucchino, my assistant, who was on the road with the team. Joey did a lot of the day-to-day paperwork. I said, "Joey, what's going on?"

"I tried to stop him," he said. "He just wanted to go off." But that was Bergy.

The next day I called Bergy. "What is wrong with you?" I said. "Bergy, please. You're not getting a contract longer than mine. If I get five years, I'll give you three, but you're never going to get the same as me."

I asked him to report back to me every day. I wanted to hear what was going on before I read it in the newspapers. He rarely did. People would ask me about Bergeron's contract. I'd tell them, "He's not getting an extension until we're ready to give him one."

The next blow-up came when Bergeron called me and asked where he stood in the organization.

"What are you talking about?" I said. "Where do you stand? You are the coach of the New York Rangers. That's your fucking job. Do it, and shut up."

He said to me, "Where am I going to be two years from now? I need security."

"So do I, Bergy," I said, "but I haven't got it, and you're not getting it." And that's how I left it.

A rash of injuries really hurt us that year. Brian Leetch fractured his foot blocking a shot against Hartford. Brian was the best player on our team and he didn't come back for a long, long time. I went out and got Mark Hardy back from Minnesota, but he wasn't any Brian Leetch.

In the next game Guy Lafleur fractured his foot blocking a shot against Boston. What a way for Guy to go out, I thought. Then Mark Janssens fractured his skull when his head struck the ice during a fight. Willi Plett suckered him bad and knocked him out cold. The team started to reel a little bit. We didn't have enough depth to stay on top.

I felt I had to do something. Our defense was really hurting. I traded Igor Liba to Los Angeles for Dean Kennedy and Denis Larocque. Dean played defense regularly and helped us.

The next confrontation with Bergeron came when he informed me he would no longer play Donnie Maloney. "I don't want him," he said. "I'm not going to play him."

Bergy, meanwhile, kept bugging me to get him a big center. I would say, "Where the hell can I find a big center?" In late December I was able to get Carey Wilson from Hartford for Maloney, Brian Lawton, and Norm Maciver. Wilson wasn't the big, strong center-man Bergy wanted, but anybody who had a center like that wasn't going to trade him.

Carey Wilson was smooth, and a good faceoff man. He could score pretty well and kill penalties. Even though it was only the third trade since the start of the season, I kept reading about that "Trader Phil" bullshit. Boy, did that piss me off. "In his fortieth trade . . ." What was I supposed to do, sit back and let the team founder? So I made some moves. And in his first game Carey Wilson had three assists in a big win over New Jersey.

I could have traded Donnie Maloney to Edmonton, Calgary, or Los Angeles, but I decided that if I was going to trade him, it would be close to New York so his family wouldn't be too badly dislocated.

I tried the Islanders first, but I couldn't trade with them, because the Islanders really didn't want to trade with us. And really, we didn't want to trade with them. They were our biggest rivals. Then I tried Hartford. Donnie was living in Westchester County, and he could commute to work. Also, Emile Francis, the Hartford GM, who had had him when he was running the Rangers, really liked him. So I traded him to Hartford in the Wilson deal. Donnie understood, but his wife, Toni, called me every name in the book. She called me names I had never heard before.

The next battle I had with Michel was over Marcel Dionne, who was slow to recover from an injury. Bergy didn't want him on the team any more. He would tell me to get rid of him. I'd say, "Marcel stays for as long as he wants."

Marcel came to me and said, "Why don't you send me down to Denver so I can get back in shape?"

"You'd do that, Marcel?" I said.

"Absolutely."

Marcel Dionne was terrific with the kids in Denver, and he worked his ass off and came back.

I didn't feel any duty to call Bergeron and tell him I was doing that. When I sent Dionne to Denver, Bergeron turned around and blasted me in the papers. "How can Phil do that to a veteran like Marcel?" he said.

Bergeron was also calling Jack Diller on the phone and questioning what I was doing. At that point I went to Diller and asked him if I could fire Bergeron.

Diller wanted to know why.

"Because he goes over my head," I said. "And I think this guy is getting too big for his britches. I want to fire him."

"Are you kidding?" Diller said. "You can't do it now. The team is going good."

"You're right, Jack," I said, "but I don't go over your head. I don't go to Dick Evans and say you're doing this wrong and that wrong, or you haven't paid the goddamn bills, and we got to fight to get into the hotel rooms." Because that had happened. The bills hadn't been paid, and we had to make a stink for one of the hotels to let us stay.

"You can't fire him, Phil," he said.

"Yeah, okay," I said. "We'll go on with him."

And I let it go.

23

THE TENSION AND THE PRESSURE were also getting to Bergeron. He was smoking all the time and drinking cup after cup of coffee. In February 1989 he was having a really tough time of it. He was extremely upset – furious – that I wouldn't give him an extension, given how well we were playing. He was furious I had sent Marcel Dionne to the minors, furious I didn't get him the centerman he wanted, furious I wouldn't trade for Michel Goulet. For him it became all about me.

In a game against Pittsburgh in the Garden, he threw a water bottle into the stands, rattled the glass, taunted the Penguins players, and began screaming at the officials like a madman.

About this time the Rangers went into a tailspin. We lost a half-dozen games and fell to third behind Washington and Pittsburgh. This came after we lost Leetch, Jim Patrick, Mark Hardy, Ron Greschner, and David Shaw. Most of our defense was hurt.

The losses kept mounting. After six losses in a row on the road, Bergeron ripped his players in the papers, saying they were scared.

I challenged Bergy to his face after he said that. "How dare you do that to your players?" I asked him.

———

April, the last month of the hockey season, is a tough month for hockey coaches. With two games left in the 1988-89 season, I fired Michel Bergeron.

I was watching the Rangers play the Red Wings in Detroit on TV, and who did I see sitting next to each other but Jack Diller, the Rangers president, and my assistant, Joey Bucchino. Joey had started out in Boston as a stick boy, and when John Ferguson got the Rangers head coach's job, we needed an assistant trainer, and I got Joey the job. From there he went on to become my assistant.

What's this all about? I thought to myself,

After the game I got a call from Joey. "Phil, I'm in Detroit with Jack Diller, and I have to tell you that Michel is saying some pretty bad things about you."

"Again?" I said. "I warned him about that. You go with the team to Pittsburgh. I'll meet you there. And tell Jack Diller I'd like to speak with him."

Diller called me. He said, "Yes, Phil. What's the problem?"

"What are you doing in Detroit?" I asked.

"Michel Bergeron called me and asked me to come," he said.

"He what?" I said. "Jack, this is bullshit. You can't do this to me."

"I just came to the game because he wanted to talk to me," he said.

"And what did he want to talk to you about?"

"He said we should have made some trades because we are going into the playoffs," Diller said, "and he doesn't think the team is good enough. He says you should have gotten Michel Goulet."

"Michel Goulet is over the hill," I said. "It's over for him."

Jack said, "Bergeron doesn't think he is."

"I'm firing Bergeron," I said.

"*What?*"

"I'm firing him right now," I said. "On the spot."

"Who are you going to put in as coach?" Jack asked.

"I'll get Wayne Cashman and Eddie Giacomin to finish the job."

"You can't do that," Jack said. "Just wait."

This was a Tuesday night, and the Rangers were playing again on Thursday.

"I'm going to Pittsburgh to tell him," I said.

"I'm coming back to New York tomorrow," Jack said. "Let's talk."

I agreed.

I hung up the phone, and Joey Bucchino called me back about an hour later. "Phil," he said, "I don't like what Bergeron just did." He was talking about his going behind my back to Jack.

"Joey," I said, "I'm going to take care of it. I'm going to fire him."

"Now?"

"Yeah," I said, "but if you open your mouth, you're history too. I'll meet you in Pittsburgh."

Joey said, "Lugonda," which means "dirt" in Italian.

"You open your mouth, and you'll be eating dirt," I said.

The next morning I was in my office in Madison Square Garden when Jack Diller came in to see me.

"Phil, I don't know about this. It isn't right," he said.

I didn't care. "I'm going to do it."

"Then I want you to coach."

I told him I didn't want to be coach.

"You have to coach."

"If you want me to coach," I said, "I want a hundred thousand dollars more a year."

"Then you have to coach next year too."

"Then I want two more years on my contract."

"I don't know," he said.

"Then I'm not coaching," I said, "and I won't fire him. Let it go." At this point I decided that making a change was more trouble than it was worth. I decided to leave everything as it was.

But I guess Jack Diller had warmed to the idea of my coaching, because he then said, "You have to fire him. You can't let a coach do this to you. I'll raise your salary from four hundred thousand a year to five hundred thousand a year and give you a two-year extension," Diller said.

That was hard to turn down. "Okay, that's a deal."

"We still want you to coach the following year," he said.

"Let me coach the rest of the year and the playoffs, and then let's see where we are, and we can discuss it," I said. "Maybe Cashman and Giacomin can do the job. Maybe I'll bring in a different coach. Maybe I'll coach. Let's just see."

Jack agreed, and with two games left in the season I signed the new contract. Then I went to Pittsburgh and fired Michel Bergeron.

"I'm making a change," I told him.

"A change in what?"

"In coaching," I said. "I'm replacing you. Right now. I warned you twice not to go behind my back. The first time I told you if you did it again, I was going to fire you. The second time you did it, they wouldn't let me fire you. But when you did it the third time, three strikes and you're out."

"Are you crazy?" he said. "You can't do that. What's the matter with you, Phil?" He then asked, "Who's going to coach?"

"I am."

"Oh yeah, you're going to coach," he said with great sarcasm. "Good luck."

"You're probably right, but we can't do any worse. And maybe I can motivate these guys." I said, "Michel, it's over, and you can take Charles Tiffeault with you. He's gone too." Tiffeault was his assistant coach. And I fired another French guy who was helping him, and I made Cashman and Eddie Giacomin my assistants.

The second-to-last game was in Pittsburgh. I walked into the dressing room and told the players, "I replaced Michel. I'm going to be the coach, and Cash and Eddie are going to coach along with me. I need you, boys. I need you to be something. We need to get going."

A change in coaches, like a change in players, often gives the team a short-term kick in the butt, but in this case we lost 5-2 and fell into third place.

I said to Eddie Giacomin, "Eddie, it's up to you to pick the goalie, because I want to tell you, there's something wrong. Froese and Beezer [Vanbiesbrouck] are not playing well."

"I know," he said. "Neither of them. But we really miss Leetch. Leetch is the key."

"I understand that," I said, "but we don't have him, so there's nothing we can do about it."

When we got back to the Garden for the final game, the fans were going crazy. We made the playoffs even though we lost that final game, and we played the Pittsburgh Penguins in the first round. My brother Tony was running the Penguins and Gino Ubriaco, one of my best friends, was their coach.

We went to Pittsburgh for the first two games because they finished the regular season ahead of us.

The most important decision I had to make was who to play in goal. I decided to start Bobby Froese, which pissed Beezer off no end. Johnny said a few things in the press and, boy, they loved it and fed off it. I didn't say anything. I just said that Eddie, Cash, and I picked Froese because he had a better record against Pittsburgh.

In that first game we were tied with the Penguins 1-1 in the second period when Guy Lafleur came down the right wing and shot. From where I sat, the puck was headed for the corner of the net, but instead it hit the crossbar and went out, and then the Penguins came back and scored to make it 2-1. They then scored another goal after I pulled our goalie. I'm convinced that if Lafleur had scored on the shot that hit the crossbar, we would have won the series. But it didn't go in.

We outshot them that day. We outshot them every game, but we couldn't stop Mario Lemieux from scoring. We tried everything, but he and Paul Coffey were too good for us. They killed us on the special teams, especially on the power play. Damn, they were good. And Tom Barrasso in goal was outstanding again.

I started Froese in the net again in game two, and with us trailing 2-1 I put Vanbiesbrouck in, and we lost 7-4. Again we outshot them heavily, but lost.

We flew back to New York by charter. I was sitting with Jack Diller. He said, "We're outshooting them. We're outplaying them. We're outdoing everything."

"But Mario, Barrasso, and Ronnie Francis are killing us," I said. "I haven't got anyone to match them."

He looked at me and said, "I hope we can win a couple of games."

"We're going to try awfully hard," I said.

When we returned to New York for game three, I started Vanbiesbrouck, and we outshot them 40-20, but again we lost, this time 5-3. Mario Lemieux killed us. At one point he was standing on the goal line to the side of our net when he took a shot, and the puck hit Vanbiesbrouck's pads and went in. Now we were down three games to none.

I decided I needed to do something drastic, and so I put in Mike Richter, our goaltender of the future. I was hoping he would give us a spectacular game and put us back in it. We didn't have anything to lose.

When the reporters asked me about it, that's when I told them: "When the Rangers win the Stanley Cup – and we will win it – Mike Richter will be the goalie."

With the Rangers down three games to none, the fans really started to boo me. They didn't care that Lemieux and Barrasso were playing out of their minds. In the final game Richter did let in one bad goal, but he played great. Again we outshot the Penguins, but again they beat us.

Our season was over.

After the game I congratulated my brother Tony and Gino Ubriaco.

"Was Barrasso good or what?" Tony said.

"Good?" I said. "He was fantastic. We should have beaten you."

"You outplayed us in every game," he said.

"I know," I said. "Tell my owners that."

That was in April. The rumors then began to fly that Jack Diller was looking for another general manager and coach. Neil Smith was the guy who was supposed to replace me. I remembered what Emile Francis had told me. Practically the only general manager who never got fired was Harry Sinden, who took his team to the playoffs and made money every year.

But why would they fire me? Hadn't Jack Diller just upped my salary by a hundred thousand a year and guaranteed me two more years in addition to the one left on my old contract? I figured I had security. Four or five times I said to Diller, "Are you going to fire me?"

"No, no, but we want you to coach next year," he said.

"Right now I have to get ready for the draft," I said. "We have to get our scouts in order. Maybe we should think about getting someone else to coach."

I got nowhere with Evans and Diller, especially Diller. I wanted to talk to him about our future plans and getting a new coach, but suddenly I wasn't able to see him, and that's when I figured my days were numbered. And it was too bad, because we had something going in New York.

I never made it to the draft. On May 23, 1989, I was sitting in my office when Jack Diller came in with two security guards.

"We're making a change, Phil," he said. "We're going to replace you."

"You just gave me a two-year extension."

"So what?" he said. "That doesn't matter to us."

"You still have to pay me."

"Absolutely," Jack said. "You'll be paid in full."

"Jack, you are a gutless wonder," I said. "You wouldn't back me, would you? I should punch you right in the face. I should whack you, right now."

One of the security guards said, "Phil, now take it easy."

"Don't worry," I said. "I'm not going to waste my breath with him. Get out of here and let me pack up." Then I said, "And tell Evans he's a gutless wonder too."

━━━

I had kept Donna shielded from what was going on with the Rangers. She was oblivious to everything. We had had a baby, our daughter Cherise, and whenever I started to talk about anything having to do with hockey, she acted as though she wasn't interested. When I got fired, the news was a shock to her.

"Oh my God, what are we going to do?" she said.

"We'll be fine, honey," I said. "Our lifestyle isn't going to change one iota." I had three years to find another job and a lot of money coming in.

I packed my things, and the two security guards escorted me out of the Garden. On my way out I popped my head into Diller's office to say goodbye to his secretary, who was great. Then I yelled in at Diller, "You chickenshit bastard. I'll get even some day."

24

THE MORNING AFTER I WAS FIRED as general manager of the Rangers, I was sitting in my basement in my home in Bedford, New York. I had three years left on my Rangers contract, so I suppose I could have played golf every day if I had wanted, but I was too young not to be doing something.

My basement, which was my refuge, had a popcorn machine and a big television and all my trophies and plaques. I sat there answering phone calls from the other general managers – Pat Quinn, Glen Sather, Cliff Fletcher, Serge Savard, Rogie Vachon, and Harry Sinden. They all expressed their condolences over my getting fired. In between calls, I was talking to myself, trying to figure out which direction I wanted to go.

Phil, you have to do something, I kept saying to myself.

People were saying to me, "You're Phil Esposito. You can always make money in New York."

"Guarantee me something," I'd say, "and I'll move back to the city tomorrow." I was hoping something would come along, because I hated living way out in the boonies and having to commute every day. Even though I had three years of money coming in, my mortgage on my million-dollar house had twenty-eight more years to run. And Donna had expensive horses. I knew the money went out pretty quickly. The pressure on me was enormous. I was scared.

I thought to myself, You ought to get a group together and get an expansion franchise. I asked myself two questions: where and how?

I had been on the marketing committee of the National Hockey League when I was general manager of the Rangers. Norm Green, who moved his team from Minneapolis to Dallas in 1993, was the chairman of the committee. Lou Nanne, who is a friend of mine, was on that committee with me. Norm Green had the habit of pronouncing the word *issue* as "ith-shoe." And every time he said that, Lou and I would crack up laughing. Norm Green would say to us, "What is *wrong* with you guys? I'm going to have to separate the two of you."

I loved being on the NHL marketing committee. I loved sitting around with a bunch of people and coming up with crazy ideas. My philosophy is to throw a lot of ideas against the wall, and use whatever sticks.

I always wanted to know, why are we just marketing the teams? Shouldn't we be marketing the stars? Why do the players have to market themselves? When I was a player, whenever we made appearances, the team made us take off the Bruins or Rangers crest, or they expected to be paid one third of our fee. So we'd take the crest off. Does that make any sense? Why wouldn't they want us publicizing the Bruins or Rangers as well?

I said this when I was GM of the Rangers. No one else agreed with me. I would say to the owners, Let's hire a marketing guru to get our players outside endorsements like car deals and soda commercials. If I could get my star player a hundred thousand dollars in endorsements, I would guarantee him half of that, and we'd get the other half. We'd put it in the contract. And the player would wear his Rangers gear, and he'd publicize the team as well.

The league refused to let me do it. The standard player's contract does not provide for such an arrangement, and the league's lawyers would not let me put one in.

But as part of our discussions, one of the ith-shoes was that of expansion. As far back as the late 1970s, when I was on the players' committee, the talk was of expanding to Florida and Texas so the National Hockey League could have a national television package. I decided what I was going to do: I would found a new NHL franchise in Florida. Where? I didn't know. How? I didn't know that either. I just knew I was going to do it.

People underestimate me when they find out I don't have a formal education. They think I'm just a former hockey player, and that they can take advantage of me. I can tell you, I *love* it when people underestimate me. If you work hard enough, you can accomplish anything.

———

I started calling people I knew to get more information. One of the people I called was Mark Perrone, who once worked with Bob Wolff, the sports agent. I knew Mark from Boston. He was the agent for Mats Sundin. I said to him, "Boy, the league really wants to expand. They are going to have to. I want to go to Florida."

"I have some friends in Florida," Mark said. "Why don't you call Henry Paul? He's Gabe Paul's son."

"Okay, let's talk to him," I said.

I called Henry Paul, and we talked, but Tampa just didn't seem the ideal place for a hockey team, primarily because they didn't have an arena where hockey could be played.

Orlando had an arena and so did Miami. Jacksonville had a subpar facility.

My first trip to Orlando started as a golfing holiday with my buddies Hooks Badia and Stuart Greenfield. I had met them at the Willie Mays Golf Tournament at my golf club, the Briar Hall Country Club off the Saw Mill Parkway, about twenty minutes from my home in Westchester. Hooks, who owned a delicatessen, is a close friend of Willie's. Another golfing buddy of ours once was a bookmaker. Stuart is in the insurance business, and another of our group is a psychiatrist who needs a psychiatrist.

I met them at Briar Hall, and we started playing regularly at seven in the morning on Saturdays and Sundays, and it turned into a great friendship. We'd eat lunch at the club, and they'd come over to the house for a few drinks. Donna loved them, and we went to parties with them.

Hooks, Stuart, and I flew to Orlando to play golf. I went to see Pat Williams, the general manager of the Orlando Magic. He once was GM of the Philadelphia 76ers. I asked Pat about the possibility of hockey in Orlando. The Magic, after all, owned the arena there.

"Hockey is not going to happen here," he said. "When I was general manager of the 76ers, I didn't want to have to deal with the Flyers. It's hard to deal with hockey. We're basketball, we own the arena, and we want *all* of the revenue. We don't want to share a penny of that."

So much for Orlando. I went and played another round of golf, and then I called Billy Cunningham, the GM of the Miami Heat basketball team. He said pretty much what Pat Williams had said. "There is no way hockey is coming to Miami."

I flew home.

A year later my buddies and I flew down to Orlando to play more golf, and that night we were playing hearts and drinking beer and having a good time when I got a call from Mark Perrone, who told me to go and meet Henry Paul in Tampa. Henry and I arranged to meet Henry at Malio's restaurant at around seven-thirty in the evening.

Rather than go back to the hotel and get clothes, I bought a pair of pants and a golf shirt at the pro shop, got in the car, and drove from Orlando to Tampa.

I walked into the back room of Malio's and met Henry Paul, Tom McEwen, a longtime sports columnist for the *Tampa Tribune*, and Michael Osterhaus, who owned radio station Q105 – the Q Zoo it was called – which was flying high, a rock station that was one of the tops in the country, and his lawyer, Peter Hobson.

McEwen was the first to speak. He asked about my plans.

"I intend to put an expansion team in Tampa," I said.

McEwen said, "The first lesson I'm giving you: you call it Tampa Bay."

"Okay, thanks," I said. And from that day I always said "Tampa Bay."

I told them the cost of the new franchise would be fifty million dollars. That's what the league was asking for. "That's too steep for me, "Michael Osterhaus said. "I can't afford to get involved." We didn't know it, but he was planning to sell his radio stations at that time. Unfortunately, he had partners who refused to sell, and it was not long before the radio market crashed, and he lost almost everything. He would have ended up with a lot of money, but his partners got greedy, and it really cost him.

"Is it worth that much?" they asked.

"No," I said, "but that's the price. You either pay it or get out of the game."

Henry Paul sat there quietly, but I took an immediate liking to him. We had dinner. We talked for about an hour and a half, and after we finished at around ten, I had to drive all the way back to Orlando because I was playing golf the next morning with the guys.

Before I left I said, "Let me ask each one of you. Can hockey make it in Tampa Bay?"

McEwen was first. He said, "Absolutely."

Henry Paul said, "I think so." Henry's a lawyer. Henry would never give a definitive answer. He won't say yes or no unless he knows for sure. But he then said, "It's a great sports town. There are great people here." Henry said he had in his possession the general partnership agreement that George Steinbrenner gave to his limited partners when he bought the Yankees from CBS. His father, Gabe Paul, had been one of those limited partners.

Henry and I decided to go after the Tampa Bay NHL expansion franchise. To help us I hired Mel Lowell, who had worked at Madison Square Garden for eighteen years, first as an accountant for the Knicks and the Rangers and later as the CEO of the building the Knicks and Rangers played in. Two years after I was fired, he left and went to work for a big corporation. I hired him and paid most of his expenses out of my own pocket.

I called everyone I knew trying to find investors. I hunted down every lead that came to me. I knew a guy named Karl Hofer, who was a general manager of some hotels. Karl had worked for the Palace, which was owned by Leona Helmsley, and you better believe she's going to fire your ass sooner or later, and that's what happened to Karl. Karl was building the Regal Royale Hotel in New York City with a guy named Jim Murphy. Karl told me to call Jim, who was the first person to give me real money – a hundred thousand dollars.

I went to a friend of mine, Rick Starr, who's a car dealer in Vero Beach, Florida, and Massachusetts. I met him in a bar when I was working as a greeter for the Sands Hotel in Atlantic City back in the early 1980s (which, by the way, was the best job I ever had in my life). Rick gave me some money, and he brought me to Frank Chase, who played hockey for Harvard and for the 1932 United States Olympic team. When I met him, Frank was eighty-five years old. Mr. Chase invested a million dollars, and he would have invested more if it hadn't been for the interference of his son-in-law.

Mel, Henry, and I were rolling. We got on the train and went to Philadelphia to meet with Tony Tavares, a bigwig with Spectacore, which was owned by the Pritzger family, and with Ed Snider, who owned the Philadelphia Flyers.

Our proposal was for Spectacore to invest fifty million dollars and own the team, and we would be the general partners. They'd be one of six or seven limited partners and become the management team. We really wanted the Pritzgers on board. We had the Pritzgers wrapped up, or so I thought.

We had a meeting at the Hyatt Hotel on 42nd Street in New York with John Pritzger, the son. John, who was in his thirties, lived in Chicago and was a big fan of the Blackhawks and my brother Tony. He really wanted to do this. This was something that would be for him and him alone. We talked. We put the papers down in front of him. He was taking the pen and getting ready to sign us over fifty million when Tony Tavares grabbed his hand and said, "John, you can't sign this until you check with your father."

Tavares looked at John. I glared at Tavares. I could have cut his head off. John put his pen down. He didn't have the balls to do it on his own.

Afterwards I said to Tavares, "Why did you do that?"

"If the old man doesn't agree to it, you aren't going to get the money even if the kid agrees to it," he said.

"But we'd have had something in writing," I said.

"Wouldn't have mattered," he said.

This was in June 1990. John said if I came back in September, he'd sign.

Meanwhile, I was going through torture in Tampa Bay trying to find a place for my new hockey team to play. We wanted to play in the Suncoast Dome, which had been built in St. Petersburg for Major League Baseball, but as yet didn't have a team. I went to see Rick Dodge, who was the city manager in charge of running the facility. I told him what we were doing, and asked if we could sign a lease so we could play in the Dome.

Rick insisted on knowing who my investors were. I told him that my investors, in this case the Pritzgers, didn't want their names made public. If we made their names public we would lose the deal. The Pritzgers had told me they were going to sign, but we didn't have signed papers, and I was going to do everything I could to make sure we finalized the deal.

"Rick," I said, "if one word is said, they're pulling out."

Rick said he would not give me a lease unless he knew who my investors were. Something smelled fishy. "Why do you need to know who the money people are?" I asked. "There are two groups trying for this team. Whichever group gets it, you got a hockey team here."

"I won't do it," he said.

Mark Perrone was so angry with Dodge he turned purple and called him names. I thought Mark was going to have a heart attack.

When Dodge refused to give me that lease, I also called him every name in the book. "You chickenshit son of a bitch . . ." I said,

"Does the mayor know what you are doing to the city of St. Petersburg? I'm going after this franchise, and I'm going to get it."

Dodge repeated, "Unless you tell us who your money people are . . ."

Later I heard that Alan Eagleson was involved with Jimmy Rutherford and the Karmanos group, our competitors for the franchise, and that Eagleson was telling Rick Dodge that the Karmanos group was going to get the franchise.

Eagleson allegedly said to Dodge, "Esposito will never get the franchise. There's no way. I'm the most powerful man in hockey. Don't do anything for Esposito." Eagleson *was* the most powerful man in hockey. But I was sure I was going to get the franchise despite him. Someone else told me later that Eagleson wanted to know who our investors were, and he was using Dodge to find out for him. But I had told the Pritzgers I would keep their identity a secret until it was a done deal, and I gave them my word.

━━━

Rick Dodge froze me out. After getting a final turndown, I was sitting with Henry Paul in his car and I said, "I can't believe this. Isn't there any place in the whole of Tampa Bay where we can put ten thousand people for a hockey game?" We needed a facility that would seat that many people.

"There might be one," he said.

"Where is that?"

"The Fairgrounds," he said.

"Where the hell are the Fairgrounds?"

"It's a little north of Tampa," he said.

"Take me there – right now."

We were on the Crosstown Expressway waiting in a line to go through the toll booth. There were two lanes, one for exact change and one with five cars in it. Henry was sitting behind the five cars.

"Henry, why are we sitting in this lane?"

"I don't know," he said. You have to understand, as crazy and aggravating as all this was, Henry and I were having fun. We laughed a lot along the way.

Henry drove to the Fairgrounds arena, and we went inside. The place looked like a big barn. On the floor sat dozens of race cars like the kind they drive at Sebring. Paul Newman, who is big into racing, was there that day. All I could do was try to imagine what the place would be like with a hockey rink in the middle. I thought, "Jesus, could we play hockey here?"

I started at one side and began to count off paces. Width was no problem: eighty-five feet wide easy. I walked to one end and started pacing again. There was room for a two-hundred-foot-long rink, but I wouldn't be able to put in any seats at either end. Still, I was sure that we could fit a rink in there, and I decided right then that this was where we were going to begin play. I knew if we could get a lease and show the NHL we could fit ten thousand fannies inside, we would get approval.

"Okay, who do we have to see about renting this place?" I asked Henry.

"The Fairgrounds has a committee," he said. "We have to go see the Tampa Sports Authority."

A few days later they removed all the cars, and I went back to the Fairgrounds with a couple of the members of the Sports Authority, who were all in favor of our renting it. I got a measuring tape and marked off where the rink would go.

"The seats come right out, don't they?" I asked.

"Yeah, they do," they said.

"How many seats are there?"

"We can get ten thousand for Reba McEntire, but that's covering the floor," they said.

"Can you put in the seats so I can see what it looks like?"

They were very cooperative. "Let's do it tomorrow," they said.

"We'll put in as many seats as we can right up to where you've marked off the rink."

I couldn't wait to get back there the next day. When I returned, the seats were in place, as promised.

"How many?" I wanted to know.

"Nine thousand, two hundred," they said.

One of the requirements for getting the franchise was that the arena had to seat ten thousand.

"We have to find another eight hundred somewhere," I said.

"We'll figure it out," they said. And they did. When I left for Sweden in August to play a series of Old-Timers hockey games, I thought we were all set with the financing in place from the Pritzgers and a place to play at the Fairgrounds.

I went to Goteborg, Sweden, along with Marcel Dionne, Donnie Murdoch, Denis Potvin, Clark Gillies, and Bobby Bourne. There were a lot of Islanders on the team. I played too. I was the oldest guy on the team. The Swedes had Anders Hedberg, Borje Salming, Stefan Persson, and Ulf Nilsson. We had a blast. We took the train from Goteborg to Stockholm. We were in one car, and the Swedes were in another, but we mingled, and we had a great time. By the time we got to Stockholm, the guys were so drunk we had to carry Marcel Dionne out. His wife was furious. She yelled at him, "Die, you son of a bitch, die." I don't know how he played the next day, but he did, and he played great.

While I was in Sweden I got a call at three-thirty in the morning from Henry Paul and Mel Lowell, telling me the Pritzgers wanted to change the deal.

"What do they want?"

"They want to be the general partners," Henry said. "They want to be the bosses."

"Can't they wait until I get back so we can talk about this?" I asked.

"They're faxing you the new contract, and if you don't sign it now, they're backing out," he said.

Mel said, "We gotta give in. We can't stand up to them."

Henry Paul said, "Phil, I'm not gonna do this. If you want to do it, fine . . ."

"Tell them to fuck off," I said. "Tell them to wait for me to get back, and then we'll talk. We're not changing the deal."

"Well, they're not going to sign."

"Then tell them to screw off," I said.

25

DURING THE SUMMER OF 1990 we kept hearing negative vibes from the league. They kept saying, "We're not sure anyone can make a go of hockey in Tampa Bay." To show the world how viable hockey could be there, we paid the city of St. Petersburg five hundred thousand dollars to put on an exhibition game in the Thunderdome between the Pittsburgh Penguins with Mario Lemieux and the Los Angeles Kings with Wayne Gretzky.

We sold a front-row ticket for ninety-nine dollars. The game took place on September 28, 1990. We printed up bumper stickers that said, "Hockey Now in Tampa Bay."

We weren't making a dime on this. We were spending the change in our pockets, but we had a dream and we promoted this game. Everyone had a great time. We really turned some heads when we drew close to twenty-six thousand customers. Without that game, I'm not sure a Tampa Bay franchise would have been awarded.

In October 1990 Henry Paul went on his honeymoon, and right in the middle of it we got a call from the Pritzgers: they were officially backing out of their deal.

Without the Pritzgers we didn't have a pot to piss in. Now I didn't know which way to turn. I had raised seven million dollars before I thought I had the Pritzgers on board, but that was no money. Worse, when I got back to New York, I got a call from Jim Murphy, who had given me $100,000 for the application fee.

Murph had been fired by the group putting up the Regal Royale Hotel, and he wanted his $100,000 back along with another $250,000 that he had helped raise. I was in total shock. I didn't know I would have to pay that money back. But later on, I was sued for the $250,000 and lost the lawsuit. I really got nailed on that one.

So we were in trouble. Where was I going to find forty-three million dollars more? I couldn't get a single Tampa Bay investor, and it wasn't for lack of trying. I made call after call, wrote letter after letter. I went to the Lykes meats people. They have made millions from their meat business. They didn't know what hockey was. The old money in Tampa Bay knew nothing about the sport. And back in 1990 there was no tech-stock money from young guys like Mark Cuban of the Dallas Mavericks or Daniel Snyder of the Washington Redskins. The technology boom had just happened, and Tampa Bay didn't have any players I was able to find.

In the end, I got the capital from Japan, and it was all because of a baseball bat I noticed leaning against the wall in Henry Paul's office.

On the bat it said, "Nippon Ham Fighters."

"Who are the Nippon Ham Fighters?" I wanted to know.

"That's owned by Tak, Tak Kojima, a friend of mine," Henry said. "Nippon means Japan, and the Nippon Meat Packers are one of the largest meat packers in the world."

"Henry, do you think we could go see this guy?" I asked. "Maybe he could help us."

Henry was reluctant. He wasn't the type of person to ask for money from friends. "I don't know," Henry said.

"Call him – now."

"I don't want to call him now," Henry said. "He's coming here in a couple of weeks."

The Ham Fighters were going to play an exhibition game against the New York Yankees in Tampa Bay during spring training.

As soon as he arrived, Henry and I took Mr. Kojima out to dinner. We took him over to the Suncoast Dome in St. Petersburg and showed him how we had put an ice rink in the baseball stadium. Mr. Kojima didn't know much about hockey, but he got caught up in it. He invited us to come see him in Japan.

He called his friend Masayoshi "Mac" Hidaka, the Ham Fighters' representative in New York, and Mr. Hidaka called David LeFevre, counsel for the Nippon Meat Packing company. LeFevre was a Clevelander who had bought Gabe Paul's stock when George Steinbrenner left Cleveland and bought the New York Yankees in 1973. After John McMullen issued his famous line, "There is nothing more limited than being a limited partner of George Steinbrenner," McMullen and LeFevre bought the Houston Astros. LeFevre, who is a partner in the law firm of Reid and Priest, had plenty of dough himself. His grandfather was Cyrus Eaton, an industrialist.

We met David LeFevre in New York at La Serena, a Japanese steakhouse on 51st Street and Madison Avenue owned by a Mr. Baba. We called him Baba-san. Mr. Baba is a hockey fanatic.

One of the dishes we ate that night was fugu, a blowfish that is poisonous if the chef doesn't cook it right. I had no idea what they were serving me. If I had known, I'm not sure I would have eaten it.

They also served a steak that was cooked on a hot, hot rock right on the table, and it was delicious. I went back many times, and Mr. Baba and I became good friends.

"I have a couple of clients who might be interested," LeFevre said. "I gather you don't mind if they're Japanese."

"I don't give a shit if they're Lebanese," I said. "They can be pink; they can be purple. I don't care, as long as they have money, because I want to do this, and I know I can get the franchise."

"Let me see what I can do," he said.

After sitting and talking for a couple of hours we exchanged phone numbers. Later I said to Mel, "If this guy doesn't come through, we're in trouble. How are we going to do this?"

"I don't know, Phil," he said. "I don't know, man."

Two days later I got a call from David LeFevre. He said to Mel and me, "Can you guys be on call?"

"On call for what?"

"To go to Japan."

"Shit," I said, "I'll go to China, Lebanon, Japan. Doesn't make any difference to me. I don't care. I'll go anywhere."

"Do you think the NHL would welcome the Japanese?" he asked.

"David, for fifty million dollars, they'd take anybody. Doesn't matter, as long as you can prove they have the money."

Mel, Henry, and I were scheduled to fly to Tokyo in November 1990 around Thanksgiving. One of the men we were going to see was a wealthy Japanese hockey lover by the name of Mr. Tsasumi. Mel and I had a routine. I'd say, "So sue me." He'd say, "No, Tsasumi." "Sounds like 'so sue me' to me," I'd say. And we'd laugh. We never did get to meet Mr. Tsasumi.

We arrived in Tokyo and took a cab to the Imperial Hotel. Offices are small in Tokyo, so a lot of business is conducted on the hotel's mezzanine level, where people bring drinks and sit and talk.

I stayed two weeks in Tokyo and got to see a lot of the city. I thought Tokyo was terrific, except for all the raw fish I had to eat. If

I didn't get worms from eating the raw fish there, I'll never get them.

One night Mel and I saw a McDonald's. We ran in there and bought two Big Macs and paid twenty bucks apiece for them. We wouldn't have cared if they had cost a hundred dollars each. I was starving. I ate that burger in three bites.

Mel had it worse than I did. He couldn't figure out how to use the chopsticks. They would put an elastic around his so they'd stay together. He would say to me, "Oh my God, look at me eat this shit."

There were two separate groups interested in our venture. The first was headed by Tak Kojima of the Nippon Ham Fighters. It turned out that Henry Paul's dad, Gabe Paul, who had been a general manager for Cincinnati, Cleveland, and the New York Yankees, and Tak were longtime friends from baseball. Tak was also a friend of George Steinbrenner, who met him through Gabe. Henry and I were trying to get Mr. Kojima to get the parent company to invest in our hockey team.

The other potential investor we went to see was Yoshio Nakamura, who also was connected to Japanese baseball and who, though we didn't know it then, didn't like Kojima. We had meetings with both factions. One night we'd go with Kojima, the next with Nakamura.

Our initial plan was to use the seven million dollars we had raised, add another seventeen million in cash, and finance the rest, though the truth of the matter was we really needed fifty-five million, including five million to buy players and operate.

One night Kojima took us to his favorite restaurant. The inside area had a pool containing live fish, and the outside was the seating area where the waiters stood. We sat on bar stools drinking sake, and while we were sitting there Kojima in his broken English, said, "Pick a fish."

I pointed to one of the foot-long fish swimming in the pool. I have no clue what kind of fish they were.

Mel looked at me.

"Pick a fuckin' fish, Mel," I said.

"Okay," he said, "I'll take that one," and he pointed.

The waiter speared the two fish and put them on our plates, wriggling and jumping. The waiter then ripped them apart with a knife right on our plates. The pieces were still wriggling.

"No way," Mel said to me. "I can't do it."

"Mel," I said, "for fifty million dollars, you're going to eat that raw fish if I have to hold you down and shove it down your throat."

"Jesus, forgive me," he said. "Help me! Forgive me." He was very funny. Mel ate the fish, and he headed for the bathroom. I was sure he was going to throw up. He denies that, but I guarantee you that's what he did. Henry, the quiet one, picked a fish, ate it, and never said a word. I ate some of the raw fish, though I don't know how. I will admit I dropped a couple pieces on the floor. Thank God they served rice. We ate a lot of rice during the two weeks we were there.

After we ate the fish, Kojima said to us, "Would you like to go to the Ginzu?"

"What's the Ginzu?" I asked.

"You'll see," he said.

We went to a nightclub that was something like our cigar bars in North America where we can go and get a cigar and smoke without having people bug you about the smoke and the smell. We went in, and they had little lockers where the patrons keep their own bottles of liquor.

Kojima said to us, "What would you like?"

"I'd like some vodka," I said. I really wanted beer, but they only served hard liquor.

"Okay, vodka," he said, and he poured a brown liquid that tasted like Scotch. I hate Scotch, but I didn't say anything, because that's all he had.

It was a karaoke bar, and we took over the joint. Henry had too much to drink, and he got up and sang, "Camptown ladies sing this song, doo dah, doo dah." You should have seen the Japanese. They were going, "Huh?" Then I got up and sang, "New York, New York." When we were done performing, we went and sat back down on the floor, where young girls on their hands and knees sat beside us peeling grapes and feeding them to us.

I really wanted to go to a geisha house. I wanted the girls to scrub my whole body with their little hands. The Japanese guys were telling me how they did this. I said, "Well, Jesus, let's go." But we never went because it was business, business, business. Every morning and night for ten days we went out with these guys to try to get money from them. Every night we took these guys to dinner, ate raw fish and drank.

I'm a salesman. If I know my product well enough, I can sell it. And I knew hockey, and I loved it. If you love something, you can sell it. And the long and short of it was, when we left Japan we had commitments for close to fifty million bucks.

The main investor was to be a company called Kokusai Green Ltd., which among other things owned golf courses in Japan. The Nippon Ham Fighters were also in with us, as was a group from the Tokyo Tower, which was built exactly like the Eiffel Tower. The head of that group was also named Kojima. We rode to the top of the tower. The guy was telling me that his company owned the White-Faced Mountains ski resorts in Virginia and North Carolina. LeFevre represented them too. They were good people. These were all good people. I thought they were all terrific.

After I flew home from Japan, David LeFevre stayed on for another five days. "I've got to wrap things up now," he said. He was also going to see the Mitsubishi people, whom he represented, about investing in our hockey team. For some reason he didn't want us there, which was fine since he was now part of our group. It turned out that when Mitsubishi found out that Kokusai Green was involved, they backed out.

David came back from Japan and told us it looked like we had a deal. We were pretty happy, but after what happened with the Pritzgers, I wasn't sure of anything.

In the meantime, I flew down to Tampa Bay and rented an apartment there while Donna stayed back in Bedford, New York, with Cherise and her horses. Henry, Mel, and I negotiated a lease for Exposition Hall at the Fairgrounds, and we began talking to some of the people I wanted to hire to make the team run.

Every nickel of expenses came out of my pocket that first year, close to $850,000, my total life savings. I figured if I was successful getting the financing for the team, I'd get my money back in the long run. Shows you how naive I was. My tunnel vision ended up getting me the team, but it also cost me my marriage. And I never did get my money back. Well, not much of it.

26

I WENT TO JAMAICA on vacation with Donna in May 1991. David Lefevre said to me, "When you come back, you'll have a hockey franchise." We needed to give the league $22.5 million on June 1. David was supposed to be holding the money. Mr. Kojima had sent Henry his $2.5 million. David LeFevre was responsible for the other $20 million.

Henry, Mel, and I continued to look for investors, just in case the Japanese didn't come through. I never realized how vulnerable people looking to raise capital can be. It's a jungle out there.

My brother Tony introduced me to a fellow named Joe Sardano, who sold MRIs, X-ray machines, and other expensive medical-supply equipment. Joe was from Montreal and a hockey fan. He had me contact a friend of his, Carroll Tessier. I told Tessier I was looking for investors, and he said, "I think I have a guy." I asked him who it was, but he wouldn't tell me.

A couple of days later he called me, and he told me the Duke of Manchester, a very wealthy nobleman from England, was interested in investing in companies in the United States. Carroll said the duke was coming to the States, and in a couple of weeks he'd come to Tampa to see me about my hockey team.

We checked the British Embassy in with Washington and found out there definitely was a Duke of Manchester. He was the second cousin to the Queen, who has all the money in the world. Carroll Tessier told us that the duke had a substantial trust fund – around $350 million. What he couldn't find out was whether he had the authority to spend it.

The day the duke came to Tampa he pulled up in a stretch limousine. He was accompanied by a woman we assumed was his wife. She was wearing a huge hat like the English wear and was dressed to the nines. Then the duke came out, and he looked like my old man, a big, barrel-chested, square-headed man. After they came to my office and sat down, the duke said, "Carroll has filled me in and I'm very interested. I'm going to do this with you. I really want to do it."

I was so excited I could barely sit down.

The duke said, "If we don't want the Japanese in the deal, you don't have to worry about that."

"They're in," I said, "unless we're told they're not, but I want you in with them."

"I have to be the boss," the duke said. "I have to be the biggest of the limited partners."

"We'll make it work," I promised.

I was staring at this guy thinking it was all too good to be true. We had talked to Washington. There *was* a Duke of Manchester. We saw his picture, and it absolutely was him. The guy was real. I wanted to pinch myself.

We went to Carroll Tessier's house in Orlando. It was large and beautiful. We had a great meeting.

Over the course of the next few months, I paid the duke's expenses out of my pocket. I paid for his plane fares coming over from England. He flew on the Concorde, of course. He stayed in the finest hotels, ate in the best restaurants, drank the best wine. It came to about fifty thousand dollars, and I paid for it all.

The night the duke agreed to sign the same deal that John Pritzger had backed out of – he was agreeing to give us $22.5 million and become a limited partner – we were overjoyed. We drank wine, champagne, and beer in our offices on Kennedy Boulevard, and at the end of the evening the duke wrote us a check for three million as a down payment. It was signed in a beautiful hand: *Lord Montague, the Duke of Manchester.*

━━━━━━

In June 1991 the NHL had an important meeting in Buffalo. We had to give the league our five-million-dollar down payment. Henry Paul had the $2.5 million from Kojima, who came to the meeting and was applauded by the rest of the owners.

David LeFevre was supposed to have the rest of the down-payment money, and I was in a state of panic because I couldn't get in touch with him. The expansion-board members were calling me, saying, "Phil, where's your money?"

"David LeFevre has my money," I said. But we couldn't find David anywhere. We began to think that David's partners were trying to squeeze us financially so he could come back with a better deal for himself and cut us out. Why else would he disappear?

Mel Lowell blasted David in front of the other NHL owners. I was appalled. "Are you sure you did the right thing?" I said to Mel.

"Phil," Mel said, "we have nothing if LeFevre has gone south on us."

None of this sat very well with some of the NHL owners. LeFevre was a friend of Boston Bruins owner Jerry Jacobs, and Mel's outburst didn't endear us to him. It also gave John McMullen, the owner of the New Jersey Devils, ammunition against us. When McMullen and LeFevre were owners of the Houston Astros, McMullen, without informing LeFevre and the other minority partners, fired talented general manager Tal Smith, infuriating LeFevre so much that David threatened a palace coup to get rid of McMullen.

The falling out was bitter, and this gave McMullen a chance to get back at David. He got up and said he didn't want our group in the league.

"The worst thing the NHL could do is let David Lefevre into the loop," he said.

Since we didn't have LeFevre's money, we gave NHL president John Ziegler the three-million-dollar check from the Duke of Manchester instead. We had not intended to use the duke's money for the down payment. We figured we would need it later. We told the NHL governors all about the duke's intended participation. Looking back, it's possible that without that check we would have been out on our asses right then and there.

We wrote a letter to LeFevre and told him we had another investor, so see ya. "Sorry, you have not fulfilled your part of the bargain, so we're going with the duke."

When David LeFevre learned that the league had accepted the duke's check, he quickly resurfaced, and he was livid. "How could you guys do this to me?" he wanted to know. "Are you trying to force my clients out, after all I did for you?"

"Well, hell, David, we did what we had to do, "I said. "We didn't know where you were."

"The Japanese are going to be the owners," he said.

"Okay, but we're going to have an added investor," I said.

"As long as my clients are in on the deal."

"Absolutely," I said. "Your guys are committed for $32 million. And I have $18 million from Montague." And I had an additional $7 million for a total of $57 million.

———

Two weeks after the league meeting I got a call from the league informing me that the duke's check had bounced.

We had been had. It turned out that the big house in Orlando really wasn't Carroll Tessier's, that he was only renting it. It also turned out that the woman with the hat wasn't the duke's wife. The whole thing, we learned, was a big con to get the Barnett Bank to lend the duke thirty-two million dollars in cash – money he was going take and run away with.

But in the end it didn't matter. Before we realized that the duke was a lunatic con man, he served us very well, even though he had no idea exactly how he helped us. When the duke entered the picture, David and his partners lost their leverage.

As soon as LeFevre found out about the duke's check going to the league, boy, did he start singing a different tune. LeFevre's Japanese investors came back so fast our heads began to spin. When the duke's check bounced, we were forced to admit to ourselves that the duke was a fraud, but we didn't tell David that. Instead, we told David that if he kept to the original deal we'd give his clients their original position back. And he agreed, because the Japanese didn't want the duke involved in the first place.

It was not long before the FBI went after Carroll Tessier and the duke. I was told that Carroll, a Canadian, skipped the country and fled to Indonesia or Pakistan or someplace. The duke ended up in jail. I think he was still behind bars when he died suddenly in July 2002.

———

At the league meeting in June 1991, David did not pay the league the twenty million dollars he was supposed to provide as a down payment. He had assurances from his Japanese investors pledging the forty-five million we owed the NHL, but the money was not forthcoming.

League president John Ziegler knew we were having financial problems, just as Ottawa, another new franchise, was also having financial problems. John wanted to expand to Florida, and because he had faith in me, the league said they would rely on those assurances, though there were questions about letting us in without paying.

Kenny Sawyer, who was the league controller at the time, asked to see Kokusai Green's financial records. From Japan came a two-page fax in Japanese which we sent to the expansion committee.

We sent a Mr. Miaki to the meeting to explain the financial statements. The only problem was that Mr. Miaki didn't speak any English. It was like a scene from the Marx Brothers or the Three Stooges, though Mel, Henry, and I hated to think of ourselves as the stooges.

Stanley Jaffe, who was the chief operating officer of Paramount, which owned Madison Square Garden, got up and started waving around the financial statements written in Japanese.

He said, "What type of joke is this? What are these people doing?" Meaning us.

And in a low voice, Mr. Miaki said, "Uhhhh. No understand."

For a long time I was as skeptical about David and his Japanese investors as the league was, and I was trying to raise money from American sources to get the Japanese out. Also LeFevre told me the Japanese wanted some local ownership, and the only guy with money I knew in Tampa Bay was George Steinbrenner. When I went to see him, he was as nice as pie. George, who at the time was under a lifetime suspension from Major League Baseball for paying a guy to give him dirt on Dave Winfield, one of his players, agreed in principle in May 1992 to lend me $2.5 million. I was hoping that having George in our corner would help us in our negotiations with the Japanese. George, who is a dog-eat-dog, show-no-mercy businessman, immediately realized our terrible bargaining position.

George said to me, "You got no ham."

"What do you mean?" I said.

"I got the bread," he said. "You have nothing."

That Christmas, George Steinbrenner sent me a package. Inside was a ham.

George wrote, "You now have only the ham."

God, he was hilarious. He made me laugh, but once we started meeting with the Japanese, he treated me very badly. I've always wondered whether George and David LeFevre had a lot to do with what happened next.

In September 1991 we were informed that the Japanese investors wanted to meet with us. Finally, we were going to meet our partners. But the meeting was intended as an execution, not a meeting. I never knew what hit me.

Henry, Mel, and I walked in to David LeFevre's conference room, and sitting on the opposite side of the table were ten Japanese investors, LeFevre, a rich Boca Raton real-estate mogul named Norton Herrick, a guy named Chris Phillips, and their lawyer, Reese Smith, who was the head of the American Bar Association. Smith said he represented "all the Japanese," but Kojima made it very clear that LeFevre and Smith didn't represent him at all. Unfortunately, Kojima represented only a minority interest among the investors.

Smith played hardball. "Either you give up your majority position," he said, "or we won't make the $22.5 million payment to the league." If we didn't give in, he said, they were going to forfeit the five million they had invested and pull out entirely. "Since we're putting up most of the money," he told us, "we're going to be the general partners." Norton Herrick commented, "They have no money. Why should we be worrying about them?"

They said the only deal they would agree to would be if they had control of the team and if Henry, Mel, and I would accept class-B stock. They had us by the balls.

Mel, Henry, and I pondered whether they *really* would forfeit the five million. I wondered: Can we afford to gamble? Without the duke's money, all we had was about six million dollars, and if we didn't give in to the Japanese investors' demands, we would have lost that *and* the franchise as well.

It's a wonder we all didn't die from the stress.

In the end I decided that we had no choice. I said to Henry, "If the deal falls through, I won't have a job, Mel won't have a job, and my brother Tony won't have a job." Tony and I were in this together. Henry, who was and is a lawyer, would have been okay. He could still make a living. But if the deal fell through we were going to be in big, big trouble.

I asked Smith and the Japanese if they would pay me my $850,000 in expenses that I had shelled out since I began the quest for a team. They said no. (Mel later sued to get paid for his stock. In late December of 1995 the three of us were forced to settle for $650,000, which we split three ways.)

Mel was dumbfounded. Henry hid his feelings. And me, I was in a daze, wondering what the fuck is going on? Why are they doing this to us?

Mel, Henry, Kojima, and I excused ourselves to caucus in private. I said to Mel and Henry, "Guys, we have no fucking choice here if we're going to be part of this. They are general partners, but we still have a piece of the team. I got my job. Henry, you got your job. Mel, you are in administration. My brother and I run the operation of the team."

We agreed. We went back and accepted their terms.

Who was to blame? To this day I'm not sure. I suspect George Steinbrenner had something to do with it, but the main culprit may have been David LeFevre, with whom I am still in business. We are partners in an East Coast Hockey League team. He couldn't get the franchise without me, so he gave me a 15 per cent interest in the team, and I didn't have to invest any money. If I ever see any money from that stake, it will be a miracle. I have nothing in writing, and that's fine. I'm part of something in hockey, and I do some work for the team.

But I do not like what David and George did to me. My brother can't forgive them, especially David. Henry Paul can't either. Do I forgive them? No. But business is business.

In the end George never did put up his $2.5 million. Once the Japanese became the general partners and he saw he wasn't going to be able to take over the team, he said, "I'm not putting in my money."

Would I do it again? Probably. Was I a fool? Was I stupid? Probably. But that's just the way it was, because if I hadn't done what I did, it never would have gotten done, and the Tampa Bay Lightning probably would not exist.

27

THE JAPANESE were happy to let Tony and me run the team once they had established financial control. And David LeFevre was smart enough to know he didn't know anything about professional hockey. The Japanese and David gave us control in the contract to run the team, and they left us alone.

It was the one consolation I had after my being screwed. I had started the franchise figuring I would have a hockey team to run for the rest of my life. Instead, I ended up just another worker. I would be allowed to mold the team in my image as long as the Japanese owned the team. But I had no idea how long that would be. And I had no guarantees.

The Japanese executives in the team offices were not bad people. I liked a guy named Mr. Nakamura a lot. I liked another guy named Sugioka. David brought in a guy who provided seats for stadiums. LeFevre had Mel write a check to him for seventy-five thousand dollars, though I never could find out what it was for. And then there was the old Japanese man with the fat head and glasses who would stay in his office all day looking at numbers. I had a lot of fun with him. I'd say to him, "What are you doing in there for ten hours?" He'd smile. At our meetings he'd pretend he was sleeping, but he knew what was going on.

Even though we had not yet been awarded the franchise, there was a great deal to be done. Since I was in charge of the hockey operation, I put my mind to all that that entailed.

We needed a name for our team. My intention was to let the fans pick the name. Then in July 1991 I was at a party at Benny Lazarra's house. Benny was one of Henry Paul's law partners, and he graciously let us use his office a lot. Benny's house was on the water facing Tampa Bay. It was about three in the afternoon and as I looked out the window I could see a huge black cloud moving across the sky. We get storms all the time during the summer around Tampa Bay, and the sky turned black, and I wondered, Is this the end of the world? Suddenly, there was a crash of thunder and the biggest bolt of lightning I had ever seen. It was on the horizon, but it looked like it was right next to me.

Behind me, a little old lady who appeared to be in her eighties said, "You ought to name the team the goddamn Lightning." The woman turned out to be Benny's mom.

"That's it!" I said. We were the lightning capital of North America. It made sense. I made up my mind: we were going to call the team the Lightning. We would still have our contest, but Lightning it would be.

I gave Mel Lowell the job of designing the logo and the uniform, but I had a lot of say about it. I wanted lightning bolts down the side of the pants and a lightning bolt on the crest. I wanted something different, so I came up with a sweater with black and white stripes under the arms, so when a player raised his arms after a goal, you could see them. That would be our special look. No one else would have that.

We interviewed a bunch of marketing firms. One marketer came in and he brought a plaque that said, "Kick Ice." I looked at him and said, "I like that." We printed up thousands of bumper stickers that said, "Kick Ice," and we went around town to parking garages and stuck them on the backs of cars. I had our people take stacks of these stickers on sales calls and smack them on whatever cars they walked past.

———

During the summer of 1991 I began interviewing possible coaches for the team. My plan was to hire a disciplinarian who could work well with older players for the first three years, and then I would replace him with Wayne Cashman, who would start as the assistant coach so he could gain more experience.

Terry Crisp was recommended to me by my friend Angelo Bombacco. I had played against Terry for years. He had coached junior hockey in Sault Ste. Marie and then coached the Flames in Calgary. He was my first choice. There were three main reasons I hired him. One, he was not expensive, and two, he had done a good job coaching in my hometown of Sault Ste. Marie. Finally, I wanted someone I knew, and I knew Terry.

I interviewed eight candidates besides Terry, but none was as impressive, and so I hired him with the proviso that Wayne

Cashman would be his assistant coach. He agreed. Of course we first had to get the franchise.

I wanted employees who would be good for the organization for the first three years, guys who could give the team as much oomph as possible, and so I hired as trainers Frosty Forristall, Jocko Cayer, and Skip Thayer. The trainers are an important part of the team. They have to be good with the players. They spend all day around the ice, and they don't get paid much. They have to be special people.

I always felt Frosty's attitude was worth six to eight points a year, and he never played a game. Frosty had been fired by Boston because of his drinking. I knew he was an alcoholic. I thought I could help him, and I got him in AA. I was with Jocko in New York. Jocko was fired two years after the Rangers fired me. Jocko's about five-foot-three, and he's missing a finger that he cut off while he was sharpening skates. I thought the two would be a terrific combination.

———

The decision of who would get the two new expansion franchises, Ottawa and Tampa Bay, was made in December 1991.

I arrived at the Breakers Hotel in Palm Beach a few days before the meeting in order to do some lobbying. I talked to every owner. I felt that Billy Wirtz, the owner of the Chicago Blackhawks, was a strong voice, and I hooked myself to him. I met with Marcel Aubut of the Quebec Nordiques three or four times. I didn't meet with Jerry Jacobs, the Bruins owner, because I didn't like him and I never trusted him after he traded me from Boston to New York. I always thought his trading me was stupid. It cost Boston at least two Stanley Cups.

The night before we were to meet with the Board of Governors, I was asked to meet with the other bidder, the Karmanos Group. Lou Beers – the biggest man I ever saw – was the lawyer for Jim Rutherford and Karmanos. Beers, who was about six-foot-five and must have weighed 450 pounds, invited me to his room at the Breakers.

I knew what he wanted. Beers's room was adjacent to that of Mel Lowell, one of my partners. We would go over to Mel's room and listen in on Beers's conversations through the wall.

We heard someone from their group say, "We got to get to this Esposito. How are we going to do that?"

"Let's offer him a deal, but let's make sure they come up with the five million dollars first."

I listened to this, and I looked at Mel and Henry Paul and shook my head.

When Beers called and asked if I would come see him, I said, "No, if you want to talk to me, come on over."

I was with Henry and Mel when he knocked on the door. He looked around. He couldn't fit in the chair, so he sat on the edge of the bed.

Beers repeated the proposal we had heard through the wall. He began, "We want to make a deal with you guys. We're both going for the Tampa franchise."

I corrected him. "Tampa Bay," I said.

"Tampa Bay," he said. "Here's what we are proposing. You guys put up five million, and we'll put up the rest later on."

"Who's going to run the team?" I asked.

"Jimmy Rutherford will be president and general manager," he said.

"Really. What will I do?"

"You will work in the organization."

"And we put up the first five million?"

"Yeah," he said.

Mel and Henry looked at me as if to say, What a lot of nerve. "If you were a little smaller," I said, "I'd grab you and throw you out the fucking window. But since I can't, get your fat ass up and get the fuck out of here! Get the fuck out of this room! We'll take our chances and see what happens tomorrow, because we're getting the franchise and you're not, and you fucking know it. You want us to pay the five million dollars and let you run the team? Get the fuck out of here." I added, "Tell your partners we'll see them when they buy some other team," which is what eventually happened.

Beers said, "You'll be sorry," and he got up and left.

If Pete Karmanos or Jim Rutherford had come to see us, we probably could have gotten something done. But they sent their lawyer, and he had no tact. He was telling us how it was going to be, and you don't do that to me. If you ask me, fine. But don't tell me what you're going to do, because my answer's going to be, "No, you're not."

Nevertheless, Mel and Henry suggested we go to Karmanos and discuss joining forces. "We're not doing that," I said. "We're going straight forward just like we planned. You don't change now."

It's that way in hockey too. If I had a breakaway and I changed my mind, the goalie would beat me. When I play golf, if I select a club, I stick with it, even if I'm not sure it's the right club. Once I pick it, I'm going with it.

We stayed up until four in the morning lobbying the other owners. Mel and Henry and I were out there talking up what we could do for the league as owners of the Tampa Bay expansion team. I got one good piece of advice from Billy Wirtz. He said, "Phil, when you're in that meeting, answer the questions honestly. Tell them what you really think, because I believe you can get it done."

———

Before we went to the meeting of the expansion committee, Jerry Helper, who worked in public relations for the league, came to our room to tell us where and when we should go.

"We got it, don't we, Jerry?" I said.

"I can't tell you, Phil, and I don't know," he said. But he knew. He didn't want to tip their hand.

Mel said to me, "If we don't get it, what are we going to do?"

"Relax, Mel, we're going to get this," I said. "We are going to be the guys." I was nervous as hell, but very confident. I went to the meeting with Mel and Henry. I didn't want David LeFevre, Mark Gannis, or Jimmy Cusack, who were involved in building the new arena in Tampa. We brought in Tampa mayor Sandy Freedman later.

The Ottawa candidate and our group went into that meeting together. I was so nervous when we walked down the corridor, turned the corner, and entered the room. All the owners were standing around a big table, and they started clapping and cheering, and chanting, "Espo, Espo, Espo." It was an unbelievable moment. John Ziegler had tears in his eyes. He came up and gave me a hug and said, "Phil, I hope you can do it. I really hope you can be successful."

We all sat down, and the other owners began asking me questions. The first question Marcel Aubut asked me was, "Pheel, do you t'ink da price of fifty million is worth it?"

"Do I think it's worth it or will we pay it?"

He said, "Do you think it's worth it?"

"No," I said, "I don't think it's worth it, but we will pay it. That's what you guys want, and that's what we are willing to do. If that's the price to get in, we'll pay it."

I found out that the group trying to get the Ottawa franchise and the other group trying to get the Tampa Bay franchise each tried to negotiate down the price. The other Tampa Bay group wanted to pay only thirty-five million dollars down and the rest later. I'm sure that's a large part of why we got the franchise.

———

That night I went to a party at Jerry Jacobs's house in West Palm Beach. He had a huge home. John Henry, who would later buy the Boston Red Sox, was there, and he and I started giggling. He said, "You guys are really loose, aren't you?"

"What are we going to do?" I said. "We'll either get it or we won't. We're ready for it, and if we get it, we'll do a good job with it."

━━━━━

The next morning we were called in, and we all went, and, boy, I was nervous then. Every group was there. Mel and David LeFevre were sitting on either side of me. Henry was beside Mel, and standing behind him was a Japanese guy brought in by LeFevre, and I don't know why. I didn't even know what he was supposed to do.

We were sitting there biting our nails, when John Ziegler stood up and said, "The franchise for Tampa Bay has been awarded to Phil Esposito and the Tampa Bay hockey group."

"All right!" I shouted like I did when I scored a goal. Henry had a smile from ear to ear. Mel put his head on the table. He was so happy, he began to cry.

David LeFevre had not yet come across with the ten million dollars from Kokusai Green. We had to pay the league five million now and another five million in June.

David turned to me and said, "What do we do now?"

I said, "You better fucking get the money." And I said to Mel, "Get on the phone and start selling tickets."

Twenty minutes later Mel was on the phone. We had an office set up that night on Kennedy Boulevard. Mel flew home to Tampa, and we were out selling tickets the next day. And people were buying them.

I flew home from Palm Beach the day after the meeting. I was by myself. When the plane landed, I was met by two burly guys.

"Phil Esposito?"

"Yeah."

They said, "Come with us."

"What's going on?"

"You'll find out," they said.

They walked me down onto the tarmac, and there to meet me were Jimmy Cusack, Mel, and Henry. They had hired a cable car on wheels, and I got on it, and we drove from the airport to down-town Tampa to our offices. When we arrived, the plaza was jammed with people.

I walked up to the podium and I talked about the franchise. The crowd began to cheer. The day was very, very special.

28

WE HAD A LOT TO DO to get ready for opening day. I had worked hard to assemble a scouting staff. I hired some of the guys who had worked with me for the Rangers, and my brother Tony hired some other guys who had been with him in Pittsburgh. During the first year all their salaries came out of my pocket. I really believed I'd get the money back. If I hadn't done it, we'd have been in as much trouble going into the draft as Ottawa was. They were screwed up and made tons of mistakes. We didn't make one mistake.

The expansion draft to stock the Lightning was held in June 1992. To prepare for it, I conducted fifty mock drafts until we knew every player available to us by heart. Tony and I would go into a hotel room with our eight scouts, and I'd say, "Okay, Tony, you represent Ottawa." I assigned John Chapman, my head scout, to be Tampa Bay. I assigned four scouts to each team. "Flip a coin and see who picks first."

The pickings were slim. The established teams were allowed to protect eighteen players and two goalies – in other words, anyone who was any good. For fifty million dollars, we were getting hosed. We were being allowed to buy fourth-line offensive players and seventh and eighth defensemen. We dissected the rosters and predicted who was going to be exposed, and we were 99 per cent right. It was amazing how close we were – unfortunately. We went around the room drafting players and talking about them. We would get to the eleventh or twelfth player, and the scouts would say, "There is nothing here to draft."

"Would you guys stop?" I would say. "That's what we have available. We have to do this."

Then I switched captains and scouts, and we would do it again. The guys would say, "Ah, Phil, again?" I'd say, "Yes. One more time."

I tried to make deals before the draft. I called every team in the league to try to trade my draft picks for existing players. I had won the coin toss held during the middle of a playoff game in Pittsburgh and was awarded the first pick in the draft, which I gladly would have traded away for a decent goalie. I figured somebody would be happy to take a second- or third-round pick. Not a single team would trade with me. Not one.

Three months later, the NHL held its draft of amateur players. I wanted our first pick to be an offensive player, because of who I am and the way I used to play. I wanted us to take Alexei Yashin, who had starred for Dynamo Moscow. The rest of my scouts wanted us to take Roman Hamrlik, a defenseman who starred for the Czechoslovakian national team. I had no problem picking Roman. I had seen him play, and he was a good one, and so I went with everyone else. We picked first and took Hamrlik, and Ottawa took Yashin, who later turned out to be a pain in the ass. He had a $3.3 million contract and demanded a renegotiation, and he sat out a whole year. To me that shows a lack of character.

We held our first training camp in Lakeland, Florida, about fifty miles west of Tampa, in an attempt to expand our fan base. That also gave us more time to fix up Expo Hall at the Fairgrounds, which needed better dressing rooms, and we negotiated for that and got it. We built a gondola for the radio and TV people, and Tony and I had a booth where we could watch the games.

I divided the squad into four teams, the way Harry Sinden did it when I was with the Bruins. Each team had a sponsor like Outback Steakhouse or Hooters. The first few days we had the teams play a round-robin scrimmage, and we watched. After the tournament, the winning team was treated to dinner. It was fun.

During that training camp, I signed Manon Rhéaume to come and play for us. Manon was a goaltender, and she was a beautiful young woman.

I found Manon through Jacques Campeau, who turned out to be another bullshit artist. When I was looking to buy out the Japanese, he told me he had money and was connected to other guys who had money, and so I flew with him to Dallas to look at a charter jet he said he owned, and he showed me where he was going to build a casino in Santo Domingo. Everybody thought I was nuts hanging around with this guy, but so long as there was even the slightest possibility he would have money, I went along. I even gave Jacques a job as a part-time scout in Quebec so he could get a visa and travel back and forth between there and the United States. I gave his son a hockey job playing in the minor leagues. Christian Campeau worked hard and did all right.

Jacques was the one who convinced me to sign Manon Rhéaume. We went up to a women's tournament and watched her play. "Play her," he said. "The publicity will be great." I agreed with him. And so when we opened camp in Lakeland, Manon was on the squad. As a result, CBS, NBC, and ABC all were there talking about the first woman goaltender ever to play in an NHL game.

Mark McEwen, the weather guy from CBS, put the pads on, and I went on the ice with Manon and Mark and one of our players, and we shot pucks at them. McEwen couldn't skate. He stood in the net, and I was tempted to shoot one at his head, but I was afraid of killing him on national TV, so I didn't.

Terry Crisp hated that Manon was on the team. So did my brother Tony, which may have been the only time they agreed on anything. Even Wayne Cashman hated it. Cash would give me the evil eye. I'd say to him, "We're doing it. That's it." A lot of the scouts hated it too. The players didn't like it much either.

I told Manon, "You have to go out with the guys. You have to be part of the team." They took her to dinner and for a few beers.

I wanted to play her because there was nothing to lose and everything to gain. This wasn't Ottawa or Toronto or Boston or New York. This was Tampa, Florida. No other person would have even tried to start hockey here. I was the right guy at the right time to do this. Was it innovative? Some people thought so. Others thought it was crazy. I knew we weren't going to win, so my idea was to promote the team in any way I could to put people in the seats. If I had staked everything on the team's record, we would have had three thousand people in the building, and most of them would have been relatives.

Manon wasn't a bad goalie, but she was gorgeous and too much of a model to stay in the game. There was no harm in letting her come to camp and play. When I told Crispy I wanted her to play half a game, he just about died.

"Oh no, we're a laughingstock as it is," he said.

"Terry, you are going to play her," I said. "And we're going to publicize it."

Even though the players didn't want her to play, they all fought to room with her. We gave her her own dressing room.

She played half a game against St. Louis during training camp at the Fairgrounds. The place was jammed. They were sitting up in the rafters. Donna and my daughters Carrie and Cherise were tickled pink that a woman was going to play. Everybody was. An unbelievable number of women came to that game. Brett Hull, who had one of the hardest shots in the game, was shooting bullets at her, and she stood right in there.

Bobby Plager, the coach of the Blues, said to me, "I've instructed my boys to shoot at the five hole," meaning just below the crotch.

"Bobby, you pig," I said.

During the game, Rob Ramage, one of our defensemen, an older guy, a class guy, wouldn't let any of the Blues players get near her. He was right there to protect her.

During practice Manon pulled a muscle in her lower back. The trainer, Larry Ness, said to me, "What do I do?" I said, "You do the same as you'd do with a guy. But you better not get a hard-on."

He was rubbing her back and her ass, and the guys were peeking through the curtain trying to see her naked.

At the end of training camp, I sent her to Atlanta as the backup goalie for our International Hockey League team. She played once in a while and was okay. They ended up winning the championship. She went on to play on the 1998 Canadian Olympic team, which Canada lost to the United States. Manon made a good living speaking and signing autographs. They made a movie about her. Sure I exploited her, but it was good for her too.

―――――

From the start I could see a rift developing between me and Terry Crisp. I should have coached the team myself. I needed a coach who would work with me and not resent me, but Terry was not that guy. Under my system, after every scrimmage I had my scouts rate the players, and I wanted Terry to look at the ratings. He refused. "What do the scouts have to do with it?" he'd say. He saw it as a threat to his authority. He refused even to talk to the scouts. He stopped coming to the meetings. He also stopped communicating with Wayne Cashman, who was supposed to be his assistant. Terry would sit by himself, and Wayne would sit by himself. I knew sooner or later I would have to fire Terry.

―――――

On opening night we jammed 10,425 fans into Expo Hall at the Fairgrounds against the Chicago Blackhawks, a pretty good team. Alan Thicke, who's Canadian, came and sang both national anthems, even though two American teams played. That night was magical. Chris Kontos, a journeyman who had played with the Rangers, the Pittsburgh Penguins, and the L.A. Kings (and who would score 27 goals and 24 assists for 51 points in his final season in the league), scored four goals, some of them beauties.

Our goalie was Wendell Young, a backup from Pittsburgh. We won the game 7-3.

I went into the dressing room after the game, and the guys gave me the puck. By the looks on their faces, they were happier for me than they were for themselves. "Guys, for as long as I live, I will never forget this night," I said. "Thank you."

I went to the tent in the parking lot afterward, and we drank champagne. Bill Wirtz, the owner of the Blackhawks, was there, and he wasn't very happy that we had beaten him.

I was with Mel and Henry and our scouts, celebrating, when Donna came up to me at about eleven-thirty and said, "I want to go."

"Everyone's staying," I said. "This is party time."

"I want to leave," she said. "Let's go." So I left in the middle of what should have been one of the happiest days of my life.

Pissed because I didn't stay, I was stopped by a cop for speeding as I was driving along Fletcher Avenue. I said, "I'm sorry, officer."

He looked at me. "Phil Esposito? How did the Lightning do tonight?"

"We won our first game," I said.

He let me go.

I said to Donna, "Let's stop at Rio Bravo and have a margarita. I don't want to go home yet."

She said okay, but she was miserable. I had my margarita, and we went home. The guys said they stayed in the tent celebrating until one-thirty, having a great time. I wish I could have been there with them.

29

THE TENSION BETWEEN CRISPY AND ME never went away.
Terry resented my presence in the dressing room. He resented that
the players liked to talk to me. And maybe I don't blame him. I don't
know what I would have done in his shoes. Maybe I was under-
mining him. Maybe I was giving the players an out. So it's possible I
was wrong. But I always thought, Why can't we work together?

Crispy used to hate it when I was out on the ice. I wouldn't go
out there during practice, but when practice was over, some guys
would be hanging around, skating around, shooting the puck, and I
liked to skate around and shoot too. I'd take a player aside and show
him how to take a faceoff. I'd show him how to come around the
outside and use his arm and his reach. Terry would get livid.

"Look at that guy," he'd say, meaning me. "Why does he do
that?"

But it was my team. Later, after the team was sold to Art
Williams, Art would go into the dressing room and bother the
players. When I tried to stop Art from doing that, he would say,
"Why? It's *my* team. I'll go in when I want." And he was right.

About two months into the season, I said to my brother, "Crispy
makes things very difficult."

The players wanted me around. And I could help them. That's
all I was trying to do. We seemed to clash over everything. He was a
coach who wanted to emphasize defense. I wanted offense. I wanted
us to go for it. If we were going to lose, we could at least lose with
flair and excitement. Give the fans something to watch, instead of
dumping the puck and chasing after it into the corners, chipping it
off the glass. God, I hate that.

At the same time, I recognized that we didn't have the personnel to go for it. So we did it Terry's way.

Our best player that first year was Brian Bradley. Brian had been a journeyman player most of his career. When he had played in the NHL, it was on the fourth line. But my brother Tony liked his skating ability. I wasn't sure about him because he was small and I was afraid he was going to get hurt, and he did eventually get hurt. But he was a very fluid skater and a pretty smart hockey player. Everybody liked Brian. I do have to say he was terrible on faceoffs. I could beat him on a draw and I was fifty years old.

▬▬▬

At the end of the 1992 season the league fired John Ziegler. The hardline owners didn't think he was tough enough in contract negotiations with the players and they ganged up on him. Gil Stein, who was one of those behind his firing, became the new league president. Ziegler's firing had a direct impact on us. He had promised us that there would not be another expansion until 1996, so we would have time to establish our territory. But in 1993 Stein announced that the league would expand to south Florida and to Anaheim. The new owners were to be H. Wayne Huizenga, the owner of the Blockbuster video chain, and the Disney Company, owner of Mickey Mouse and Donald Duck and about a billion dollars in capital. Wayne wasn't doing too badly for himself either.

We were blindsided. Not only did the NHL go back on its word that they wouldn't expand, but they liberalized the expansion rules so that the existing teams could protect only a handful of players and one goalie. That meant there were a lot of terrific players – especially goalies – available to both south Florida and Anaheim, which would quickly make them a hell of a lot better than we were. I'll never forgive the league for that. That was unfair to both us and Ottawa.

I was angry but there was nothing I could do about it. David LeFevre and I were driving back from West Palm Beach, and I said, "David, what just happened?"

"I don't know," he said. "But we got railroaded."

———

Since the number of penalties was on the rise in the NHL, I figured it was incumbent on me to trade for some veteran players who could score on the power play. As a result, I traded for Petr Klima, who I figured could quarterback our power play. I also figured that since Klima was Czechoslovakian, he'd help Roman Hamrlik, another Czech, become a better player. I also traded for Gerard Gallant, a tough, hard-nosed left winger who scored a lot of points, and for Denis Savard. Savard was old but he had been one of the great players of all time, very fancy, a great forward. Each of them had scored 30 goals in a season. Some guys in our organization thought I was just giving these guys a chance to play out the string in sunny Florida, but I also knew that Terry Crisp dealt with older players better than he did with younger players. And I knew the young guys we had drafted were not ready to play.

We had to be competitive to draw fans in our market. This wasn't Ottawa, where the team could stink and still draw sixteen thousand a night. I was hoping these vets would add some stability and scoring to our young team. I knew we couldn't win with the goaltenders we had, Pat Jablonski and Wendell Young. I wanted to make a deal with Bobby Clarke. I figured that Clarkie owed me one. After Bill Torrey was named president of the Florida team, Bobby called me a couple of times to ask me to put in a word with Torrey about getting him the GM job. I called Torrey half a dozen times to recommend Clarkie for the job, and he got it.

Florida had acquired John Vanbiesbrouck, Mark Fitzpatrick, and Daren Puppa in the expansion draft to play goal. I knew Clarke didn't need all three goaltenders. I called him and offered him a draft pick for one of his goalies. Puppa had been the backup goalie in Toronto, and my brother Tony loved him. He was big, and he had played pretty well when he was in Buffalo. The night before the draft Clarkie agreed to trade him to me for a draft pick.

Tony said, "Phil, we got our goalie." And Puppa was an excellent goalie when he was healthy.

Players' salaries were beginning to skyrocket, making it rough on all the GMs. This was the year Ottawa gave Alexandre Daigle a five-year, $12.5 million contract. I couldn't believe they paid that much money for the guy. The GM who signed him ended up losing his job. Almost all the GMs who overpay end up losing their jobs. The only one who keeps his after doing something stupid like that is Bobby Clarke.

That same year the Kings paid Wayne Gretzky $25.5 million for three years. If there was one player in the history of the sport who was worth that kind of money, it was Wayne, because of what he did for the game of hockey. Not just for what he did on the ice, which was phenomenal, but what he did for the game. He deserved the money.

Unfortunately there were agents who would come in and say to me, "My player is a tenth as good as Gretzky, therefore you should pay him $800,000 a year, since Gretzky is getting $8 million."

I'd look at him and say, "Yeah, my balls are one tenth as good as Gretzky, and they aren't getting $800,000."

I just could not handle it when an agent did that. When I was playing in Boston with Bobby Orr, Donnie Awrey tried to pull that. Donnie said, "I'm one-third as good as Bobby Orr. If he's getting $100,000, I should be getting $33,000." That was years ago, when $33,000 was a lot of money.

I remember saying to Donnie, "What are you talking about?"

"I am one-third as good as Bobby," he said.

"How is that relevant?" I asked. "*Everybody* is one-third as good as Bobby Orr. Everybody. Come on."

I never compared myself to anyone. I didn't believe in that. When an agent did that, it got my back up, and it became more difficult for him to get his player signed. But if an agent came in and said, "Look, my player isn't Wayne Gretzky, but, you know, he's a pretty darn good player, and he deserves to be making more than fair market value." Now you're talking to me on a level that I can understand.

When Ottawa gave Daigle that ridiculous amount of money, it affected everyone. I had a lot of trouble signing Chris Gratton, our first choice in the amateur draft, third pick overall. Gratton was nineteen, and at that time I wasn't even sure Gratton was going to be good enough to play for our team that season. How many nineteen-year-olds can come in and make an impact? Not many.

If we hadn't signed him, Gratton would have gone back into the draft. Two years later we drafted Shane Willis in the third round of the draft and had to let him go because we couldn't sign him. He wanted too much money.

We signed Gratton five minutes before the deadline. He and I were at a function at the Chamber of Commerce in St. Petersburg. I was with him outside and I had his agent on the phone, and Chris agreed and the agent agreed, and I had Henry Paul on the other line, and he notified the league right before the deadline.

I can honestly say that the first couple of years the Japanese owners left me alone and let me do my job. They sent a guy, Yoshio Nakamura, to be their liaison. There isn't much I can say about Yoshio. Mel Lowell nicknamed him "The Commander." If you remember the movie *Bridge Over the River Kwai*, the Japanese commander in that movie looked just like him. That's the truth. I'd go into his office, and he'd be half-asleep.

I liked Yoshio a lot. He was very nice, and he left us alone. To this day I have no idea what relationship he had with the owners. I think he was representing Kokusai Green. I have no idea what his job was. He was just there.

On opening night of our second season we played the Florida Panthers in the Thunderdome (which was the new name for the Suncoast Dome), and that night we sold twenty-two thousand tickets. Unfortunately, we were really bad. It was a huge, important game for the franchise, and we lost 5-0. I was very embarrassed. I was appalled at how bad we were.

I was not a happy man, and of course I blamed Terry, which was unfair. I second-guessed him on some of his moves. Our power play was awful. I wanted Terry to let Cash be in charge of the power play, but when Terry refused I felt I couldn't step in.

I should have coached and managed the team myself the first three years. That way the team and the whole franchise would have been the way I wanted, and the team would play the way I wanted them to play. I wanted a team that was offensive-minded, that would go for it, with special teams that would make the power play go. Even if you don't have talent on the power play, you have to find a way to make the other team pay at least 20 per cent of the time when it commits a penalty. And I believe in my heart I would have made that happen. I would not have had the players go through all those stupid drills Terry put them through. I would have scrimmaged, and when I saw a player out of position, I would have blown the whistle, stopped, and asked him, "Why are you here?" And I would have taught them how to make the power play go.

At the start of our second season I really thought we were close to making the playoffs. The reason we didn't make it was simple: we were twenty-third on the power play. I just couldn't make Crispy understand that though we didn't have the talent to play the other team five-on-five, we could have made up for it by beating them five-on-four.

I wish I had had the time to be the manager and the coach those first few years. I should have done it. Wayne Cashman could have run all the practices, and I would have taken care of the special teams and the power play. I would have let Tony take care of the offense. But I was involved in marketing, and I just had too much else to do.

One time I went out on the ice and worked with Rob Zamuner and Chris Gratton on faceoffs. They were so bad on them I couldn't stand it any more. There is a knack on faceoffs. It's not all ad lib. Position is very important. I tried to help Rob and Chris. Of course, Terry didn't like it at all.

By January 1994, our team was last in the league in scoring. I called a meeting with Terry, Wayne, and Tony to see what we could do. "How can we change this?" I asked. "Can we become more offensive?" None of the others thought we had the talent to do it. I disagreed with them all.

Terry never once asked me to help, and he should have. I could have taken it upon myself, but I didn't want to interfere. I rarely traveled with the team because I got the sense Terry didn't want me to. He never made me feel comfortable. You can make your friend the coach, but you can never make the coach your friend, because you know that sooner or later you're going to have to fire him. It's gonna happen, because you're going to protect your ass. Somebody has to take the fall.

———

Around that time we announced that we were going to build a beautiful new arena in Tampa. The decision was made by David LeFevre and the board of directors over the objection of some pretty powerful Tampa businessmen.

We needed a modern facility if we were going to compete over the long run, and so we went to the Tampa Sports Authority for financial help. They were going to commit millions toward the building of a brand-spanking-new arena we were going to locate near the waterfront and the convention center to help revitalize the downtown. The city had spent ninety million dollars on an aquarium, and it figured if it had a hockey arena, hotels would be built, and eventually they could host large conventions. It was a smart thing to do.

We held a press conference and showed the design of the building, which was to be constructed of glass and steel, very modern and beautiful. Sandy Freedman, the mayor of Tampa, was standing there with me, and all sorts of people were in the audience.

"I can't wait to see this giant erection go up," I said quite innocently.

Sandy looked at me and said, "Phil!"

"Oh, well, you know what I meant," I said. "Folks, come on now. This is going to be a beautiful building."

Sandy Freedman and most of the politicians had wanted the arena to be built away from downtown, next to the football stadium on Dale Mabry Boulevard. The main proponent of the waterfront site was Ed Taranchik, who sat on the Sports Authority. Ed wanted the arena downtown in the worst way. He wanted to be mayor, and if he revitalized downtown, he had a good shot. He thought he could stop us from building by the stadium by taking his case to the NHL. He would get on the phone and complain about us to Jerry Helper, who had left the NHL to work for us. What Taranchik didn't know was that Helper was close to Mel Lowell. Taranchik would call Helper and say, "I represent the county government, and we don't want the stadium where they want to put it. We want it downtown. Can't you postpone expansion for a year?"

Helper would say, "I'll see what we can do," but instead of passing on his complaints to NHL president John Ziegler, Helper would get on the phone and call Mel and tell Mel what Taranchik was up to.

The next day I'd confront Taranchik. "Ed," I'd say, "What are you doing? Have you lost your goddamn mind? We want and need that building built." But Taranchik never gave up. He got David LeFevre on his side, and ultimately he got the mayor and the commissioners to come on board. In retrospect, downtown was the best place for it.

We had been offered a site for our team right next to the Thunderdome in St. Petersburg, but we said no. The truth is that we never thought baseball could survive in the Thunderdome. We didn't want to stay in St. Pete. Tampa's demographics were way, way better. Hockey fans are usually between the ages of twenty-nine and fifty-two, and St. Pete's demographics were between forty-five to sixty-five. Also, St. Pete had grown as large as it was going to get. There was no room for expansion. All the land had already been developed. And because the Tampa Bay Buccaneers football team was successful, the fans from St. Pete had no problem crossing the bridge to see the games in Tampa. We figured if they'd come to see football, they'd come to see hockey.

But before we moved to the Ice Palace, we set attendance records in the Thunderdome. In front of twenty-six thousand fans, we beat Eric Lindros and the Flyers 6-3. We started to play better. The key was Daren Puppa. He was keeping us in games.

We had a shot at making the playoffs, but we folded at the end when Puppa and Petr Klima got hurt, and that killed us. When Klima went down, our power play went south. We didn't have a good backup goalie, and what's worse, Florida made the playoffs and went all the way to the final. When that happened, I endured a lot of criticism. The fans did not want to hear any excuses about the changes in the expansion rules. That's another reason why I was so pissed. If we had had their expansion rules, we would have made the playoffs too.

Toward the end of the 1993-94 season, there were some shenanigans going on behind my back. Rumors were floated in the local papers that David LeFevre was going to fire me and replace me with his good friend Neil Smith of the Rangers. I suppose David could have gotten the Japanese to agree to it, but I really don't think they would have. I confronted him. "What is this bullshit with Neil Smith?" I asked.

"That's not true," he said. But Jerry Helper had in fact written a release saying that Smith was going to be named general manager. David is a very cool customer. I really think he was trying to force me out. I don't know why – I was doing okay – but that's what I believe. Later on he tried to make amends.

We didn't make the playoffs that second year, but we gained eighteen points from the first year. For me, however, things were not going the way I wanted. The team wasn't playing the way I wanted it to. The organization wasn't treating me very well. I had to fight a lot. With the stress these people put me through, it's a wonder I didn't die of a heart attack.

30

DURING THE 1993-94 SEASON I was offered a job with ESPN. One reason I considered taking the job was that I thought it might save my marriage, which was on the rocks.

My marriage to Donna had started to go bad years earlier when we left New York City and moved to Bedford, New York, in the sticks of Westchester County. Donna insisted we move to Bedford, because she loved horses. I had to get up early and drive an hour and forty-five minutes to go into the city for my job running the Rangers. When I was done, I had to drive an hour and forty-five minutes home, and by the time I arrived, it would be midnight.

When I moved to Tampa in 1991 to work on getting the Tampa Bay franchise, she stayed back in Bedford, and we spent even less time together. When I first moved to Tampa, I lived in an apartment on Bayshore Boulevard with my brother Tony.

I was then approached by the company that had developed Marco Island. It was building a development in Lutz, north of Tampa, called Cheval. The head of the company asked me and General Norman Schwartzkopf to be their spokesmen. He gave us each houses, and he used us to help sell the rest of them. A number of the Lightning hockey players bought houses there. The guy was smart to do what he did.

Despite our problems, Donna and I had one spectacular week together. Once I felt we were going to get the franchise, I arranged for us to get away together to Jamaica. We were there seven days, and I had the most wonderful time with that woman. But when we returned, the old problems also returned. We weren't communicating much and really weren't getting along.

I couldn't afford the thirty-five hundred dollars a month mortgage on the Bedford house any more. I couldn't get it through Donna's head that I was no longer a player and soon would no longer be making five hundred thousand dollars a year. My savings were spent getting the Lightning started. I needed to sell that house in Bedford. She really didn't want to sell it, but I wanted her to live with me in Tampa, and basically I sold it out from under her. We got $1.4 million for it.

I also owned another Bedford property across the street from our house with two other investors. I didn't know it, but the other two guys, friends of mine, hadn't paid their share of the mortgage. The sale was supposed to leave us with a profit of $680,000, but the sheriff swooped down and seized the profits right there at the sale when the bank repossessed it. I didn't even know there had been a lien.

The closing had been delayed three days. I didn't know why. I don't know how the bank even found out I was selling. I was devastated, but I couldn't do anything about it.

Donna was not only furious with me for selling the Bedford house, she was also mad that I had let my friends take advantage of me. When she and our daughter, Cherise, came to Tampa, she was very unhappy. And so was I. I was tired of going to horse shows, tired of trying to take care of her and her sister and her family and her horses and her animals.

All intimacy had virtually stopped. She rarely came to Lightning games. I'd come home late at night, and she'd be sleeping, and I'd just sit there in front of the TV and make myself popcorn and watch a movie and think about the game, or I'd be on the phone to a general manager out west.

I'd get up in the morning and go to the office without even saying hello, come back again at suppertime, and there'd be no dinner because she was out at the barn. Her sister Jo Anne still lived with us, and I would have to cook dinner for the two of them, Cherise, and me.

In the meantime I met my current wife. I wasn't looking for any new attachments, but life can be like that. By this time I was no longer the hard-living, hard-drinking, stay-out-all-night guy I had been as a player. I was fifty, and those days were behind me. I had come to Tampa to start a hockey franchise, and that had become the focus of my life.

But one day when I needed a haircut I asked Henry Paul if he could recommend someone. "I go to a girl named Bridget Lee," he said. I asked him if he could get her to come over to my house, because I wanted to color my hair a little bit too.

Henry came over with his wife, Rozella, and his hairdresser, Bridget. I came to the door wearing weightlifter's sweatpants with paint spots all over them. I had on a white T-shirt and was wearing my flip-flops, which I like to wear around the house.

Bridget, as it turned out, was drop-dead gorgeous. She was tall and beautiful and wow. She looked me up and down, and as she did, I said, "I have my ballroom pants on. Plenty of ball room."

She laughed, and I knew we were fine. Later on she told me that was one of the craziest things anyone had ever said to her.

We started kibitzing back and forth, and I remember Rozella saying, "You guys are fine. I'm outta here." She later told me, "I couldn't stay. The sparks and sexual tension were in that room."

But we didn't do anything. I asked her if she would go out to dinner with me the next Friday.

"Aren't you married?" she asked.

"Yeah, I am," I said. "Come over to the house. I'll cook you dinner."

"I don't think so," she said. "I'm engaged. I don't think I can."

"Look," I said, "I'll expect you at seven-thirty. If you come, you come. I'll have the food ready. If you don't, I'll eat more."

When Friday at seven-thirty came, I got a call from the security guard that someone was coming up to see me.

"Please let her in," I said. We had dinner, and we drank a bottle of wine, and we just talked and talked and talked, until about ten o'clock, when she had to go. From that moment on, there was no doubt in my mind that we were going to have a relationship.

It took a little while for Donna to find out about Bridget. The final straw came when we were in New Jersey at the National Horse Show, which was usually at the Garden, but that year was held at the Meadowlands. We were staying at a hotel, and we went to a party and had a great time. We went back to the hotel room, and we had a great time that night too.

The next morning I called Bridget to make a hair appointment.

Usually I pay the hotel bill, but this time Donna got it, took it down to the lobby and paid it. I wondered about that, but I didn't ask her about it, and she didn't say anything. Then we went to Boston and checked into another hotel. During our stay I called

Bridget again. Donna picked up the bill, took it downstairs and paid it. Turns out she was checking the phone charges to see who I was talking to.

She confronted me when we returned to Tampa. She asked me whether I was fooling around. I said, "Yeah, but not with Bridget." She called me a liar, and she told me to get out.

"Let's talk about this," I said.

She screamed, "No, I want you out of this house." I could hear Cherise, who was eight, crying in the background.

"If I leave," I said, "I'll never come back." She was calm until I started packing a bag. I remember packing my shaving kit. Then everything became a blur.

Donna started throwing things at me and yelling, and one thing led to another, and she pulled one of my golf clubs from the bag and started hitting me with it. I put my arms up to keep from getting hurt, and then I pushed her and she fell, and I headed for my car. She came after me with the golf club.

I got into my Toyota Supra and locked the doors, but I couldn't get away before she started whacking the car with the golf club, putting dents in it. The Irish-Sicilian in her had gone crazy. I took off and went to a hotel.

She was out when I came back to get my clothes. All my suits, jackets, everything, were in the swimming pool. My underwear lay on the grass. I left it all, and I never went back.

Shit happens. I loved Donna, but I couldn't live with her any more. I couldn't stand the lifestyle any more. My life was the Tampa Bay Lightning. It wasn't horses and going to horse shows and raising animals.

By this time Bridget was married. Her husband was a man named Ray. I told her, "My wife and I split. She threw me out."

"Are you sure you want to do that?" she said.

"Yeah," I said. "I've had enough."

Up until that point we had gone out for dinner a few times. We hadn't fooled around yet, but we sure did afterwards.

I'm not saying I'm an angel. I was a married man. I should not have been playing around with a woman who was married.

Bridget hadn't intended to leave Ray. She went with him to San Antonio, Texas, to help him set up a new home. She was debating whether to go with him or to stay with me, when something happened that made her leave and go to her mother's. She divorced him, never asked for a thing, never got a thing. So it wasn't a slam dunk with Bridget and me.

But the truth is she loved me and I loved her. We went through some tough times together, but through it all we had fun, and that's the key to it all. We talked. We communicated. My life is in such good order now.

I live much more simply now. And I'm going to spend the rest of my life with Bridget. I am very, very lucky to have found her.

31

AT THE END OF JUNE 1994 our scouting staff decided to take a flyer and draft four hockey players out of Russia. Head scout (and former Rangers player) Donnie Murdoch and Jake Goertzen recommended them.

I didn't know who they were. I never saw them play. I was told that two of them, Dmitri Klevakin and Alexei Baranov, were going to be good ones. I said, "Why are we drafting these goddamn Russians?"

Donnie said, "We don't have to sign them. They can stay in Russia, and if they ever develop, we can sign them then."

I said, "This is your job. This is what you're supposed to do. Okay."

Far too often the general manager gets the credit for the draft choices, and he certainly gets the blame when they don't pan out.

We also took a Russian by the name of Yuri Smirnov in the ninth round. I stood up and said, "We're going to take from the wonderful family in Russia, Smirnov, the vodka . . . I mean, the player . . ." People laughed. None of the Russians ever made it to camp.

Our top pick that year was Jason Wiemer. Our scouts thought he had tremendous leadership potential. When we interviewed him, he was well dressed, beautifully coifed, and very well spoken. What we didn't know what that he was a party guy. When he got to Tampa, I would get calls at night from the police. He was only nineteen, under drinking age, and after the team would return from a road trip late at night, instead of going home he would go over to the Hideaway on Howard Avenue and tend bar and have a blast.

He was just a kid, and I asked him not to do that, because I didn't want him to get busted for it. When he did it again, I figured we ought to get him out of town. We needed real toughness, and Jason is one of the toughest guys in the league, but at nineteen he wasn't playing that tough, and he partied a little too much. He went from us to Calgary to Florida to the New York Islanders. And he's only twenty-seven. That tells you something about him.

Jason would have been far better off starting in one of the minor leagues, but because of the players' agreement, it isn't an option. Everyone was afraid that if the NHL teams signed the young kids and sent them to the American Hockey League, the International Hockey League, or to the Eastern Hockey League, it would kill Junior A hockey in Canada. So when you sign a young kid in the first round out of Junior A, you either have to keep him on your roster or send him back to Junior A until he's twenty, and then you can send him to the minors. Sending Jason back to Junior A would have been a waste of time for him.

Later, when we signed Vincent Lecavalier at age seventeen, we kept him on the Lightning roster rather than send him back to Junior A. He scored thirteen goals his rookie season, and he struggled mightily for two or three years to score twenty a year. On the other hand, Brad Richards was sent back to Junior A, and when he came back he played very well. If I had to do it over again, I would have sent Lecavalier to Junior A. We weren't going to win anyway.

———

Despite the rumors that Neil Smith was going to take my job as general manager, and despite the fact that the Lightning was for sale and that the new buyer would likely replace me, I decided in August 1994 to turn down the very lucrative job offer from ESPN and stay with the Lightning.

I was flattered to have gotten the offer. The money was about as good as I was making with the Lightning. Behind the scenes there had been some preliminary talks with Bill Davidson about buying the team. Davidson owned the Detroit team in the International Hockey League. He had Rick Dudley as GM and Steve Ludzig as coach, and I knew I'd be gone if he came in. But the deal didn't seem to be going anywhere, and besides, the Lightning was my baby. Even though I wasn't having fun, even though our budget was too small, I decided I was going to stay and do my best to build something.

———

We only got to play half a season in 1994-95. The players didn't have a collective bargaining agreement, and they were going to go on strike. The owners made a final offer. I thought the players were stupid not to take it; but they were adamant in refusing to accept a salary cap. They turned the offer down, and on October 1, 1994, commissioner Gary Bettman called for a lockout of the players. We played only forty-eight games that season, after play resumed January 19, 1995.

Another impasse is coming in 2004. This time the work stoppage might mean we'll miss the whole season. The players remain adamant over the salary cap, while the owners continue to lose money. Why is it that the media, the fans, the players, the coaches, and the general managers begrudge an owner who has invested two hundred million dollars in a sports franchise making 4 per cent on his money? Why is that bad?

When I was general manager of the Lightning, I told everyone I was willing to open our books so they could see how much money we were losing. No one was interested. Everyone thought I was lying.

This past year only three teams made money. The Dallas Stars are a cash cow. They have sixty million dollars in revenue from their suites alone. Last year the Columbus team made twelve million dollars. The third team is a big secret. I'd be hard-pressed to believe it wasn't the Boston Bruins.

During the lockout, the Lightning players came to me and asked if they could use the ice rink to practice. I said to them, "I can't give it to you, because if I do, I'm in breach." But I wanted them to stay in shape, so I said, "I will rent it to you." But they never paid me. Basically I winked at them and let them have it.

———

If the lockout hurt the Lightning, it was nothing compared to what would happen to the team beginning November 22, 1994, a black date in both American and Lightning history. That's when it was announced that president Yoshio Nakamura was being replaced by Saburo "Steve" Oto.

I went to Oto's office the day he arrived. I said to him, "Welcome aboard." I never in my wildest dreams thought he would end up as much a pain in my ass as he was. He just about ruined our franchise.

Oto, who was Japanese, had gone to Brigham Young University and UCLA. He had worked for Deloitte-Touche and was appointed by the chairman and majority owner Mr. Okubo to count beans. All he cared about was our bottom line.

In the three years that Yoshio Nakamura was president he never bothered the hockey part of the operation: I ran things the way I felt best. That all changed when Oto replaced him. Within three months Oto, who didn't know the first thing about hockey, began telling me who the good players were and who was bad.

Oto and I attended a meeting of the owners in Chicago. I was sitting with Bill Wirtz, Ed Snider, Jerry Jacobs, and the other owners, men who had been in the game a long time, and with the general managers, guys like Harry Sinden, Bobby Clarke, and Serge Savard, who had all played the game and been in it for years, and Oto got up and began lecturing them on how he thought the game should be improved. What he said was so stupid, I was embarrassed for him.

Later I said to Oto, "Why are you talking? What you said was stupid."

He said, "We got to make the game better. Hockey got to get better."

I said, "Those guys have been doing this for fifty years. You want to tell them how to run the game? Come on."

Bruce McNall called me over and said to me, "Good luck with that guy."

I said, "Tell me about it."

———

The first major rift I had with Steve Oto came in March 1995. My plan had been for Terry Crisp to coach for three years and then to move up to the front office as my assistant. I wanted Wayne Cashman to replace him and hire his own assistant coaches. My brother Tony was supposed to become vice-president of hockey operations. Terry was going to be the top guy for pro scouting.

Oto wouldn't hear of it. From what I heard, Oto and Terry got to be real friendly and their wives became friendly as well. They played golf together, went to dinner together, and so on.

Oto said, "Terry wants a new contract."

I said, "But Steve, my game plan was for three years, and Terry knew it. This is what we're supposed to do."

He said, "No, no. He wants to coach. I've talked to him. You have to get him signed."

I said, "But I don't want him to coach."

He said, "I don't care. He's going to coach." Oto also said that he wanted Terry to pick his own assistants.

I gave Terry a contract extension, and because Terry didn't want Wayne Cashman as his assistant, Oto forced me to fire him, which hurt me deeply.

This is where I made my absolutely biggest mistake. Oto had no authority over me. He couldn't fire me. I owned 8 per cent of the team. What was he going to do? I should have flown to Japan and talked to Mr. Okubo.

Oto's interference didn't stop there. In June 1995 I was about to make one of the most important trades in the history of the Lightning. I had arranged with Mike Keenan of St. Louis to trade Daren Puppa and a draft pick in exchange for their outstanding goalie, Curtis Joseph. Puppa was terrific when he was healthy. He later got the Lightning into the playoffs, but he was too injury-prone. Curtis Joseph, on the other hand, was unbelievable. I was determined to move Puppa and get someone more durable. But before I could trade Puppa to St. Louis, I first had to sign him for $1.6 million or less in order to fit him into the Blues' budget. We were taking him to arbitration. I had offered him a two-year deal worth $1.2 million and $1.3 million. He wanted $2.2 million each year.

The night before the hearing, I said to Henry Paul, who was going to argue our case before the arbitrator, "Are you ready?"

He said, "Boy, am I ever."

I took Cherise to see a movie, and I turned off my cellphone. We then went to Wendy's to get something to eat and I checked my messages. One of them was from Tony. He said, "Call me. It's very important."

I called Tony. "What's so important?"

He said, "They gave Puppa the money."

"Who gave Puppa the money?"

"I got a call from Steve," he said. "No arbitration. Oto gave Puppa the money."

I said, "How much?"

He said, "I don't know, but I'm telling you, he gave him the money."

I went ballistic. That night when I got back home I called Oto. I said, "What did you do?"

"Where have you been?" he asked.

"I was with my daughter," I said. "What did you do?"

"We decided we didn't want unfavorable publicity. We gave Puppa the money," he said.

"How much?"

He said, "2.2 million, and $2.4 million."

"You're fucking kidding me," I said. "Do you know what you have just done?"

"What?" he said. "I saved us a lot of aggravation and trouble."

"You don't understand," I said. "If I had beaten Puppa in arbitration, I was going to trade him for Curtis Joseph. You do not understand what you just did. If I could have gotten Puppa for $1.6 million or less, Mike Keenan was going to take Puppa for Curtis Joseph."

I called Keenan back trying to salvage the deal. I said, "Mike, I'll tell you what we'll do. We'll pay you the five hundred thousand dollars' difference." I had no permission to do this, but I knew I had to do what I had to do.

He said, "Nah, it's too complicated. I can trade Joseph to Edmonton."

"I really want the guy," I said. "Please. I've already talked to Joseph's agent. I can get him signed. Let's do it."

"I don't know," Keenan said. "I'll call you back." I knew he was going to get on the phone with Edmonton and see what he could do. Sure enough, when he called me back he told me he had traded Joseph to Edmonton.

Mike Keenan said to me, "I don't understand. Why did you give him $2.2 million?"

I said, "I didn't give it to him. My ownership did."

He said, "He isn't worth the money."

I said, "That's right."

Mike said, "I'm sorry. It wasn't worth the aggravation. I didn't want to have to chase you for the money." That happens a lot of times. So we lost out on getting Curtis Joseph.

With Puppa in goal, the Lightning made the playoffs with one game left in the regular season. We edged out the New Jersey Devils, who had won the Stanley Cup the year before. Our opponents in the first round were the Philadelphia Flyers. We split the first two games, winning the second one in overtime on a great goal by Brian Bellows. But before the start of game three, Daren Puppa bent over to tie his skates for the morning practice, and he couldn't straighten back up. At that point we were dead meat. But our future was still very bright.

━━━

Perhaps the lowest day of my career running the Lightning was October 20, 1996, during opening night of the Ice Palace. That's when I found out how far my status had fallen.

Oto and NHL commissioner Gary Bettman went onto the ice for the puck-dropping ceremony, and that was fine. But Oto didn't even assign Tony and me a place to sit and watch the game. When I asked him about it, he said, "Go sit in the crowd."

I said, "I can't do that. The people will drive me crazy."

Right in front of me Bettman said to Oto, "Steve, you should have a place for your general manager to watch the game." Tony and I ended up sitting in the press box.

I couldn't believe it. It was so embarrassing. I was the one who had started the franchise. I had a lot of help, but it was my idea, my dream, my team that I had put together, and I was very proud of that. In fact, of all the things I've done in hockey, it is my biggest achievement. And I wasn't even given a seat for the opening game in the new arena. How humiliating.

━━━

Not long after the Ice Palace opened, David LeFevre left the organization. I don't know whether he quit or was fired. Whatever LeFevre did was always a secret. He did a terrific job getting the Ice Palace built, but once he completed it, he left. David doesn't talk much about it, but I sense that Oto interfered with what he was doing, and he just decided he had taken enough crap from the guy. After he left, I didn't see LeFevre very much at all. Steve Oto took over as the governor of the team.

━━━

Late in 1996 Robbie Zamuner came to me to tell me that Terry Crisp was making their lives miserable with his screaming and yelling. He said, "Phil, it's pretty hard to play for this man. He's killing Chris Gratton. He's killing Alex Selivanov. He's killing Roman Hamrlik. Crispy yells and screams at them from the bench so much these guys don't know whether to shit or go blind."

I commiserated, but there wasn't anything I could do about it.

━━━

In November 1996, my hopes were raised when Gavin Maloof came to town to look into purchasing the Lightning. Gavin's father, Grant, had owned the Houston Rockets basketball team. Accompanying Gavin was a little guy, Tony Guanci. How he got in with the Maloofs I have no idea.

Gavin and I walked around the Ice Palace. He was impressed. I talked to him about a few of my marketing ideas. I said, "We haven't been able to get a hundred thousand dollars for ads on our dasher-boards, but if we had rotating dasherboards, we could sell space for twenty thousand dollars to local mom-and-pop companies, and we could generate a lot of income."

He seemed to like what I had to say. He asked me, "Would you stay if we bought the team?"

I said, "Absolutely. This is my dream. This is my baby."

Gavin left, and for a long time I heard nothing from the Maloofs. When Daren Puppa hurt his back again in April 1997, and the Lightning just missed making the playoffs, all I could think of was how things would have been different had we had Curtis Joseph.

Then in May, I went to Pittsburgh for the amateur draft, and who showed up but Steve Oto and Tony Guanci. Tony and I were seated around a large table along with Terry Crisp, head scout Donnie Murdoch, the scouts, the marketing people, Jerry Helper and the public-relations people when they arrived.

Guanci said to me, "What you need is just two good players like the Anaheim Ducks." Anaheim had Paul Kariya and Teemu Selanne. "That's all you need," he said.

"Are you fucking crazy?" I said.

Guanci kept talking on and on, and Oto said, "The truth is, you have to get rid of a few guys because we can't afford to pay them. The Maloofs and nobody else is going to buy this team because we're carrying too much salary."

At the time our salary was about eighteen million dollars, the lowest in the league or close to it. I finally said, "Listen, would everybody please leave." After the scouts and assistants left, I said, "This is not the time, and this is not the place. We're trying to get ready for a draft tomorrow morning."

Tony Guanci said, "You should trade some of these guys at the draft. You should trade Roman Hamrlik so you can get rid of his $2.3 million salary. He's a lousy player."

I said, "What the fuck do you know about hockey? Tell me what you know. And Oto too. What the fuck do you guys know about hockey? This is ridiculous. I've had enough. I will trade Hamrlik, okay? Go. Leave me alone. Get out of here."

I decided I would satisfy them and trade Hamrlik at the draft table. When they left I got on the phone with Jimmy Rutherford, the GM of Hartford/Carolina. We were talking Hamrlik for Marek Malik, a big defenseman, and another player whose name I can't remember. When I told my brother about the deal, he said, "You cannot do this trade."

I told Rutherford I'd get back to him.

I had barely fallen asleep that night when the phone rang. I looked at the alarm clock. It was 2:50. In the morning. Steve Oto was on the other end of the line.

"I have to talk to you," he said.

"Come on up."

He came up with Chris Phillips, who was supposed to be Okubo's eyes and ears. If Phillips had had any spine he would have gone to Japan and told Okubo what was going on.

Oto said, "Listen, Phil, it's a must that you trade Hamrlik. We can't afford to pay him."

"Steve," I said, "I'm trying, but I will not give him away. I won't. I can't. This is June. We're not paying anyone right now. We do not have to trade him right now."

"If this team is sold, and the Maloofs want to buy it," he said, "they don't want Roman Hamrlik and his $2.3 million contract."

"I'm trying," I said. "I will try to trade him."

It was civil, and he left.

It was 3:15 in the morning, and I called Jimmy Rutherford back. I said, "Jimmy, if you give me Rod Brind'Amour, I'll trade you Hamrlik."

He said, "I can't give you Brind'Amour. I'll give you Malik," and the other player whose name I can't remember.

I said, "Jimmy, I can't do that. It's not enough, and you know it."

He said, "That's my best offer."

I said, "I'll talk to you tomorrow."

I called my brother to tell him what was going on. I went back to sleep, and at seven in the morning my brother came in to see me. I got up and showered. The scouts were putting together their final lists. When I told them what was going on, they were so depressed they didn't know what to do. Jerry Helper said, "Phil, I feel for you. I don't understand it. What's going on?"

I said, "Jerry, I don't know." And I believe at that moment Jerry decided he was going to leave, and it wasn't long before he did leave and went to Nashville.

Donnie Murdoch said, "This is wrong. This is crazy. What is the matter with them? We can't do this." The guys were all arguing about what Oto and Guanci wanted me to do.

I said, "Listen, I'm not trading Hamrlik unless we get a good deal." And I didn't trade him. Instead, I got rid of Shawn Burr, Rudy Poeschek, and Bill Houlder. I loved Shawn Burr. I liked Rudy too, but Rudy couldn't play any more. I figured by trading the three I could save close to two million dollars in salary, and Oto would get off my back about trading Hamrlik.

I then got a call from Gavin Maloof. He said that Tony Guanci had left a list of players he wanted me to get rid of.

I said to Guanci, "You don't own this team. The Maloofs haven't even put up a penny." I said to Oto, "How can you let him tell us what to do?"

A month later I read in the papers that the Maloofs had backed out of the deal. Now I was out three guys who I could have used. But Hamrlik was still there, which was good for us. I thought that perhaps I was done with Oto's meddling for a while. I couldn't have been more wrong.

32

IN EARLY AUGUST 1997 Chris Gratton, arguably our best player, signed an offer sheet with the Philadelphia Flyers giving him nine million dollars up front, plus an average of two million a year over five years for a total of nineteen million dollars. I knew it was far more money than we could afford to pay him.

I got on the phone with Steve Oto. "I don't know what's going to happen," I told him, "but we're in deep shit public-relations-wise." I even went behind Oto's back and called the Sunshine Network, which broadcast the games, to see if they would put up the nine million dollars so we could keep him. Not that Chris Gratton was worth it, because he wasn't, though he was a kid I really liked. He has developed into a terrific player, but back then he wasn't worth that kind of money.

It would turn out that Bobby Clarke had made a huge mistake. A year later he traded Gratton back to Tampa Bay and ate the nine million. Anybody else would have lost his job in a heartbeat.

But once Gratton signed the offer sheet, the only move for me to make was to bluff Clarkie by telling him I was going to match his offer and then try to make the best deal possible in a trade.

I called Clarkie up and told him that I thought he was a fuck for doing this to me. I said, "But we're going to match. Maybe we can work out a deal. I'll call you back."

I had until midnight Pacific time, or three in the morning Tampa time. It was three in the afternoon in Tampa. I didn't have a lot of time. About an hour later I called Clarke back and said, "I'll give you Gratton for Rod Brind'Amour and Mikael Renberg."

He said, "I can't give you those two guys. I can give you Karl Dykhuis and Renberg."

I said, "No, I need Brind'Amour to replace the center I'm losing."

He said, "We're going to put Gratton on the wing, and I want him to play on a line with Brind'Amour."

I said, "Gratton is not a winger." I told Bobby no.

Clarke said, "I'll give you Brind'Amour, Dykhuis, and Renberg, and you give me Gratton and a second-round draft choice." I was thrilled. I had made lemons into lemonade.

"Do we have a deal?" I asked.

Bobby said, "We have a deal, Phil."

I said, "I'll call you back and get everything done."

I left the office and went to see my daughter. My cellphone was on. No one called. I figured it was a done deal.

As I drove my daughter home, I got a phone call. It was about eight at night. Steve Oto was calling.

"I made a deal," he said.

"What are you talking about?"

He said, "Ed Snider and I made a deal."

"What did you do?" I said.

He said, "We're going to get Dykhuis, Renberg, and Dan Kordic for Chris Gratton."

I said, "Dan Kordic can't play hockey. He's big and tough, but he can't play. That's absolutely stupid." I told him to fuck off, and I hung up.

Right away I called Bobby Clarke. He was in a restaurant. I said, "Bobby, what's going on?"

He said, "What? Nothing. We got a deal."

I said, "Eddie Snider said we had a deal with Dykhuis, Renberg, and Kordic."

He said, "Phil, I don't know anything about that. I really don't."

Clarke called Snider. I got ahold of Oto. The four of us held a conference call. I said, "Bobby, come on. We don't want Dan Kordic. You promised me Brind'Amour."

Clarke said, "Okay, we'll give you Brind'Amour, Renberg, and Dykhuis."

I said, "Fine."

Ed Snider, the owner of the Flyers, said, "Absolutely not. We made a deal. The deal is done, Bobby, and that's going to be the deal."

"We're not taking Kordic," I said. "We'll take Renberg and Dykhuis. We're not taking Kordic. We don't want him."

Afterward Oto said to me, "Why not?"

I said, "Four hundred thousand dollars for a guy who can't play? I'm not going to do it."

Snider is no stupido. He knew Oto was unknowledgable, and he called him up directly. If Oto had just stayed away from where he didn't belong, we'd have had Rod Brind'Amour, who would still be on the Tampa Bay Lightning.

Two players, Curtis Joseph and Rod Brind'Amour, would have made a huge difference. We'd have made the playoffs every year. I had Dino Ciccarelli. Imagine Dino and Brind'Amour playing on the same line. Ah, that fucking little bastard. His screwing up those two deals right there changed the complexion of the franchise. The Lightning is just now starting to get back on track. And I got blamed for it. I took a lot of shit for that deal. And I'm through taking it.

———

As a result of Oto's meddling, even before the team assembled for the 1997-98 season it was missing Shawn Burr, goalie Rick Tabaracci, Chris Gratton, Bill Houlder, Rudy Poeschek, and John Cullen, who came down with lymphoma. We were really struggling. Early in the season we lost five games in a row, and that's when I read in the *Tampa Tribune* that Terry Crisp was going to get fired because Steve Oto had lost faith in him.

I had no plans to fire him. A few months earlier we had given him a three-year deal at five hundred thousand dollars a year. Why fire him now? We had played only a dozen or so games. The phone rang. It was Oto. He said, "Phil, you were right. I think we have to replace Terry."

"This is the wrong time," I said.

"I think you better," he said. "Let's fly up to Boston." Oto was insistent.

It was a Saturday and Oto and I flew to Boston and we watched the team tie the Bruins 1-1. After the game, Terry didn't sit with us on the flight from Boston to New York but went to the back of the plane instead. And he avoided us on the flight back to Tampa.

"What's wrong with him?" asked Oto.

I said, "Guys know. He knows what we're here for. And I don't agree with it. I don't think we should do it now. We signed him. We're stuck with him." I said, "Who's going to coach?"

"You are," he said.

"Like hell I am."

He said, "Find a coach."

"Let's wait on this," I said.

We flew back to Tampa Bay. The next day was Sunday, and at ten in the morning I got a call from Chris Phillips. He said, "Steve wants to see you right away."

"It's ten o'clock Sunday morning."

He said, "Steve wants you to come in to the office."

I drove in, and I said to Oto, "What's the problem?"

"I want you to fire Terry Crisp right now and put Rick Paterson in charge," he said.

I said, "This is crazy, but if that's what you want."

I went downstairs and told Terry. I had no problems firing him. None. But the timing was incredibly stupid.

I let Ricky Paterson, Crispy's assistant coach, take over, and I started interviewing for a new coach. If Ricky had had any success at all during the six-game road trip, I probably would have named him the new coach, but during his first game in Los Angeles Brian Bradley got hurt, and he never played another game in the NHL. He hurt his wrist and suffered a concussion, and he never came back. That was a big loss. Brian was our best player. We lost most of the games on that road trip.

I interviewed Terry Murray. His agent, Robin Burns, said he wanted $750,000. That wasn't going to work. Next I called Teddy Nolan. His agent also was Robin Burns, who said that Teddy wanted $750,000. No dice. I called Barry Melrose, who was doing TV commentary for ESPN. I said, "I can't afford to pay much." Barry said, "Phil, I don't want to take a pay cut to coach again."

Then Neil Smith told me about Jacques Demers. Neil said, "Jacques is a go-getter. He'll make the team good from the beginning."

I called Jacques and asked him to drive over from his home in Jupiter. He was doing radio for the Montreal Canadiens, and we agreed that I'd give them an eighth-round draft pick if I signed him. We met in Henry Paul's office so no one would know about it. I liked Jacques immediately. He was enthusiastic. Jacques also was represented by Robin Burns, and Burns again asked for $750,000. When I spoke to Jacques privately, I told him I could pay him $350,000 tops to coach. Jacques said he'd take it. Burns was furious. Like I could care.

Meanwhile, Oto kept the pressure on me to lower the team salary. He was all over me to trade players. To add to the pressure, he was calling the local reporters and complaining about me, saying I was disobeying orders and not being a good soldier.

He was driving me crazy, but I'm at my best when things are at their worst. Mentally, I got tough. I knew it was just a matter of time for me. I knew that sooner or later the team would be sold, and I would be gone. It wasn't fun any more. The team had gone backwards because of Oto's interference, and there was little I could do to stop it. The owners wouldn't give me money to pay players. The budget was terrible. In the past I would make a list of all the players. I'd write down how much each player wanted and what I thought I could get each player for. I would present the list to get my budget. And if I saved money on one player, ordinarily I would use that money to pay another player who might do a little better than I expected. In the end it would all balance out, and it was rare that the numbers did not end up very close to where I predicted they would. But in 1997-98, I went to Oto to brag that I had saved five hundred thousand dollars on one of the players. He said, "That's terrific. And that will come off the budget."

"What?"

He said, "That comes off the budget."

"Steve," I said, "I'm going to need that five hundred thousand to pay another player."

He said, "Oh no, no, no, no. That savings comes back to the club."

"What, are you crazy?" I said. "If I stay under my budget, what do you care?"

But this time he did care. They were running the team on a shoestring, and it was making my job very, very difficult. By mid-January 1998, everyone was in the dumps, including Jacques Demers. We lost a lot of games. We were clearly the worst team in the league.

Jacques said to me, "Phil, the team is bad. There's no talent."

I said, "We have no goaltending. But what am I supposed to do? I can't trade, and I have no money. I can't get a player. Where am I going to get him? I'm sorry. That's just the way it is."

Magically, I was able to get Stephane Richer from Montreal. Jacques thought Stephane really would help us by scoring some goals, and he did for a while, but he was a flake. There was always something wrong with him, whether it was his knee or leg or toe or elbow. Something always was bothering him. He was a hell of a player though.

Dino Ciccarelli asked me to trade him. He said he couldn't take it any more, and I said okay. "Where would you like to go?"

He didn't really care.

"I can trade you to Florida," I said.

"Fine."

I sent Dino and Jeff Norton to the Panthers for Jody Hull and a goalie, Mark Fitzpatrick, who was a nut. We also couldn't afford him, and I shipped him to Chicago.

By mid-March 1998, *Sports Illustrated* was reporting that the team was on the brink of ruin. And I was the one taking the biggest beating. But it was all because of Oto. Another article stated the team would be sold by the summer. Then in early May 1998 Steve Oto left as quickly as he arrived.

33

MY GUESS WAS that Oto was messing up the sale in some way, and to replace him Kokusai Green sent Chuck Hasagawa, a crisis manager, and a very nice guy. When Chuck came in, he said, "Run hockey the way you think is right."

"Thank you," I said. "That's what I did my first three years."

"The team is for sale, no doubt about it," he said.

In one of my last great deals, I traded Bryan Marchment, a player who wanted two million dollars and who we were not going to be able to sign, to San Jose for their lottery pick in the draft. And as it turned out, San Jose won the lottery, and I got their pick.

The two top players were Vinny Lecavalier and David Legwand. When I saw them play, Vinny was by far the better player. He was bigger and smarter. They said he was skinny, but he was seventeen years old. Sure he was skinny. He's twenty-two now and weighs 205. In another couple of years he will play at 225.

Nashville took Legwand, and he turned out okay. Lecavalier is turning out to be a star.

———

The Japanese sold the Lightning on May 18, 1998, to Art Williams, who bought it for $118 million. If ever there was a human being who was out of his element in our sport, it was Art Williams. He had no business buying this team. He had no business being involved in sports.

Art fancied himself a coach, because he had coached high-school football before he made his fortune in insurance. His net worth was about $1.7 billion.

Art had the notion he was a motivator. During the press conference announcing the sale, we were in the Ice Palace in the restaurant area overlooking the parking lot, and he brought out T-shirts that he gave to everyone. On the T-shirt it said, "I'm a Stud, Not a Dud."

Williams was in the habit of sending us weird faxes intended to motivate us. One morning I got a fax that said, "The gazelle gets up in the morning and starts running. The lion gets up in the morning and starts chasing the gazelle. If the gazelle stops, the lion eats him. Go. Go. Go."

This man was weird, weird, weird.

When Art Williams bought the team he offered Jacques Demers

the general manager's job along with his coaching job, but Jacques turned him down. Jacques said, "I can't do both. I don't know how." Art told Jacques to sit with me and watch me. He said, "Learn what Phil is doing."

All summer Jacques hung around the office. Tony would say to me, "What's he doing here all the time?"

I got along with Jacques. In August he and I went overseas, because we were going to Austria during training camp. Jacques's wife was supposed to come, but she got breast cancer, and that was pretty traumatic for everyone.

Jacques and Art became close. Jacques said to me, "Art calls me. I know he's not supposed to call me and ask me about the team, but he's the owner. What can I do?"

Art would call me about players Jacques wanted me to sign. One day Art said, "Phil, I want you to sign Benoit Hogue for $1.5 million." I said, "Art, Benoit Hogue is okay, but he is not a player who can help us."

I called Jacques. I said, "Do you want Benoit Hogue?"

"I like him," he said.

"Jacques, come on," I said. "He's going to cost $1.5 million. Where is he going to play on this team?"

He said, "I don't know."

So I called Art back and I said, "Art, Hogue is not the right guy for us. We can spend the money more fruitfully. I'd like to try to get a goalie. We have to get a goalie."

Art said, "Jacques really likes him, and I think you should sign him."

I said, "That goes way over my budget."

"Don't worry about that," he said.

I said, "It's your money. I don't agree with it, but I'll do it."

I shouldn't have gone along, but I did as I was told, and I signed Hogue. When that SOB fired me, he had the colossal gall to say that I was over budget.

Williams always wanted to go into the dressing room to talk to the players. Jacques didn't want him there. The players certainly didn't. But it was my job to tell him.

I said to him, "You can't. I won't let you."

"You won't let me?" he said. "I own this team."

"No, I won't let you."

He said, "I'll go where I want."

"I'm not going to let you into that dressing room."

Art kept me specifically for the purpose of getting everybody signed. The last player, Vinny Lecavalier, signed at midnight at the deadline. As soon as he signed, I knew it was over for me.

We lost the opening game of the 1998-99 season at Florida, and Daren Puppa played, and then we went to Carolina. We were losing 3-1 in the second period. I went downstairs, and I said to Jacques, "Come on. This is ridiculous." And Jacques went in and read the players the riot act. As the players came out of the dressing room I stood there glaring at them. I didn't say a word. I just looked at every player. And they went out and tied the score 3-3, and Puppa was unbelievable. It was my last day with the Lightning.

Art Williams didn't even have the balls to confront me and tell me I was fired. And then he had the nerve to withhold my twenty-five-thousand-dollar pension. I had to sue him for it. I hired a lawyer, and we went around and around, and he finally gave it to me.

I don't know what I did to this man. He obviously didn't like me. I felt it was my team, not his. But as George Steinbrenner told me, "He who has the ham rules." And I didn't have any ham.

Eight months after he bought the team for $118 million, Art Williams sold it to Bill Davidson for $96 million. I was on the phone a lot with David LeFevre, because we were working hard trying to raise money to buy the team back. David called me and said, "Phil, I talked to Art Williams. I asked him to give us until February 20. I told him we needed to do some due diligence and look at some things." David told me that Art said, "No, I'm selling this team by Valentine's Day, because I promised my wife I'd sell it as a Valentine's present."

On February 14, Valentine's Day, 1999, he sold it to the Davidson people for $96 million. The papers reported it as $100 million. If Williams had waited just six more days, he would have gotten $125 million from us. Ira Kaufman, a reporter for the *Tampa Tribune*, said to Williams, "You lost $18 million in eight months." And he replied, "Me losing $18 million is like you losing $1,800."

———

After getting divorced from Donna, I was very happy living with Bridget. I didn't think about marriage. As far as I was concerned, we were married. I didn't need a piece of paper to tell me that. But every time we went away together, to a celebrity golf tournament or a similar kind of function, I would introduce her as "my lady," because I didn't feel comfortable saying she was my girlfriend.

It was 1997, and Bridget and I flew to Las Vegas. I said to her, "Why don't I just say that you're my wife. What's the difference? Everyone does it."

She said, "But I'm not your wife."

"I'm not about to say that you're my girlfriend," I said. "I'm fifty-five years old."

"Are you ever going to marry me?" she asked.

"Yes," I said. "Any time between now and the year 2005. I will. I just don't know when."

That winter I wanted to buy Bridget a gift for Christmas. I have a friend who works at Silverberg Jewelers in Tampa. I told him, "I want to buy an estate ring, over a hundred years old. I don't want it to be too big and I don't want it be too small. I'll design it myself. If you ever come across one, let me know."

I figured it would take him two years. But about five months later he called and said, "Phil, I think I have the ring for you." I went over and looked at it. It was perfect. I told him how I wanted it designed. I told him, "I want it ready before May 29, because I'm taking Bridget to Jamaica for her birthday, and I'm going to bring it with me to give to her."

He made the ring to my specifications, and he finished it in time. We went to Negril and stayed at a resort there. When they showed me our room, I didn't like it. I said, "I want to overlook the other side."

The desk manager said, "But there's a nude beach on the other side."

I said, "Good. I'll be right in the middle of it." Beyond the nude beach was a point where lovers got married. I got a suite that overlooked the ocean. It was beautiful.

Bridget and I went to dinner the night of her birthday, and when I gave her the ring, she was flabbergasted.

"Will you marry me?" I asked her. It had been three years since we were engaged.

When we got back from Jamaica, Bridget and I set a date, and on July 31, 1999, we were married at our place in Boca Grande. I know I will be with her forever.

———

The phone has stopped ringing. No one calls any more. Usually when the door closes in your sport, it closes shut, and very seldom does it open up again. Some guys do get recycled, and I don't know how they do it. Are they good guys who are quiet and keep their mouths shut? Do they just go along? I'm not like that. If I have something to say, I have to say it. I don't want it to eat me up. I give ulcers. I don't get them. That's the way I look at life.

The New York Islanders called me to see if I was interested in running their team. It was a simple phone conversation that didn't go very far. I said, "I'd be interested if the situation were right." That was the end of it.

And I'm surprised. No one has called Tony either. Tony and I didn't do a bad job here in Tampa Bay. I had owners come to me and say, "I don't know how you did it, putting together a team on such a low budget. You did a hell of a job." But when they look to replace a general manager, no one calls. I don't know what we did wrong. A lot of people think I'm too strong, too much of a bonehead, a hard-head, but I'm not, and proof of that is what I did for Steve Oto. I did what he told me to do – which was a huge mistake.

Here's what I'd like: make me the general manager. Give me a five-year deal at a million dollars a year. I would go to the press conference to announce my signing, say something to piss off one of those owners who think they know it all, and he could fire me. And that would be fine with me. I'd pay the taxes and say, "God bless the U.S. of A."

Index

Adams, Jack, 47
Adams, Weston, Sr., 73
Alexis, Kim, 147
Algoma Contractors, 18-19
Allison, Mike, 177
Anaheim Mighty Ducks, 268
André the Giant, 92-93
Aubut, Marcel, 191, 234, 237
Awrey, Don, 67, 71, 81, 94-95, 103, 248

Badia, Hooks, 208-9
Bailey, Garnet "Ace," 63-64, 79
Ballard, Harold, 186-87
Ballard, Yolanda, 187
Baranov, Alexei, 259
Barber, Bill, 193
Baron, Art, 173-74
Barrasso, Tom, 203-4
Barsanti, Harvey, 20
Bateman, Justine, 170
Baxter Birney, Meredith, 170
Beers, Lou, 234-36

Beliveau, Jean, 46, 87
Bellows, Brian, 266
Berenson, Red, 80
Bergeron, Michel, 191-202
Bergman, Gary, 106
Bettman, Gary, 261, 266-67
Biletnikoff, Fred, 94
Billets, Kevin, 191
Bombacco, Angelo, 14, 18-20, 23, 233
Bombacco, Jerry, 20, 35, 87-90
Boston Bruins, viii, 1, 4, 22, 57-98, 122-29, 141-43, 155, 172, 274
Boston Red Sox, 79, 81-82, 237
Bourne, Bobby, 215
Bourque, Ray, 172
Bower, Johnny, 50
Bowman, Scotty, 80, 144, 156
Bownass, Jack, 29
Bradley, Brian, 246, 275
Brando, Marlon, 148
Breinin, Warren, 169
Brenneman, Johnny, 29-30

Brewer, Carl, 84
Brezhnev, Leonid, 113
Brind'Amour, Rod, 270, 272-73
Brooke, Bob, 178
Brooks, Herb, 159, 178
Bucchino, Joey, 195, 199-200
Bucyk, Johnny, 56, 65, 67-68, 79,
    82, 85, 98, 134
Buffalo Sabres, 162-63
Buffy, Vern, 72
Burns, Robin, 275
Burr, Shawn, 270, 273

Caan, James, 148
Calder Trophy, 41
Calgary Flames, 233
California Golden Seals, 92, 132, 141
Campbell, Ken, 25-26
Campeau, Christian, 241
Campeau, Jacques, 241
Canada Cup, 144
Canada Post, viii
Canada-Russia series, 20, 99-104,
    107-20
Canney, Danny, 58, 68, 123, 134
Carleton, Wayne, 67, 79
Caron, Alain "Boom-Boom," 33,
    36-37
Carpenter, Bobby, 183, 187
Carter, Gary, 177, 190
Cashman, Wayne, 1, 4-5, 67, 70-71,
    75-76, 79, 85, 91, 95, 97, 103, 105,
    110, 119-20, 129, 131, 138-39, 172,
    175-76, 181-82, 185, 191, 200-202,
    233-34, 242-43, 250-51, 263-64
Cavacuello, Gino, 7, 12

Cayer, Jocko, 234
Chadwick, Bill, 166-67
Chapman, John, 239
Chase, Frank, 211
Cheevers, Gerry, 56, 59, 61-63,
    66-67, 75-76, 79, 99, 122, 132, 144
Cher, 151
Cherry, Don, 130-34, 155
Chicago Blackhawks, viii, 14, 22, 25,
    36-53, 80, 127, 154, 188, 244
Ciccarelli, Dino, 273, 277
Ciotti, Norman "Sockeye," 20
Clarke, Bobby, 106, 113, 247-48, 263,
    271-73
Coffey, Paul, 203
Cohen, Joe, 173-74
Coleman, Sandra, 27
Conigliaro, Tony, 148
Cooke, Jack Kent, 84
Cosell, Emmy, 145, 155
Cosell, Howard, 145-46, 155, 167
Cournoyer, Yvan, 102-3, 115-16
Crawford, Bobby, 183
Crisp, Terry, 27, 233-34, 241, 243,
    245-47, 250-51, 263-64, 267-68,
    274-75
Crozier, Roger, 41-42, 169-70
Cuban, Mark, 217
Cullen, John, 273
Cullen, Ray, 26
Cunningham, Billy, 209
Cusack, Jimmy, 237-38
Czechoslovakian hockey team, 118

Daigle, Alexandre, 248-49
Dallas Mavericks, 217

Dallas Stars, 206, 262
Daly, Joe, 72
Davidson, Bill, 261, 280-81
Davidson, John, 135, 140, 150-51,
     156-57, 160
Delvecchio, Alex, 14, 39
Demers, Jacques, 275-76, 278-80
DePauli, Chester, 20
Desordo, Roger, 20
Detroit Red Wings, 14, 38, 47,
     193, 199
Diller, Jack, 178, 188-92, 197,
     199-201, 203-5
Dionne, Marcel, 187-88, 197-98, 215
DiPetro, Joe, 34
Doak, Gary, 67, 81
Dodge, Rick, 212-13
Dryden, Ken, 87, 102, 104, 114-15,
     117, 156
Dudley, Rick, 261
Duff, Dick, 46
Duguay, Ron, 145, 147, 151-52
Dykhuis, Karl, 272-73

Eagleson, Alan, 48, 83-84, 98-101,
     107-9, 116, 118-19, 133, 149-51,
     169, 186-87, 213
Earl, Don, 72
Eastern Hockey League, 28
Eaton, Cyrus, 218
Edestrand, Darrell, 155
Edmonton Oilers, 157-58, 177-78,
     189-90
Edwards, Donnie, 163
Emms, Hap, 22
Erixon, Jan, 179-80

Eruzioni, Mike, 117
Esaw, Johnny, 104
ESPN, 261, 275
Esposito, parents, 7-19, 24, 30,
     33-35, 162
Esposito, Carrie Lynn, 71, 122, 242
Esposito, Cherise, 170, 205, 223,
     242, 256, 258, 265
Esposito, Donna Flynn, 1-3, 85,
     93-98, 101, 120-22, 124-27,
     129-30, 133-34, 136-37, 140-41,
     145-47, 152, 155, 160, 163, 165,
     170-71, 205-6, 208, 223, 242,
     244, 254-58, 281
Esposito, Laurie, 35, 100, 122
Esposito, Linda, 30, 32, 35-37,
     48-49, 52, 55-56, 59, 71, 82-83,
     86, 90, 95, 97, 108, 111, 120-22
Esposito, Marilyn, 56, 85, 88
Esposito, Phil: hockey records,
     awards, and trophies, vii-viii,
     4, 71-72, 84-85, 159, 171;
     childhood, 7-17; adolescence,
     17; on juvenile hockey teams,
     18-21; on junior hockey teams,
     21-25; on intermediate hockey
     teams, 25-28; marries Linda,
     30, 32, 35-36; works in steel
     mill, 24, 34-35, 52, 55; signs
     with Blackhawks, 29-30; plays
     for Blackhawks, 36, 38-52;
     traded to Boston Bruins, 52-55;
     plays for Bruins, 57-82, 86-87;
     boat cruising experiences,
     87-90; meets and marries
     Donna, 93-97, 120-22, 145;

plays for Team Canada,
98-120, 149-50; leg injury, 1-2,
123-28; traded to New York
Rangers, 129-31; plays for
Rangers, 132-60; operates
nightclub, 151-52; retires,
161-64; assistant coach for
the Rangers, 164-65; plays
Old-Timers hockey, 86, 165-66,
215; color commentator for
Rangers, 40-41, 166-69, 173;
general manager and coach
of Rangers, 168-69, 173-85;
establishes Phil Esposito
Foundation, 169-70; elected
to Hall of Fame, 171; receives
Order of Canada, 171; fired as
general manager of Rangers,
204-6; forms Tampa Bay
Lightning, 207-39; visits Japan,
219-23; general manager of
Tampa Bay Lightning, 239-54,
259-81; breakup of marriage to
Donna, 254-56; meets and
marries Bridget, 254-59, 281-
82; fired from Tampa Bay
Lightning, 280-81
Esposito, Tony, 7, 9-11, 16-20, 30,
35, 53, 56, 80, 85, 88, 99-100, 101,
103, 105, 113, 119, 126, 155, 202,
204, 211, 224, 230-31, 239, 241,
245-47, 250, 255, 263, 265-67,
269, 279, 283
Evans, Dick, 178, 188-92, 197,
204-5
Expansion draft, 51-52

Fairbairn, Billy, 97
Fairchild, Morgan, 151
Farrelli, Jimmy, 29
Favell, Doug, 60
Fawcett, Farrah, 151
Ferguson, John, 87, 107, 138-39,
141-42, 148, 153, 199
Finnish hockey team, 144
Finos, Enos, 34
Fitzgerald, Tommy, 92
Fitzpatrick, Mark, 247, 277
Fleming, Reggie, 39-40, 63
Fletcher, Cliff, 206
Florida Panthers, 247, 250, 253, 277
Flynn, Dick, 120-21
Flynn, Jo Anne, 93-97, 145-46,
152, 256
Foreman, George, 146
Forristall, Johnny "Frosty," 1, 58,
66, 74, 83, 116, 134, 234
Fox, Michael J., 170
Francis, Emile, 133, 135-38, 153, 175,
197, 204
Francis, Ron, 203
Frayne, Chucky, 20
Freedman, Sandy, 237, 252
Froese, Bob, 182, 189, 202-3

Gadsby, Bill, 39
Gallant, Gerard, 247
Gannis, Mark, 237
Giacomin, Eddie, 97, 175-76, 185,
191, 200-202
Gilbert, Gilles, 128
Gilbert, Rod, 103, 106, 135, 138,
141-42, 146, 175

Giles, Curt, 178
Gillies, Clark, 215
Giovanatti, Clem, 7, 20
Godfather, The, 148
Goertzen, Jake, 259
Goldsworthy, Bill, 104, 106
Gordon, Jimmy, 166-68
Goulet, Michel, 194, 198-99
Gratton, Chris, 249, 251, 267, 271-73
Greco, Benny, 12, 19, 21
Green, Norm, 206-7
Green, Ted, 57-59, 67, 71, 77-78,
    81-82, 122, 132, 142
Greenfield, Stuart, 208-9
Greschner, Ron, 136, 147, 151-52, 198
Gretzky, Wayne, 15, 64-65, 85,
    157-60, 163, 177, 179, 189-90,
    216, 248-49
Grosso, Donnie, 31-33
Grosso, Lorne, 20
Guanci, Tony, 268-70
Guevremont, Jocelyn, 107
Gusev, Alexander, 103

Hadfield, Vic, 103
Hall, Glenn, 36, 39, 42, 80
Hall, Murray, 38
Hamilton Red Wings, 28
Hamrlik, Roman, 240, 247, 267,
    269-70
Hanlon, Glen, 177
Hardy, Mark, 196, 198
Harnett, Frank, 99
Harris, Ron, 28, 123-24
Harrison, Jimmy, 69, 154
Hartford Whalers, 180, 197

Harvey, Doug, 37
Hasagawa, Chuck, 277
Hay, Billy, 36, 47, 49
Heaney, P.J., 15
Hedberg, Anders, 215
Helmsley, Leona, 211
Helper, Jerry, 236, 252, 254, 268, 270
Henderson, Paul, 28, 102, 106-7,
    113-14, 116-17, 120
Henry, John, 237
Herrick, Norton, 229-30
Hewitt, Foster, 102
Hidaka, Masayoshi "Mac," 218
Hobson, Peter, 209
Hockey Night in Canada, 14
Hodge, Ken, 1-2, 21, 27, 53, 57, 63,
    65, 67, 69, 71, 75, 79-81, 83, 85,
    91, 98, 127, 129, 134, 138, 142,
    172, 183
Hofer, Karl, 211
Hoggarth, Ron, 162-63
Hogue, Benoit, 279
Houlder, Bill, 270, 273
Houston Astros, 218, 226
Houston Rockets, 268
Howe, Gordie, vii, 14, 18, 39-40, 47,
    92, 159, 165-66
Hryhorchuk, Ross, 7
Huber, Willie, 176
Huizenga, H. Wayne, 246
Hull, Bobby, 20, 36, 38-46, 48-52,
    64, 72, 80, 84, 99, 159, 165
Hull, Brett, 242
Hull, Dennis, 27, 42
Hull, Jody, 277
Hunter, Tommy, 49

Ice Palace, Tampa, 251-53, 266-67
International Hockey League, 260-61
International Ice Hockey Federation, 150
Ivan, Tommy, 30, 41, 51, 183

Jablonski, Pat, 247
Jacobs, Jerry, 137, 226, 234, 237, 263
Jaffe, Stanley, 228
Janssens, Mark, 196
Jarrett, Doug, 42
Jennings, Bill, 137, 145
Johnson, Tommy, 70, 74-75
Johnston, Eddie, 3, 56, 66, 69, 78, 83, 91
Johnstone, Eddie, 62
Jordan, Michael, 190
Joseph, Curtis, 264-66, 268, 273

Kariya, Paul, 268
Karmanos Group, 213, 234-35
Karmanos, Pete, 236
Kaufman, Ira, 281
Keenan, Larry, 62
Keenan, Mike, 264-66
Kennedy, Dean, 196
Kharlamov, Valery, 104
Kisio, Kelly, 177-78, 189
Kitchener Rangers, 29
Klevakin, Dmitri, 259
Klima, Petr, 247, 253
Kojima, Tak, 217-18, 220-21, 223, 225, 229
Kokusai Green Ltd., 222, 228, 238, 249, 277

Kontos, Chris, 244
Kordic, Dan, 272-73
Krumpe, Jack, 166, 173-74
Krumpetich, Paul, 19
Kulagin, Boris, 117-18
Kuryluk, Merv, 31
Kutcher, Nicky, 12, 19
Kuzkin, Victor, 103
Kyle, Gus, 31, 33, 37

Lachowich, Richard, 20-23
Lafleur, Guy, 192, 196, 202
Lafreniere, Jason, 190
Laidlaw, Tommy, 187
Lambert, Lane, 177
LaNoche, Johnny "Clipper," 19-20
Laperriere, Jacques, 31, 33
Lapointe, Guy, 106, 156, 161
Larocque, Michel "Bunny," 156
Larocque, Denis, 196
Larouche, Pierre, 182-83
Lawton, Brian, 196
Lazarra, Benny, 232
Lecavalier, Vincent, 261, 278, 280
Lee, Bridget, 256-59, 281-82
Leetch, Brian, 196, 198, 202
LeFevre, David, 218-19, 222-23, 225-32, 237-38, 247, 251, 253-54, 267, 280
Legwand, David, 278
Lemaire, Jacques, 171
Lemieux, Mario, 15, 65, 179, 203, 216
Liapkin, Yuri, 117
Liba, Igor, 196
Lindros, Eric, 16, 253

Lindsay, Ted, 39, 47-48
Longarini, Carlo, 20
Los Angeles Kings, 84, 136, 155, 187,
    190, 192, 216, 244, 248
Lowe, Kevin, 158
Lowell, Mel, 210, 215-16, 219-21,
    223, 225-26, 228-38, 244,
    249, 252
Ludzig, Steve, 261
Lutchenko, Vladimir, 103, 115

Maciver, Norman, 196
MacLeish, Rick, 128
Madison Square Garden, 132,
    184, 190
Mahovlich, Frank, 102-3, 106, 114
Mahovlich, Peter, 103, 106, 112,
    114-16
Maki, Ronald "Chico," 38, 45, 74
Maki, Wayne, 77-78
Malik, Marek, 269-70
Maloney, Don, 148, 154-55, 159,
    161-62, 196-97
Maloney, Toni, 197
Maloof, Gavin, 268-70
Maloof, Grant, 268
Manchester, Duke of. See
    Montague, Lord, Duke
    of Manchester
Maniago, Cesare, 31, 33
Mantle, Mickey, 14
Marchment, Bryan, 278
Marcotte, Don, 79
Marotte, Gilles, 53, 141
Martin, Pit, 53
Masters of Hockey games, 169

McEwen, Mark, 241
McEwen, Tom, 209-10
McKechnie, Walter, 85, 149
McKegney, Tony, 178-80
McKenney, Don, 65, 71
McKenzie, Johnny, 63, 67-68, 77,
    79, 82
McMullen, John, 218, 226
McNall, Bruce, 190, 263
Melrose, Barry, 275
Memorial Cup, 23
Messier, Mark, 177-79, 189
Miami Heat, 209
Middleton, Rick, 142
Mikita, Stan, 36, 47, 49, 69-70,
    80, 103
Miller, Kelly, 183
Minnesota North Stars, 78, 206
Mio, Eddie, 160
Miron, Bonnie, 17
Monahan, Leo, 92
Monday Night Football, 167
Montague, Lord, Duke of
    Manchester, 224-27
Montgomery, Elizabeth, 43
Montreal Canadiens, 38, 47, 50, 70,
    86-87, 155-56
Morris, Mercury, 91
Muldoon, Pete, 50
Murdoch, Don, 140-41, 147-48,
    154-56, 160, 215, 259, 268, 270
Murphy, Jim, 211, 217
Murphy, Ron, 65, 70
Murphy, Terry, 19
Murray, Terry, 275
Muscatello, Donny, 7, 12, 20

Naccarato, Abbie, 20
Nakamura, Yoshio, 220, 249, 262-63
Namath, Joe, 161
Nanne, Lou, 20, 207
Nardini, Pat, 20
National Hockey League (NHL), 51, 55, 62, 158, 189, 206-7, 210, 246-47, 260
National Hockey League Players' Association, 47, 99, 150, 169-70
Neilson, Jimmy, 123
Ness, Larry, 243
Nesterenko, Eric, 49
New Jersey Devils, 226, 266
New York Islanders, 282
New York Knicks, 190
New York Mets, 177
New York Rangers, viii-ix, 1, 4, 14, 40, 50, 72, 79, 98, 123, 129, 132-64, 170, 173-205
New York Yankees, 79, 218
Newman, Paul, 214
Nilsson, Ulf, 154, 215
Nippon Ham Fighters, 217-18, 220, 222
Nolan, Ted, 275
Norris, Bruce, 47
Norris, Jack, 53
Norris, Jim, 47, 51-52
Norton, Jeff, 277
Nowak, Hank, 131
Nykoluk, Mike, 153

O'Donnell, Fred, 1-2
O'Neal, Ryan, 151

Ogrodnick, John, 193-94
Okubo, Takashi, 264, 269
Orlando Magic, 209
Orr, Bobby, 1-4, 20, 48, 56-57, 59, 65-67, 71-72, 77-79, 81-85, 91, 93, 99-100, 123-24, 130-33, 150, 172, 248
Orr, Peggy, 67
Osterhaus, Michael, 209-10
Oto, Saburo "Steve," 262-77, 283
Owens, Jesse, 52

Pace, Frank, 134-36
Pacino, Al, 148
Paiement, Wilf, 149
Parent, Bernie, 102, 128, 171
Parise, Jean-Paul, 103-4, 113-14
Park, Brad, 103, 106, 116, 133
Paterson, Rick, 274-75
Patrick, Craig, 157, 159-62, 164-65, 173, 179, 182
Patrick, Jim, 198
Pattison, Jim, 129-31
Paul, Gabe, 208, 210, 218, 220
Paul, Henry, 208-11, 213-18, 220-23, 225, 228-32, 235-37, 244, 249, 256, 264-65, 275
Paul, Rozella, 256-57
Pavelich, Mark, 176
Perrone, Mark, 208-9, 212
Persson, Stefan, 215
Pezzuto, Fuzzy, 20-21
Phil Esposito Foundation, 169-70
Philadelphia 76ers, 209
Philadelphia Flyers, 127, 155, 159, 182, 188, 191, 193, 253, 266, 271

Phillips, Chris, 229, 269, 274
Pilote, Pierre, 36, 39
Pilous, Rudy, 25
Pittsburgh Penguins, 72, 198, 202-3, 216, 244
Plager, Barclay, 33
Plager, Bob, 33, 242-43
Players' Association. *See* National Hockey League Players' Association
Plett, Willi, 196
Pocklington, Peter, 177-78, 189
Poddubny, Walter, 177, 185, 190
Poeschek, Rudy, 270, 273
Polano, Nick, 31
Porter, Cole, 17
Potvin, Denis, 215
Pratt, Tracy, 37
Pritzger family, 211-13, 215-17
Pritzger, John, 211-12, 225
Pulford, Bob, 51
Puppa, Daren, 247-48, 253, 264-66, 268, 280

Quebec Nordiques, 191, 234
Quinn, Pat, 191, 206
Quintanen, Janie, 17

Ramage, Rob, 243
Ramsey, Mike, 163
Ramsey, Russ, 52
Ratelle, Jean, 103-4, 133
Ravlich, Matt, 87-90, 99
Reay, Billy, 36, 38-39, 41, 43-45, 47, 51
Redmond, Craig, 192

Reid, Tommy, 161
Renberg, Mikael, 272-73
Rhéaume, Manon, 241-43
Richard, Henri, 47, 87
Richard, Maurice "Rocket," 128
Richards, Brad, 261
Richer, Stephane, 276-77
Richter, Mike, 182, 189, 203
Ridley, Mike, 183
Risebrough, Doug, 156-57
Roberts, Jimmy, 63
Robinson, Larry, 156
Rochefort, Normand, 190
Rosen, Sam, 40-41, 168
Rowe, Dr. Carter, 3, 124-25
Roy, Patrick, 79, 177
Ruotsalainen, Reijo, 40-41, 176
Russian hockey team, 101-4, 112-18
Ruth, Babe, 72-73, 79
Rutherford, Jim, 213, 234-36, 269-70

Sabourin, Gary, 135
Sacharuk, Larry, 135-36
St. Catharines Blackhawks, 24-28
St. Louis Blues, 80-81
St. Louis Braves, 32-33, 37
St. Paul Fighting Saints, 37
Salming, Borje, 149, 215
Salming, Stig, 149
Samuelsson, Kjell, 182
Sanderson, Derek, 67, 76-77, 79-81, 93, 98, 122, 132, 139
Sandstrom, Tomas, 178, 182-83, 189
Sanko, Jimmy "Chubby," 19-21
Sardano, Joe, 224

Sarnia hockey team, 23-24

Sather, Glen, 178, 183, 189, 192, 206

Sator, Ted, 173, 178-79

Sault Ste. Marie Greyhounds, 157-58

Sault Ste. Marie Thunderbirds,
   28-31

Savard, Denis, 247

Savard, Serge, 87, 101, 103, 118,
   156-57, 206, 263

Sawchuk, Terry, 39-40, 50

Sawyer, Ken, 228

Schmautz, Bobby, 134

Schmidt, Milt, 22, 53-57, 61-62

Schock, Danny, 57

Schock, Ronnie, 57

Schwartzkopf, Norman, 255

Sebetski, Gunther, 150

Seiling, Rod, 103

Selanne, Teemu, 268

Selivanov, Alex, 267

Shack, Eddie, 58, 67-69

Sharf, Lisa, 43

Shaw, David, 198

Shero, Fred, 153-56, 159

Shire, Talia, 148

Sinden, Harry, 57-58, 64-65, 68,
   70-71, 80, 96, 100, 102-4, 107-8,
   114, 117, 129-30, 133-34, 137, 172,
   183, 204, 206, 241, 263

Smirnov, Yuri, 260

Smith, Dallas, 1-2, 59, 67, 77, 133

Smith, Emmitt, 20

Smith, Gary, 112

Smith, Kate, 127-28

Smith, Neil, 183, 204, 253-54,
   261, 275

Smith, Reese, 229-30

Smith, Tal, 226

Smythe, Conn, 92

Snider, Ed, 186, 211, 263, 272-73

Snyder, Daniel, 217

Soetaert, Doug, 177

Songin, Tommy, 171-72

Soviet hockey team. *See* Russian
   hockey team

Spectacore, 211

Stanfield, Fred, 27, 53, 57, 67-68,
   79, 183

Stanfield, Jack, 27

Stanley Cup, 47, 50, 81-82, 92,
   96-98, 189

Stapleton, Pat, 103, 109, 116

Starr, Rick, 211

Stein, Gil, 246

Steinbrenner, George, 210, 218, 220,
   228-30, 280

Stemkowski, Peter, 51, 133,
   135-36, 141

Stephenson, Wayne, 159

Sterner, Ulf, 105

Stewart, Ronnie, 136, 138

Sulliman, Doug, 162

Sullivan, Red, 29

Sundin, Mats, 208

Swedish hockey team, 104-7, 149

Tabaracci, Rick, 273

Talbot, Jean-Guy, 153

Tallon, Dale, 107

Tampa Bay Lightning, ix, 4-6,
   239-54, 259-81

Taranchik, Ed, 252

Tavares, Tony, 211-12

Team Canada, 98-120, 149-51

Tessier, Carroll, 224-25, 227

Thayer, Skip, 234

Thicke, Alan, 244

Thomas, Wayne, 160

Tiffeault, Charles, 201

Tkaczuk, Walter, 97, 123, 135-36,
    141, 143, 153-54, 175

Toronto Maple Leafs, 14, 50

Torrey, Bill, 247

Tremblay, J.C., 62

Tretiak, Vladislav, 101, 103-4, 106,
    113, 115, 117, 171

Trudeau, Pierre Elliott, 101, 118-20

Ubriaco, Gene, 99, 202, 204

Vachon, Rogie, 206

Vadnais, Carol, 75, 79, 92-93, 129,
    132-34, 137

Vanbiesbrouck, John, 177-78, 182,
    188-89, 202-3, 247

Vancouver Blazers, 129

Vancouver Canucks, 179-80

Vasiliev, Valeri, 117

Vasko, Moose, 36, 39

Vickers, Steve, 97, 123, 138, 141,
    153, 175

Walton, Mike "Shaky," 76, 91-92, 95

Washington Capitals, 182

Washington Redskins, 217

Webster, Tommy, 180-85, 188, 191

Werblin, Sonny, 145-46, 153, 155,
    159, 161-62, 166-67

Westfall, Eddie, 67, 79

White, Bill, 103

White, Kevin, 82

Wiemer, Jason, 260

Williams, Art, 245, 278-81

Williams, Pat, 209

Williams, Ted, 162

Williams, Tommy, 67, 70

Willis, Shane, 249

Wilson, Bob, 22-23, 72

Wilson, Carey, 196

Windsor Spitfires, 180

Winfield, Dave, 229

Wirtz, Bill, 186, 234, 236, 244, 263

Wolff, Bob, 93, 208

World Championship (1977),
    149

World Hockey Association, 122,
    132, 158

World Trade Center, 64

Worsley, Gump, 70

Yakushev, Alexander, 114

Yashin, Alexei, 240

Young, Howie, 42

Young, Jimmy, 134

Young, Wendell, 244, 247

Zamuner, Rob, 251, 267

Zeidel, Larry, 142

Ziegler, John, 186-87, 226, 228,
    237-38, 246, 252